BRASS VALLEY

The Story of Working People's Lives and Struggles

in an American Industrial Region

BRASS VALLEY

**The Story of
Working People's
Lives and Struggles
in an American
Industrial Region**

The Brass Workers
History Project

Compiled and edited by

Jeremy Brecher, Jerry Lombardi,

and Jan Stackhouse

Temple University Press

Philadelphia

Temple University Press, Philadelphia
19122

Published 1982

Printed in the United States of America

Library of Congress Cataloging in
Publication Data

Brecher, Jeremy.
    Brass Valley: the story of working peo-
ple's lives and struggles in an American
industrial region.
    Includes bibliographical references and
indexes.
    1. Brass industry and trade—Connecti-
cut—Naugatuck River Valley—History.   2. Trade-unions—Brass industry
employees—Connecticut—Naugatuck
River Valley—History.   3. Brass industry and trade—Connecticut—Naugatuck
River Valley—Employees—Interviews.
4. Naugatuck River Valley (Conn.)—Social conditions.   5. Naugatuck River Valley (Conn.)—Economic conditions.
6. Ethnology—Connecticut—Naugatuck
River Valley.   7. Naugatuck River Valley
(Conn.)—Biography.   8. American Brass
Company—History.   I. Lombardi, Jerry.
II. Stackhouse, Jan.   III. Brass Workers
History Project.   IV. Title.
HD9539.B8U538   331.7′6733′097467
82-5770
ISBN 0-87722-271-1   AACR2
ISBN 0-87722-272-X (pbk.)

Publication of this book has been assisted
by a grant from the Publication Program
of the National Endowment for the
Humanities.

The portraits of the interviewees are by
Jerry Lombardi, with the following
exceptions:
Portrait of John Driscoll courtesy Connecti-
cut State Labor Council, AFL-CIO.
Portrait of John Monagan courtesy John
Monagan.

Brass Workers History Project Community / Labor Advisory Panel

Al Avitabile
Ed Borowski
Leo Briguglio
Romeo Caputo
Rachel Doolady

Frieda Ewen
William Freeman
Quentin Garatoni
Hyotha Hofler
Helen Johnson

Sandra Kay
Eddie Labacz
Mike Laban
Dorothy Larson
Bobby Lombardo

Peter Marcuse
Sid Monti
Art Muzzicato
Alannah Nardello
Claude Perry

Ann Smith
Fred Smith
Russell Sobin
John Yrchik
Daniel Zuraitis

PREFACE

"The Things That the Old-Timers Won, We're Fighting for Again"

I was always interested in unions to an extent, but I never really got into the history. I remember one time I picked up a book on labor history. I didn't know what it was, but it was on sale, so I figured I'd buy it. It was hard reading, but it was hard to put down. I learned about all kinds of struggles that I never read about in the history books. I'm saying: What is this, fiction? I couldn't believe it. All over the place—it wasn't just isolated here and there—they had general strikes, they had to take over factories, just to get common decency, just to get the basic rights.

After that, I kept trying to read more about it, because it seemed there was a whole facet of my history, my personal history, that I never heard of in school. I heard of people like the Carnegies and Rockefellers, the libraries they made and their foundations, but I never heard about how many people they killed to get the money to do this. It was a shock. Though I was a history buff in school, I never read any of this history.

Now it seems to be getting back to the point where we're fighting the struggles over again. We're fighting the old fights. Fighting overtime. Fighting for our wages—they're trying to take our money away. Fighting to keep up with the price of oil. It seems like it's gone around a circle. The things that the old-timers won, we're fighting for again.

I'd like to see something my daughter can read to find out where she came from, just like I read these other history books and saw where the labor movement came from. My grandfather worked in the brass industry, my father worked in the brass industry, and I'm working in the brass industry. Now I'll have something my daughter's children will be able to read and find out where their ancestors were coming from. To me that's what it's all about.

Quentin Garatoni
Rod Mill
Anaconda Industries
Ansonia, Conn.

CONTENTS

ACKNOWLEDGMENTS

We would like to thank:

The Advocate Press: Dennis Pearson, Co-manager

John Ambrozaitis, Jr.

Michael Ames of Temple University Press

Anaconda Industries: Kathy Nyhan Judd, Librarian; Rod Thorpe, Director, Metallurgy and Research

Ansonia *Evening Sentinel*

Emil Antinarella

Stanley Audietis

Elizabeth Baker

Baker Library, Harvard Graduate School of Business Administration: Florence Bartoshesky, Director, Manuscripts and Archives Division; Liz Grisaru, Marjorie Kierstad, staff

Marie Balco

Eddie Becker

Bergin Center

Eva M. Bergin

Danny Bialek

Robert Bisaillon

The Rev. John Blackall, St. Cecilia's Church, Waterbury

Marty Blatt

Sandos Bologna

Bridgeport Brass Co., Seymour: Carl Drescher, Plant Manager

Nancy Brigham

Cecelia Bucki

Paul Buhle

Sarah Cappella

Romeo Caputo

Angie Cardosa

Babe Carpentieri

Century Brass Products, Inc.: Jack Lynch, Vice President, Mill Products Division; Emil Howes, Director of Personnel; Robert F. Dunn, Vice-President, General Products; Les Hawley, General Products Division; Ruth Hutt, Manager, Office Services; Irene Salvatore, Office Services Department

Century Employees Recreation Association

John Brown Childs

Frank Cipriano

Connecticut Humanities Council: Ron Wells, Executive Director; Bruce Fraser, Associate Director

Connecticut State Labor Council, AFL-CIO: John Driscoll, President

Connecticut State Library, Archives and Genealogy Division: Eunice di Bella

Tim Costello

Tom Curtin

Customized Computer Systems, Inc., New Haven

Jill Cutler

Anna Davin

Doreen Del Bianco

Derby Historical Society: Dorothy Larson, Director

Derby Senior Center: Helen Lewis, Executive Director; Theresa Tiano, Information and Referral

Michael De Santis

Irving Dichter

Shirley Dichter

Mary Diogostine

Tony Diogostine

Keith Dix
Rachel Doolady
James Dougherty
James Early
English History Workshop
Frieda Ewen
Art Finelli
Margaret Foley
William Freeman
John Fussell
Quentin Garatoni
Ovide Garceau
Jonathan Garlock
John Gatison
Tony Gerace
Diane Gold
Heidi Gottfried
Jim Green
Anita Gregorski
Neil Griffin
Dennis Guillaume
Arlease Gutridge
Fran Harvey
Christy Hoffman
Hyotha Hofler
Henry Hook
Fritz H. Hummel
Peter Hylwa
Corinne Iacovino
Leonard Insogna
The staff of the Institute for Labor
    Education and Research, New
    York City: David Gordon, Jane
    Hammond, Judy Hilkey, Mike
    Merrill, June Sager, Sally
    Silvers, and Cydney Pullman
Fr. Daniel Johnson
Helen Johnson
Carlos Julia
D. A. Kaplan
Sandy Kay
Fred Kelly

Lydia Kleiner
Walter Kloss
Joyce Kornbluh
Mike Laban
Patricia Land
Peter Langston
Lithuanian Club of Waterbury,
    Inc.
Dom Lobo
Daniel Loffredo
Terry Longo
Jewel Lucarelli
Lorraine Lugar
Gustave Luschenat
Staughton Lynd
Anne Mackinnon
George Magnan
Neil Maloney
Bill Mancini
Fran Marcuse
Peter Marcuse
Massachusetts History Workshop
The staff of the Mattatuck
    Museum: Ann Smith, Director;
    Marie Galbraith; Dorothy
    Cantor; Audrey Grossman; and
    Jeannette Malich
Joseph P. Micci
MIT Library
Hon. John Stuart Monagan
David Montgomery
Dolores Monti
Sid Monti
Bill Moriarty
Louise Moshe
Henry Murray III
Alannah Nardello
National Archives and Records
    Service
National Endowment for the
    Humanities
David F. Noble

Jim Noonan
Jim Overton
Palladino Center
David Palmquist
Pennsylvania State University
    Library Historical Collections:
    Ronald L. Filipelli, Archivist
Domingo Pereira
Claude Perry
Robert E. Phillips
Joe Pilkington
Marshall J. Rachleff
Peter Rachleff
Mariano Ramos
Sid Resnick
Susan Reverby
Bobby Richards
Genevieve Rodriguez
Mary Rosengrant
Roy Rosensweig
Steve Sapolsky
Ron Schatz
Barbara Schulgasser
Scovill Mfg. Co.: Paul F. Beetz,
    Jr., Director of Corporate
    Relations
Seymour Senior Center
Dottie Shami
Bob Sherry
Silas Bronson Library
Bertha Silva
Russell Sobin
Erasmus Sparks
Crystal Steele
Marty Stolar
Chris Stone
Kathy Stone
Ed Thompson
UAW: Art Shy, Administrator of
    Educational Activities
UAW, Region 9-A: Ted Barrett,
    Director; Jerry Rocker,

Assistant Director; Richard Days, Education Director

UAW Amalgamated Local 1827, Eddie Labacz, President

UAW Amalgamated Local 1251, Art Muzzicato, President

UAW Collection, Walter P. Reuther Library, Wayne State University, Detroit, Michigan: Walter Pflug, Assistant Director

UAW Local 1078, Bobby Lombardo, President

UAW Local 1604, Ed Borowski, President

USWA Local 6445, Fred Smith, President

University of Connecticut– Waterbury Branch: Al Avitabile, Acting Director

Victor Vaitkus

Valley Legal Assistance

Valley Photo Co-op

Dave Vasek

Mike Vernovai

Janet Vigezzi

Mario Vigezzi

Mrs. Adelaide Walker

Waterbury Citizens Action Group

Waterbury *Republican-American*: Gene Martin, Editor

Waterbury Retired Workers Council: Richard Woodruff, Executive Director

Seymour Weingart

George Wheeler

Nathan Witt

Western Historical Collections, University of Colorado Libraries: John A. Brennan, Curator; Cassandra M. Volpe and staff

Work Relations Group

Mary Yost

John Yrchik

Joseph and Mary Yrchik

Daniel Zuraitis

The research for this book has been made possible in part by a grant from the National Endowment for the Humanities.

INTRODUCTION

This book is the story of one group of working people, the brass workers of the Naugatuck Valley in western Connecticut, told with the collaboration of those workers themselves. It tells how people came from many parts of the world to this, as to so many industrial regions in America; the conditions they experienced at work and in their communities; the ways of life they created for themselves; and the problems they continue to face today. It tells of the many ways that they tried to get together to meet their needs and solve their problems, and it shows the kinds of opposition that their efforts to make a better life have met.

For more than 150 years, the American brass industry was centered along the Naugatuck River in Connecticut. At its peak, more than 50,000 people were employed in it, or closely related industries, in what came to be known as the "Brass Valley." While every community is unique, the Brass Valley has witnessed many of the main social groups, movements, organizations, and developments of American working-class history. In many ways, the story of its workers is a history of the American working class in microcosm.

Until recently, most history has been the history of elites. The experiences of ordinary people, and how these experiences have affected the course of society, have largely been ignored. This book joins a growing body of materials that seek to redress that imbalance by presenting the history of non-elite groups.

Most people in our society are either workers themselves or come from working-class backgrounds. Some have had their family lore passed down to them, but virtually none have access to histories of working-class communities like those in which they were born and in which they may still live and work. This book seeks to make available to people their roots—not just in their own families, but in the diverse and common experiences of working people generally.

No doubt its most unusual feature is that it has been written with the collaboration of many working people in the community it describes. Not only did they serve, through oral history interviews, as a prime source of information, but they took part in many ways in shaping the form and the interpretations of the book. The process by which this collaboration took place is described in detail in the Appendix.

We have tried to show the connections among aspects of life that are too often dealt with in isolation. We examine the entire working class of a community, not just the members of one family or one ethnic group, men or women, Black or white. While much labor history has been concerned with either the work place and the struggles there or with cultural and social issues in the rest of the community, we stress the intimate connections between the world of work and the rest of life. We try to present the normal patterns of everyday existence, *and* to show how, at times, great mass struggles have developed out of them. We bring this history right up to the present to emphasize the relevance of the past to the problems our society faces today.

There is a dialogue about the history of working people in our society, but it tends to go on in academic forms hardly accessible to those it is about. Thus, we have designed this book to be of interest and of use to the communities it describes and to others like them. Working people have been brought into the historical dialogue as col-

laborators on this book; we hope, in addition, they will enter the dialogue as readers. The attempt to understand the conditions of one's life and the forces that have shaped them is a fundamental aspect of human dignity. It is also one of the prerequisites for controlling those forces.

One thing unites the people who are presented in this book: their lives have been shaped by the necessity to spend most of their waking hours working for others, under conditions they do not control, for purposes they do not determine. They live in a system that treats them as tools. Alex Lopez, who came to the Naugatuck Valley from Puerto Rico with the most recent wave of immigrants, and who

has worked in a Waterbury brass mill for the past twenty-eight years, expressed a feeling about this that virtually all the working people described in this book might well share: "A foreman from another department would come and say, 'I want to borrow a man.' 'Hey, you, go with him.' They did that to me. I didn't say much in those days; I didn't know what to say. But I didn't think that was right. It was just like they borrowed a pencil. A person is a person, not a thing."

P A R T I

Prelude to the Brass Industry

The first residents of the Naugatuck Valley were the Mattatuck Indians. They were supplanted by English settlers, who spread throughout the Connecticut hinterland. Print Collection, Art, Prints and Photographs Division, The New York Public Library, Astor, Lenox and Tilden Foundations.

The great economic growth of the United States in the nineteenth century gave rise to many specialized industrial districts. Detroit became a center of the carriage industry, Pittsburgh of the steel industry, New Britain of the hardware industry. The Naugatuck Valley of Connecticut, where people began making fashionable brass buttons around the start of the nineteenth century, soon became the center for the manufacture of brass and brass products— from snap fasteners and hinges to clocks and watches to electrical wire and artillery shells.

The original brass enterprises began primarily as household activities of local families. As the production expanded, small facto-

TABLE I
Connecticut Domination of Brass Manufacturing, 1890

Product	Rank (Conn.)	No. of operatives (Conn.)			No. of pieceworkers (Conn.)			Capital Expenditures ($)		Value of products ($)	
		Men*	Women*	Children	Men*	Women*	Children	U.S.	Conn.	U.S.	Conn.
Brass	1	713	0	0	15	0	0	1,209,000	1,108,000	1,765,000	1,523,000
Brass and copper, rolled	1	1,119	68	15	216	166	16	8,042,000	4,768,000	8,381,000	4,170,000
Brass castings & finishing	1	2,391	162	0	491	263	20	18,663,000	7,109,000	24,344,000	7,428,000
Brassware	1	3,006	673	81	1,035	894	20	10,866,000	9,148,000	13,615,000	10,712,000
Buttons	3	214	93	15	127	401	19	3,089,000	915,000	4,217,000	928,000
Clocks	1	1,227	249	20	1,043	176	12	5,727,000	4,485,000	4,229,000	3,117,000
Watch and clock materials	2	129	23	0	0	0	0	661,784	192,300	787,310	260,090

*Over 16 years old.
Source: Compiled from U.S. Census data by Peter Rachleff.

ries were built and the owners often formed partnerships, which combined skills in production, marketing, and finance. These developed into companies controlled by one or a few families—almost all descended from the early Yankee settlers.

The brass masters' families formed a tight-knit group that controlled many aspects of both the community life and the industry. They established trade agreements which set prices and fixed market shares. They combined forces to develop sources of copper in the West. They cooperated in civic ventures ranging from the building of a railroad to the construction of a hotel for visiting dignitaries.

Farmers resting in a hayfield. By the early 1700s, farming communities had been established up and down the Naugatuck Valley. Print Collection, Art, Prints and Photographs Division, The New York Public Library, Astor, Lenox and Tilden Foundations.

Alongside farming, family members and perhaps a few hired hands would run blacksmith shops or make boots and shoes, textiles, or, as in this case, tinware. Courtesy, American Antiquarian Society.

Yankee peddler. The poor condition of the roads confined early Connecticut tinsmiths to selling their products from door to door in their own communities. Eventually they hired peddlers who went further afield, first on foot, then on horseback, and finally in specially designed wagons. Print Collection, Art, Prints and Photographs Division, The New York Public Library, Astor, Lenox and Tilden Foundations.

Early brass rolling. In 1790, Henry Grilley and his brothers began casting pewter buttons in their home in Waterbury. Two years later, they began manufacturing buttons from sheet brass; this was perhaps the first rolling of brass in the United States. They sold the buttons door-to-door; later, the buttons were added to the stock in trade of the tinware peddlers. By 1819, Connecticut produced four-fifths of the metal buttons made in the U.S.

Because button making depended upon hand labor, button companies could produce far more brass than they needed. So in the 1820s the brass button companies began rolling brass to sell on the open market. Thus brass rolling, the characteristic emphasis of the Connecticut brass industry, became established. Courtesy Scovill Collection.

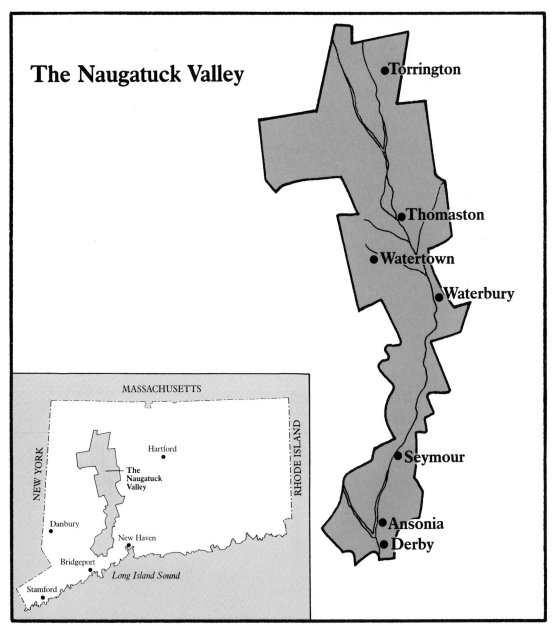

The Naugatuck Valley

- Torrington
- Thomaston
- Watertown
- Waterbury
- Seymour
- Ansonia
- Derby

MASSACHUSETTS

NEW YORK

RHODE ISLAND

Hartford

The Naugatuck Valley

Danbury

New Haven

Bridgeport

Long Island Sound

Stamford

Drawn from an original by Hyotha Hofler.

The brass industry, centered in Waterbury, spread up and down the Naugatuck River from Torrington to Ansonia, with outposts in Bridgeport, Bristol, New Haven, and elsewhere. By 1880, three quarters of all rolling and manufacturing of brass and copper in the U.S. was done in this region.

P A R T I I

From the Establishment of the Brass Industry to 1920:
The Era of the Immigrant

THE PEOPLE

1. English Skilled Workers: Importing the Industrial Revolution

The first "brass workers" were Yankee families who produced buttons in their homes or shops as an adjunct to their other occupations of farming, spinning, blacksmithing, storekeeping, or peddling. As their production increased, they may have occasionally hired relatives or neighbors to help out; their production was still too limited to require a greater work force.

While "Yankee ingenuity" contributed to the rise of the brass industry, the basic skills which made growth of the industry possible had to be imported. The "industrial revolution" in England was revolutionizing the brass button industry as well as others in the early nineteenth century. American button manufacturers could not compete with English producers either in price or in quality—they lacked the skilled workers who knew the new production techniques developing in England.

Starting in 1820, the Waterbury entrepreneurs began to import skilled workers from Birmingham. Toolmakers, rollers, die sinkers, casters, platers, and burnishers were all brought to the Valley.

According to a story widely known in the Valley, skilled workers were smuggled out of England by brass manufacturer Israel Holmes. "Mr. Holmes transported his craftsmen in casks from England. They were thus smuggled on board ship. After arrival on this side, the workmen again entered their casks to be drawn ashore at night and transported to Waterbury."

Charming as this story may be, it is folklore, not history. As P. W. Bishop, a business historian who worked extensively in the Scovill papers of that era, pointed out, the law against migration of workers from England was repealed in 1825, four years before Israel Holmes' famous journey.*

The skilled workers enjoyed a high level of power and autonomy. One roller at Scovill, the first of the Waterbury brass companies, frequently left Waterbury to visit a brother in New Jersey. The Scovills and their customers were forced to wait until his return for their rolled metal. When his brother, who had also been hired as a roller, was discharged, one of the Scovills wrote, "I have wanted this to happen a long time but have been fearful of having the mill burnt or something else happen."

The English workers tried to maintain the secrecy of their skills.

*P. W. Bishop, "History of Scovill Manufacturing Company," manuscript in Scovill collection, Baker Library, pp. 175–78.

Wire drawers at Holmes and
Hotchkiss, for example, refused to
let apprentices approach machines
that were in operation. In Wol-
cottsville (now Torrington), the
kettlemen demanded and got a
separate building that was off limits to Americans.

The majority of the imported
Englishmen became American citizens and permanent residents of
the area. By the mid-1830s, local
workers had learned the craft
skills, and production was no
longer entirely dependent on the
English workers. But the jealous
guarding of craft knowledge as a
basis for skilled workers' power remained for more than a century.

*Four generations of Gabriels. It was common for several family members to be
employed at the same company. Joseph Gabriel, Jr., 11, is pictured here with his
father, grandfather, and great-grandfather, all employees of Scovill. When this photo
was published in the* Scovill Bulletin *in 1920, the caption claimed that "Joseph, too,
hopes some day to join the ranks of the Scovill Manufacturing Company." Courtesy
Scovill Collection.*

2. The Immigrant Work Force: "They Leave the Place of Their Birth and That's against Their Will"

The growth of the brass industry—and the American economy
as a whole—corresponded to a period of enormous economic and social disruption throughout Europe.
From Ireland to Russia, traditional
forms of peasant agriculture were
giving way to capitalist farming.
Population growth and various
forms of private enclosure of com-
munal lands were leading to the
impoverishment of millions of
rural people. At the same time,
democratic and nationalist movements were developing, only to

meet severe repression from local
despots or imperial powers. Millions came to the United States.
Some planned to work, save
money, and return to their homelands; others hoped to make the
new country their home. Successive waves of immigrants came
from England, Scandinavia, Germany, Ireland, Italy, and the various countries of the Austrian and
Russian Empires. Somewhat similar conditions brought immigrants
from French Canada into the New
England area as well. Many dozen
nationalities were represented in
the immigration to the Valley. This
chapter can only focus on a few of
them.

Every aspect of the lives of the

early brass workers was shaped by
their relationship to work. The
very fact that they lived in the
Brass Valley was a result of the fact
that they could find work there.
When the work dried up, large
numbers simply left the area to
seek it elsewhere or to return to
their homelands. Families were
disrupted as large numbers of
single men—and, in some cases,
single women—came to America seeking work. The ability to
reunite families depended on
whether or not there was work. Individual opportunities depended
upon the availability of work.
When unskilled jobs were plentiful
and those requiring education
scarce, most children of mill work-

TABLE 2
The Changing Composition of Waterbury's Population, 1890–1930

Place of birth	1890	1900	1910	1920	1930
Native-born, native parents	19,068	30,941	47,643	61,821	
Connecticut	14,984				
New York	1,597				
Massachusetts	1,022				
Foreign-born	9,578	15,368	25,498	29,894	
Ireland	5,402	5,866	5,838	4,507	
Canada	1,362	2,266	1,901	1,521	
Germany	887	1,195	1,433	1,010	
England	692	938	1,175	1,086	
Italy	308	2,007	6,567	9,232	
Poland	n.a.	277	n.a.	1,629	
Russia	n.a.	1,265	5,600	3,209	
Lithuania	n.a.	n.a.	n.a.	3,674	
Native-born, foreign parents	10,862	n.a.	n.a.	n.a.	
Native-born, "mixed" parents	584	1,083	1,359	7,484	9,322

Source: Compiled from U.S. Census data by Peter Rachleff.

ers left school early and followed their parents into the plants.

Nonetheless, the workers were also people who were trying to make a life for themselves under conditions they did not control. They created their own ways to survive and to realize their own values in an industrial world in which they were treated as little more than "labor."

THE ETHNIC GROUPS

The Irish
Starting in the 1830s, large numbers of Irish immigrants, faced with famine and the deliberate clearing of peasants from the land, came into American industrial areas, including the Naugatuck Valley.

Frank Keane's mother came from Ireland, alone, when she was about fifteen, and went to work as a do-

mestic. His father came from Ardford, in County Kerry, to Waterbury, where he worked at Chase and Scovill. Born in 1919, Keane grew up in an Irish neighborhood which he remembers fondly. "I lived in a ghetto, really—an Irish ghetto. It was a very exciting and dynamic environment. A strong work ethic bound the community together, and a fine family, very adequate housing and warm neighbors and friends made for a thoroughly rewarding childhood." Most of his brothers and sisters worked at Scovill at one time or another. Keane worked there, too, on summer vacations. He earned a B.S. at Holy Cross College in Worcester, Mass., and a Master's Degree in Education at Trinity College in Hartford. For many years he has taught history in the Waterbury school system, and for the last twelve years he has been

TABLE 3

Foreign Stock in Waterbury, by Parents' Place of Birth, 1890–1920

Place of birth	1890	1900	1910	1920
Foreign stock (aggregate)	28,646	45,859	73,141	91,715
1st generation	9,535	15,310	25,498	29,894
2nd generation	10,862	18,169	28,590	38,695
1st and 2nd generation (aggregate)	18,140	29,717	54,088	
Ireland	11,690	14,226	15,413	
Germany	1,627	2,369	3,061	
Canada	1,463	2,777	2,621	
England	916	1,398	1,971	
Scotland	460	662	865	
Italy	389	2,815	10,302	
Russia	n.a.	1,890	8,028	

Source: Compiled from U.S. Census data by Peter Rachleff.

Chairman of the History Department at Kennedy High School. He enjoys traveling, and in 1979 was awarded a fellowship to study at Jagiellonian University in Cracow, Poland. In the summer of 1981, he toured the countries in Eastern Europe. He and his wife, the former Mary Blake, are the parents of four children. Keane is the brother-in-law of Jim Cusack, introduced on page 72.

Frank Keane: If you travel through Ireland, you see these little stone houses that they just left in the 1840s and 1850s. They just got up, stuffed stuff in a sheet, threw it over their shoulders, and walked down to some port city. Tried to get out of there.

By 1876, Irish immigrants and their children made up more than 43 percent of Waterbury's population. They originally settled on a hill called the Abrigador (now known as Pine Hill) and spread in the area of Baldwin Street, near the Scovill factory.

John Monagan's grandfather was a hand caster at Scovill; his Uncle Bill was head of the casting shop. His father was a physician and surgeon in Waterbury for many years. Monagan remembers the discrimination his father faced because he was Irish: "When my father graduated from the University of Pennsylvania as a doctor, he couldn't get on the staff of Waterbury Hospital. That was in 1899. When

he graduated from Bristol High School, the establishment had a hell of a time because he was the top person in the class, and they didn't want to let him be the valedictorian. All this gradually changed. My uncle Bill could be a member of the country club. That would be about 1916." A dozen members of his family in three generations worked at the Scovill plant, and Monagan was employed there for two summers himself. A graduate of Dartmouth and Harvard Law School, he has been a member of the Connecticut Bar since 1938, and has practiced law in Waterbury for many years. He served as President of the Waterbury Board of Aldermen, as a Member of the Board of Finance for three years, and as Mayor of the city for five years. He was Congressman from the Fifth District for seven terms and a member of the House Committees on Foreign Affairs and Government Operations. After leaving the Congress, he was the senior Washington partner of a New York law firm for eight years. He now lives in Washington, where he is doing historical and biographical writing and serving as the President of the Former Members of Congress, the Congressional Alumni Association. He is married to the former Rosemary Brady, and they are the parents of five children.

John Monagan: This song is written about the people who are coming to work in the brass mills of Waterbury. The "half past ten from Tralee town" was the train that left Tralee, which is in County Kerry, Ireland. It went to Queenstown, which is now Cobh, where the greenhorns would get on the boat and come to the U.S. It is a real folk song out of the experiences of the brass workers, written by a onetime Waterbury fireman, Faker Sullivan. I used to hear it sung by Packy Moylan, the detective lieutenant.

Scovill's Rolling Mill
by Michael (Faker) Sullivan

The half past ten from Tralee town to
*   Queenstown on its way*
Brings thousands of our boys and
*   girls off to America.*
They leave the place of their birth
*   and that's against their will*

And they labor for their bread in
*   Scovill's Rolling Mill.*

You may work at the pickle tub, you
*   may work in the yard,*
You may work at the scratching
*   machines, for that's not very hard.*
And when Wednesday comes around
*   again, your belly with beer you'll*
*   fill*
And you'll spend the money you
*   earned hard in Scovill's Rolling*
*   Mill.*

"Good morning, Mr. Wilcox."
*   "Good morning," he will say.*
"Have you e'er a job for me Willie at
*   a dollar and a half a day?"*
He will give you a bag and a piece of
*   wire and your eyes you'll begin to*
*   rub,*
For your daily occupation is beside
*   the pickle tub.*

You may work at the muffles. They
*   say that it is swell,*
But take a tip from me, boys, I'd
*   rather be in hell.*
If he gave me a job to sweep the
*   floor, I'd do it with a will.*
But I'll be damned if I'd work at the
*   pickle tub for Wilcox in the Mill.*

You may go down to Randolph's.
*   You may go over to Booth's.*
You may go down to Benedict's and
*   Chase's is no use.*
And when pay day comes around
*   again, your belly with beer you'll*
*   fill*
And you'll curse the day you sailed
*   away to Scovill's Rolling Mill.*

You may go down to New York, my

boy, and hear the ocean roar.
You imagine you see Mother standing
*   at the cabin door,*
Crying "Darling Jack, come back
*   again and the old farm you can*
*   till,*
Then no more you'll roam from your
*   native home to work in the Rolling*
*   Mill."*

And when your health and wealth
*   are gone, and you think you'd like*
*   to go home,*
Your friends will get a raffle up to
*   ship you across the foam,*
Where your Mother will greet you
*   with a smile and tears her eyes will*
*   fill.*
She knows your health was broken
*   down in Scovill's Rolling Mill.*

And when you arrive in Ireland, the
*   boys and girls to see,*
They will ask you all about the land
*   you call the brave and free.*
You will answer them quite modestly
*   though it's against your will.*
You know your health was broken
*   down in Scovill's Rolling Mill.*

And when you are six months in
*   Ireland and feeble is your walk,*
The friends you knew while in your
*   youth, to them you'll scarcely talk.*
Your dance is gone, your voice is still,
*   six feet of earth you'll fill*
And they'll lay you away in the
*   burying ground due to*
*   Scovill's Rolling Mill.*

Frank Keane describes growing up in the Irish community of Waterbury early in the twentieth century.

Frank Keane: There was a big immigration from southern Europe and eastern Europe, but there were still plenty of Irish coming over at that time.

I'm first generation here. My mother and father were born in Ireland. The first job my father had was laying Belgian block in the streets of Baltimore. He tells me he walked from Waterbury to Baltimore, and I believe it. I guess it wasn't so unusual at that time. He came to Waterbury and worked up at Chase's. Ultimately he worked at Scovill. I worked on the same machines with him in the mill.

My mother came over shortly after that. She came out alone. She was a young girl, maybe fifteen years old. It had to be some kind of a trip. She had a brother who

Anne O'Brien. Born in Ireland in 1863, she came to the U.S. at age ten and worked at Scovill until 1920. Courtesy Scovill Collection.

preceded her to Waterbury. Life was difficult, so she made the trek herself.

My mother went to work as a domestic. She was a maid or a cook, as most young Irish girls were at that time. It might have been for a Goss or a Sperry [prominent brass industry families]. She didn't work after she got married. There were eight children in the family.

Generally speaking, it was almost marrying outside the church if an Irishman from County Kerry married one from Queens County. It wasn't a case of being Irish; it was a case of, "Where're you from?" It hung over until my generation. All the people from one county, I think Kerry people, were buried from Mulville's. All the Queenies, Queens County, would be buried from Bergin's.

South Street in Waterbury might be Queenies or Kerries. Down around my own area, upper Baldwin Street, they were mostly Kerries. You had some people from other counties. But the main rivalry in Waterbury seemed to be between the Queenies, from Queens County, and County Kerry. For some strange reason, that's where the bulk of the Irish in Waterbury probably came from. There was a built-in nationalistic spirit in a local sense.

There were clubs, but not Queenie- or Kerry-type clubs. You had the AOH, or the Hey-Ho-Haich as they said—the Hiber-

nians. Or the Irish-American Club, which became a political association.

The Irish could speak the language. So they had an edge on just about all the other groups.

The Italians

By 1920, Italians formed the largest group of foreign-born in much of the Valley, with 9,232 people born in Italy in Waterbury alone.

Giovanni Parziale. In World War I a recent immigrant and Scovill employee, Parziale returned to Europe in the uniform of the United States army. Courtesy Scovill Collection.

James Tiso was born in 1890 in Italy. As a youth, he worked as a farm laborer, and learned to drive teams of horses. He came to America with his family shortly before World War I. They lived in Pennsylvania for a while, where many Italians were being hired to lay and maintain railroad tracks. One of his brothers was killed there in a train accident. Shortly afterward, the family settled in Waterbury. His younger brother, Liberto Tiso, was shot dead by police and company guards during the 1920 strike in Waterbury. After working in a number of Waterbury factories, Tiso went to work at the Chase tube mill, from which he retired after thirty-five years of service. Tiso lives in a house he owns in a Waterbury neighborhood where the Italian language is just as likely to be heard as English. At the age of 90, he still maintained a vegetable garden that filled his entire back yard.

James Tiso: My father came in 1901 to America. He came into New York. From New York he went to Pennsylvania. From Pennsylvania he came back to Italy. In Italy, the same story. We were poor. He stayed three more years. No money at all. Ten cents a day. He worked like everybody else. Slave. On a farm. Pick and a shovel. Cut the woods.

When he went back to America, he first brought my brother, who was seventeen years old. "Maybe me and my son make a dollar, we go to Italy, we buy a little piece of land, we live better"—he figured that way. But the devil figured another way. He came to America, brought my brother, my cousin, another cousin; he bring five people on his shoulders. He was the boss, responsible for the kids.

He stopped in New York. The Italian office got the people from across. This guy says, "You go this way; you go that way." He sent those people off on the roads, up in the mountains, do work on a farm, cut the woods, mine the coal. We had to pay a dollar. The dollar we didn't have, but when we made a dollar, we had to send it. That's where the people started—a crook. To work, you've got to bring your dollar.

My father had been in Pennsylvania. My cousin lived in New Jersey. He cleaned up the table at the bar, swept, washed, fifty cents a day. Another cousin, the same thing.

In 1913, I was getting big myself. I was fifteen or sixteen. Work like a slave. They sent me a letter. My aunt was in Italy with me, my brother, and my brother the baby. They sent for us to come to America. We all come at one time, in 1913.

Caroline Nardello's family came from Italy in 1900; she was born in 1902. "My mother went to school. She learned to read and write and sew. She never went to work in the country. In the old country my father was a musician, but when he came here he was a shoemaker. He used to play in the band in Waterbury. He'd go to all the parades. When my mother came here, she worked for a while in a dressmaking shop on South Main. After that she started having children— she had eleven children." Caroline Nardello began working at American Brass in 1916 when she was 14. She has worked at many other plants in the Waterbury area, including Plume and Atwood, American Ring, Waterbury Paper Box, and Waterbury Clock. Her sisters worked at "the box shop." Her brothers worked at Oakville Pin and Scovill. (Caroline Nardello is the mother-in-law of Alannah Nardello, introduced in the Appendix, page 273.)

Caroline Nardello: One time [my mother] worked at American Brass, but not long. Leaving all the kids home was kind of hard for my mother. I kind of took care [of the kids]. I was the oldest. We used to jump rope and play hide-and-seek. We used to jump in the leaves. But before you'd know it, I'd have to go home and help with the children.

Work was very bad in those days. If you got a job, you'd work for a while; then there was no work.

My father had his own shoe shop for a while. Then he'd go back to work in American Brass for a while. The work was kind of bad. The bosses in those days were kind of tough. He'd quit, then go back.

The men used to be out [socializing] more than the women in those days. On Sunday my father and four or five men used to play cards. Not for money, just to pass away the time on a Sunday afternoon. That's about all there was to do in those days.

They didn't have any cars while I was growing up. We always had to walk. We didn't mind walking in those days. We wouldn't take the trolley, we'd walk, even in the snow and everything.

I guess we had more fun than my mother did. She came here as a young girl and settled down; she got married. She never really had any fun until I got big and used to take her to the minstrels. The mothers didn't have time, because they always had the supper on the stove, the ironing, taking care of babies. She had to work hard. My mother had the time to go visiting.

Art Finelli's father, Antonio Finelli (also known as Jack O'Brien) came to the U.S. from Italy when he was ten or twelve. One of nine children, Art was born in Waterbury in 1919. In 1939, he went to work at Scovill in the Anodizing Room and Lacquer Wash. After military service, he went to work at Chase's, where he worked for many years as a crane operator, jitney driver, carpenter, and in the

scrap room. He was active in the union, and was somewhat unusual among local union leaders in being a well-known Republican for much of that time. He was the president of the Chase local during the difficult period of the company's demise. He is happily retired and lives in Waterbury with his wife. They have two sons, one of whom works at Scovill as a C.P.A.

Art Finelli: My father came here as a very young boy. He learned how to speak English well. When he first came, he helped drive a mule with the mail in Boston. Then he worked in the coal mines in Pennsylvania. Then he settled in Waterbury because he had some friends here. He went to work in Scovill's.

At that time he worked in the trucking department. There was no such thing as jitneys or forklifts. Then it was just brute force.

No horses—the human being was the horse.

There used to be the "Romans" coming from Italy. They were the big, strong guys. My father used to get them all jobs in Scovill's. He became a foreman and he was able to get all these people to come to work. They were happy to find work.

[My father got into management because] he could talk English. He was a selectman in the city of Waterbury for about four years. This is 1928 up to about 1934. He was a Republican.

If a guy came over from Italy and went into the shop and became a citizen, my father took him down and made him a Republican.

The Lithuanians
Waterbury's next-largest ethnic group was the Lithuanians. Most of them settled in the "Brooklyn section," which, until the 1880s, had been predominantly Irish.

Daniel Zuraitis and Peter Kukanskis were interviewed together at the Lithuanian Club in the Brooklyn section of Waterbury. Both can be found there at odd hours, engaged in an extensive remodeling of the club's hall.

Daniel Zuraitis was born in Waterbury in 1928. For the past few years he has been collecting photos and other materials from the Lithuanian community, which he displays at the Lithuanian Club. "It was a Lithuanian trait to have

took them to the dump. Like every ethnic group." Most of his uncles worked in the brass mills. His father was a general contractor, and Daniel Zuraitis followed him into the business.

Peter Kukanskis was born in the Brooklyn section of Waterbury before World War I and lived there for much of his life. His father was a plumber. Peter Kukanskis had hoped to go to college, but the Great Depression put an end to his plans; he followed his father into plumbing instead. He is proud of the fact that he can still speak Lithuanian.

Daniel Zuraitis: The family was dispersed in the old country because, as soon as they reached about seven years old, they were shipped out to different farms. There was still a serf system really. Everyone that didn't have land rights [did that]. They were apprenticed. My uncle Frank was apprenticed as a klumpenmaker, a wooden-shoemaker. Vincent was apprenticed, when he was seven or eight years old, to a man who traveled and traded—traded horses, cattle, chickens, and whatever. He tended the stuff the man bought. My dad was a gooseherder. That was his thing at seven years old. My uncle Sam's thing was that he was apprenticed to a gypsy circus that toured Germany, Poland, Lithuania, Latvia, and Estonia.

The way I understood it, anybody traveling through the town-body traveling through the town-

their group pictures taken periodically and send them to people overseas to show them they were still alive and well. They all had boxes, and the second generation usually put them in the attic or the cellar. The next generation just

ship that was looking for additional help [would take them]. They were cheap. All they had to do was feed them; they didn't have to pay them. And if times were tough, the parents looked for somebody to take a kid.

The apprenticeship wasn't the concept that we have today. This was really a locked-up society. This is my impression from what I was told.

My uncle Frank was the first to come, I think in 1894. He had come out of a church in Lithuania and there was a guy signing contracts with people who would work in America, promising that the streets were paved with gold and the like. So he signed up.

When Frank signed up there was a two-year work hitch in the

Joseph Zuraitis, Daniel Zuraitis' father. Courtesy Daniel Zuraitis.

Vincent and Frank Zuraitis, Daniel Zuraitis' uncles. Courtesy Daniel Zuraitis.

forests of Washington and Oregon. So he came, steerage, through the canal and up. He worked this [two-year] contract and found out that he had to work another contract, because the first contract only paid for his way and food. So he worked four years. Then it took him approximately a year to work his way across the country. Six of them ended up in New Jersey and worked in the car barns building trolley cars.

As soon as they had a few dollars, the first thing was to bring another brother over. So he brought Vincent. I think that was 1903. Two of them were working, and they were saving up to bring Joseph, my father, over. Then three of them were working, saving up to bring Sam and John and Patrick over.

My dad came in 1907. My mother came in 1910. Most of them came to avoid the draft. They were Lithuanians, and they refused to serve in the czar's army. Lithuania at that time was under Russian occupation. As soon as they got anywhere near draft age, they just left for other parts.

They had to have fake documents in order to cross the borders. Most of them left out of Bremen, Germany. There were al-

ways [ways] of falsifying [documents] or sneaking out at night.

My mother's parents were fairly affluent; they were burghers. They took in boarders or people who were passing through, so they had extra rooms to rent. My mother and her sisters came. Her oldest sister left to work in England as an upstairs maid for wealthy families. The next two girls were Anastasia and Ona, my mother. Their mother had died at my mother's birth. The father had remarried. She had family. She couldn't stand the father's kids. So they just wanted out. The father bought them the tickets.

My father and his brothers came to Waterbury in 1909. While in New Jersey, they had secured land in Oakville [just north of Water-

Ona Zuraitis, Daniel Zuraitis' mother. Courtesy Daniel Zuraitis.

bury], a dollar down and a dollar a month. So they were under the impression that they had a big farm up in this section of the country. That's how they came to Waterbury. Frank ended up in the brass mills. Sam ended up in the brass mills. Vincent ended up working for himself. My father ended up as a general contractor.

Coming here and not finding the streets paved with gold, they did find the opportunity to work and save, and they found that the church was off their back; the government really stayed off their back. They felt the freedom that they never experienced in their life overseas.

Peter Kukanskis: My dad belonged to this club, and he also belonged to the 103 Club they had. That was the Lithuanian Citizens Political Club. My mum belonged to one or two Catholic societies that the women had. They were always active in all these affairs, because that was the only gathering—your own group, your own people.

They used to put on theaters and plays here. They'd have dinner dances every so often. Wrestling matches.

Zuraitis: The women used to get together, too. When there wasn't an activity they could go to, they would gather at one house, and they would do what they call "tear feathers." They would make the featherdowns for gifts for the next person that was getting married. They'd save their feathers, and the girls would get together one night and gossip and pull the feathers. Goose and duck.

Kukanskis: They had it tough, the old folks, when I think of it. Not knowing the language. Different people used to be here, like the Irish, the ones that had been here a little longer. They called them Polacks and [said], "Get out of here!" It was tough, but it never hurt anybody. They took it with a grain of salt.

Like any Europeans, [the Lithuanians] came here to get away from the rule of the czar or the kaiser or somebody or another that they were dominated by. I suppose they came here with the intention of staying here, the big-

gest part of them. There were quite a few who went back and lived there; they made a few dollars here and they went back.

As soon as somebody worked and saved a few bucks, they had to have a thing of their own. So out in Bethlehem and Morris, most of the farmers are Lithuanians. I was a little shaver, I remember. Right down on Riverside, to the old market, all these farmers would come in with the horse and buggies. Sell whatever products they had just to get a couple of dollars. There'd be mobs of them down there. They were all friends of different people. This one would buy from that one. That one's cheese is better; that one's eggs are bigger. It was what they raised on that farm.

Poles and Russians

Poles and Russians formed a large part of the immigrant work force, especially in the lower valley towns such as Ansonia and Seymour. The discussion below was recorded one evening at the house of Joseph and Mary Yrchik in Seymour. Joe Yrchik, John Chubat, Sam Kwochka, and Frank Pochron are all retired workers at the Seymour Brass Co. (now part of Bridgeport Brass) and sons of Polish and Russian immigrants who worked there before them.

Joe Yrchik's father came to the U.S. around 1912 and started working at Seymour Manufacturing Company in 1914. His mother

came around the same time, following her brother to the area.

Joe Yrchik was born in Seymour in 1916. He got out of school in 1936 and followed his father into Seymour Mfg. He spent three years in the service, then returned to Seymour Mfg. He was a steward in the union for two years, but then decided not to run again. He retired in 1980 with 43½ years at the company.

Mary Yrchik, also Polish, comes from Naugatuck. Their son, John Yrchik, is introduced on page 20. Their daughter is a speech therapist in California. In addition to working in a plant, Joe Yrchik was a supernumerary policeman in Seymour for thirty-two years. "That's what helped to get the kids through school. Thirty-two years was a long time to work two jobs."

John Chubat was born in

Seymour in 1911. Just before World War I, the entire family went back to Russia to see John Chubat's grandfather, who was sick and dying. When the war broke out, his father tried to run away, but was caught and drafted into the Russian army. Then he was caught and imprisoned by the Germans and spent five years in a German camp. In 1919 he was released, a broken man. John and his mother lived in the forest, in fox holes, in the Russian winter. "During the Revolution, the soldiers fed us. But after that, we had nothing to eat. We ate grass, clover, leaves from the trees. I was skinny. More children died than in the war. I contracted a sickness like malaria. Three times they pronounced me dead. When I came to, there was a candle in my hand."

When John Chubat was eigh-

teen, his mother wrote to her sister in Seymour to bring him to America. "We had no money—they would have to send me the money and guarantee to take care of me." He came in 1929 and got a job at Seymour Mfg. in 1930. "It was very hard because it was Depression times and because I couldn't speak a word of English. That was my handicap. I was skilled; they saw I had a talent for work on the drawbench. In those days the operator had to go to the blacksmith shop and make his own dies. I grasped measurement fast. The second year I went to night school. It was for citizenship. The teacher said she couldn't teach me anything else. It was very difficult. In the shop I couldn't learn English—everybody spoke incorrectly or colloquial English. People would laugh at how I spoke my English, but that didn't bother me. My foreman saw how ambitious I was to learn English. He bought me fifteen volumes of books in English as a present for me. He was very strict, but he felt sorry for me. I still have them."

John Chubat was married in 1939. He was in the shop continuously for forty-four years. He can read and write Russian and Polish and understand Ukranian. "I have two cultures. This is my country, and I would never go back for a million dollars." He belongs to the Three Saints Russian Orthodox Church in Ansonia, where he has been a parishioner for fifty-two years. He retired in 1973, and lives on the Seymour border in Oxford.

Sam Kwochka was born in Seymour in 1916. His father came to the U.S. in 1914. His uncle was in Seymour, served in the American army during World War I, and sent Sam Kwochka's father the money to come over. His family came from Austria, but spoke a dialect of Russian. His father was a builder, with skills in carpentry, plumbing, and electricity; he worked in the annealing depart-

ment at Seymour Manufacturing.

Sam Kwochka started work in 1929 in charge of a crew of paper boys for the New Haven *Register*. In 1934 he worked digging and installing artesian wells. In 1934–35 he worked for the Seymour Water Company. With no other work available, in 1935 he went into the Seymour Mfg. Co. He gave up the opportunity for more schooling

and stayed in the mill to help out his family. He retired in 1979. He lives in Oxford, on the Seymour line.

Sam Kwochka speaks Russian, Polish, and Lithuanian. He married in 1948 and has a daughter, a schoolteacher, who lives in Naugatuck. He writes in an elegant, almost calligraphic script, and speaks with an eloquence to match it. His knowledge of the history of the Seymour Mfg. Co., technological and otherwise, is encyclopedic.

Frank Pochron was born in Seymour in 1917, and spoke Polish instead of English until he entered first grade. He got his first job at Seymour Mfg. Co. in 1936. He worked four-and-a-half months on the slitters. The plant superintendent's office needed a typist and clerk and didn't want a woman. He had finished high school and could type, so he got the job. He

was in the first group drafted out of Seymour in World War II and was in the army about five years. He came back and went into time study—he went into management before there was a union, and so never belonged to it. He went to night school and took courses in time study. He got married and had a daughter, who is now a Ph.D. in medical research in New York City. He retired in June 1980 and lives in Seymour. Culturally he is quite similar to the others in this discussion, but his attitudes about some work issues can be markedly different.

John Chubat: In 1905 my father came from Russia. He worked in the wire mill. He went back to Russia in 1914. The war broke out, and he couldn't come back. He was drafted into the czar's army. I came here in 1929.

[The Russian immigrants] got jobs here because there were all the heavy industries. Our people had the jobs of rollers, wire drawers, cheap labor. They worked thirteen hours a day, seven cents an hour.

Frank Pochron: In Poland years ago, when you turned eighteen you had to get into the service. My father was in the cavalry. You could buy them out of the service if you paid a certain amount. At that time they said the roads in the United States were paved with gold. So they came over here to try to make a little better living and not have to be under that strict military stuff. He was here for a while, then he went back to Poland. He said it isn't all that it was cracked up to be. Then he came back here again. He said, "Well, I think I'd be better off." They wanted to come here, make their money, and go back to the old country.

Most of them used to settle around Chicago and that territory. When they knew somebody around this territory, they used to try to drift down this way. My mother drifted down through here.

Sam Kwochka: In Seymour were Italian, Lithuanian, German, Irish. On one side of town there were Germans. The Polish and the Russians were on the West Side.

Chubat: When I came here first, there was nobody who spoke English at all. When I went to work, they all spoke Russian or Polish, Italian, Lithuanian. They didn't have much schooling in Europe; some were illiterate.

Our people were a proud race. They didn't go for charity, a bag [of groceries]. They worked and they educated their children. Today they have doctors, lawyers in their families. They started from the rock, from nothing.

Pochron: I couldn't speak English until I went to the first grade. Then it was broken English. My mother couldn't go to schools in Poland because Russia took over.

Chubat: All these people spoke about seventy-five different dialects in the Russian language. How could you understand?

Pochron: They tried to learn the English language, but it was difficult. You got into your own communities, you had your own clubs, and you spoke your own language, so they never had an opportunity to speak English. My father went to night schools down here. That's how they learned English.

Cape Verdeans
One of the more tightly knit of the immigrant groups came from the Cape Verde Islands, between Portugal and Africa.

Roberto Alves (a pseudonym) came to the United States from the Cape Verde Islands in 1921. He started working at American Brass in Ansonia in 1926, and worked there until he retired in 1962.

Roberto Alves: In the old country there were no shops; it was all farm work. Raise a cow, pig, chicken; work the plow. In 1914, no rain, everything dry. In 1916 you had rain. From 1917 to 1921 no rain at all. Everything was dry. You've got to go someplace to make a living. So I came to this country.

Many, many people left [the islands]. Before, they came to this country. After America closed in 1922, nobody came. Now they've started to come [again].

When I came to this country in 1921, there was no work; all the shops were closed. When I worked in the cranberry bog, I worked ten hours for fifty cents—three dollars a week. That was no good. I didn't like it. Picking cranberries. On your knees, on the ground. Some people didn't have any jobs.

[When I first came here] it was very strange. When first I came here I was not satisfied. The country was all right, but I got five cents an hour, worked ten hours for fifty cents. You've got to eat, pay rent, buy clothes, shoes. But shoes at that time were pretty cheap; for three dollars you could buy a good pair of shoes. You'd buy suits for twenty-five dollars, the best one. Everything was cheap.

There were a lot of Cape Verdeans [when I came to Ansonia]. A lot of Portuguese. [In my place there were] twenty-four men in five rooms. Some worked nights, some worked days. The more money you made, the more you saved. I sent money back. When I got through work I'd come home, wash, eat, and go to bed, sleep.

I was a gauger, a roller. I started work as a helper. I took the place of a man who retired. It was tough work, a heavy job.

[There were no Portuguese foremen or group leaders] because before us there were the Irish and the English. No Polish, no Italian, no Lithuanian. Now you've got the union; since you've got the union, you've got everything. But before,

English, Irish, that's all—all rollers. After the union, there were no Portuguese foremen, but you could get the better jobs.

"My grandfather was a trader. He had a lot of people working for him. Cotton and things like that. My mother and all her family were sent to college. He educated all his children. My father always said he wanted his children to grow up to be something." Bertha Silva was born in 1908 in Scotland Neck, North Carolina. Her father was a shipyard worker who worked in places as distant as the Brooklyn Navy Yard and Portsmouth, Virginia. Silva grew up in Virginia and came to Connecticut on her own. When she was fifteen she went to work as a domestic for the Coes in Ansonia. "I didn't care to work for them. I did everything. I

helped cook. I was a mother's helper. I was paid about seven dollars a week, that's all. I had Thursdays a half-a-day and Sundays, a half-a-day off." She wanted to become a nurse but was dissuaded from it. "I loved to dance. I went back to New York. My sister's husband was a bandleader. I joined the show: Lou Lesser's Blackbirds. After that we were on the road. We went to Poughkeepsie and the show was busted, so I came back to New York." After returning to Ansonia, she married a Cape Verdean, Vital Silva, who worked in American Brass. They lived in the North End, in the tightly-knit Cape Verdean community, where they raised eleven children. In the mid-1960s, Silva was active in the housing protests of North End Community Action (NECA), and though not a welfare recipient herself, in an organization for welfare mothers. She is not fond of Ansonia: "I'd have left Ansonia a long time ago, but money was the problem. My daughter and I had planned to go together. I got on my knees and prayed to God, never let me die here, because I hate this town."

Bertha Silva: The Portuguese fellows—[the companies] didn't bring them over here; they came on their own. Like my husband. He came to New Bedford. He didn't want to go to service in his country, so he came here. He was only eighteen when he came here. They put them in the army in Por-

tugal when they become eighteen. They only get room and board; they don't get any pay.

You had to have somebody to be responsible when you came to this country. This fellow who was a friend of his father's stood for him when he came here. That's how he came here.

After [her husband] learned about the country, he went all around. One thing about them, if they didn't have any work in this town, they would go somewhere else. They would never stay in one place. He was in Newport News; he worked there on the docks. Then he came back to Connecticut. He traveled all around.

He was treasurer for the Santiago Club [composed of people from the island of Santiago]. He was secretary of the Holy Name Society. They were Portuguese clubs; they didn't have any Americans in there. We used to have fights, because every Sunday that's where he'd be. He'd never be home, he'd always have to go to the club, check up. He was on the sick committee of the Holy Name Society. When people were sick, he had to go and see about them.

[The Santiago Club] used to have a convention at the city hall in Ansonia. On Santiago Day. They would have a whole week convention. And on Labor Day, they would have a parade.

[The Portuguese] went by their traditions. They gave many dances up there [in the North End]. They gave their own dance up there

Vital Silva, husband of Bertha Silva, in 1915, shortly after arriving in the U.S. from Cape Verde. Courtesy Bertha Silva.

every Saturday night. When they had a baby christening, they would start one Saturday and celebrate the whole week. When my kids were christened, they came from everyplace: Providence, New Bedford, Bridgeport.

When somebody died, they would celebrate two or three days. They set up a table after the burial. Stay all night. If taverns were open, they'd go from tavern to tavern.

Whenever one would die, you'd get in touch with the headquarters. The headquarters would go house to house and tell people. When the time came to bury them, they would be sure to be there the night of the wake.

NAMES

Many immigrants tell of the involuntary transformation of their names.

Born in 1953, John Yrchik worked summers at Bridgeport Brass in Seymour, where his father (introduced on page 15) also worked. He is now a graduate student in sociology at the State University of New York in Binghamton, studying the effects of technological change on auto workers. He says he has never experienced discrimination due to his Polish background. John lives in the Washington metropolitan area with his wife, Eileen Sypher, a Connecticut

native and a professor of English at George Mason College.

John Yrchik: They came by Ellis Island and got their name wrecked. The name was originally spelled Gyrczyk. My grandfather pronounced it, and it came out Yrchik. The only one in the United States with that particular spelling.

Peter Kukanskis: A lot of the Lithuanians that came here didn't know how to write or read. "What's your name?" "Aliskouskis." "Geez, how do you spell it?" "Aliskouskis!" So whoever is in charge writes it. So three of us are brothers, but we have three different last names because of the way he writes it down. I know a few of them. "What's your name?" "Stotskoskis." "Stokes, that's good enough. Bill Stokes." Then they'd write down the name Stokes. And they held onto those names: Stokes and Martin and a few of them. Because that's how they signed them up in the shops.

ETHNIC TENSIONS

Ethnic groups in the Valley tended to remain distinct entities long into the twentieth century.

Frank Keane: This was no melting pot. When you came into town, if you were Italian you moved up to Town Plot or way up to the North End. They were Italian people, and it was Little Italy. If you were French, you moved down to the South End. That's where the French church was and all the French-speaking people. If you were Irish, you moved to Washington Hill or out in the East End of town. You were with your own. The idea of mingling—no way. This was in my time, too.

Each immigrant group was, in turn, subjected to discrimination and harassment by those who came before.

John Monagan: There was quite an immigration [of Irish] in the 1840s. There were some stirring times then, because you had the Know Nothing nativist movement. [A movement which opposed immigration and immigrants working in the U.S.] Its basis was largely economic, as so many of those movements are. The Irish were coming in and getting jobs, so on that level of the community there was a lot of opposition. There was a time in the 1840s when an earlier John Elton gave out arms to the Irish to defend themselves against the attacks of Dave Mix's Know Nothing group.

There was a cleavage between laborers who would be competing for the same jobs, and you had bad depressions in 1873, 1892, and 1893. There was a religious difference [between Yankee and Irish], there was a racial difference, and there was a tendency on the part of the Yankees to view the Irish the way some earlier immigrants looked at Puerto Ricans or Chicanos in the not-too-distant past.

Charles R. Walker was born in 1893, the son of a Concord, N.H., doctor. After serving in World War I, curiosity led him to take a job as a laborer in a Pennsylvania steel mill. In 1920 he came to Ansonia and worked for a year at American Brass. He kept a detailed diary, which provides intimate details of many aspects of daily life in the brass mills. In 1927 he published a novel, *Bread and Fire*, based on his experiences in Ansonia. He later became an authority on industrial relations, directing the Yale Technology Project and writing *The Man on the Assembly Line* and other well-known books. He found ethnic conflict very evident in Ansonia in 1920:

"H. Hickman relates a dispute with a 'Mick' in the mill. Herb says he concluded it by saying:

"'The English are the dominant people in the world—ain't they? You admit that. That's what God made 'em for. They dominate over Ireland don't they? Well, that's why I was sent over here from England to dominate over you. You're an Irishman, ain't yer?'"

Conflict was often rooted in competition for jobs and positions of authority.

Caroline Nardello: No Italians were on the police force; they were all Irish. There was one Italian fellow who was a fireman. That's the only Italian fireman I remember. The rest were all Irish. Now they've got everything—Irish, Lithuanian, Polish, any kind. In those days, [the Irish] used to run the city.

The Laskys were among the first Lithuanian families in Waterbury. Ed "Hap" Lasky's mother left Lithuania for the U.S. in 1888. His father left Lithuania in 1885, worked in the mines in Pennsylvania for a year, then came to Waterbury. His father, who spoke five languages, worked as a brazed tuber at American Brass. Hap was born in 1898, and remembers the violent Waterbury trolley strike of 1902. He worked in the brass mills as a boy, then became an electrician, and was a founding member of Local 660 of the International

Brotherhood of Electrical Workers; he eventually became an independent contractor. In 1920 he married Helen Flaherty, of Irish extraction, who had worked at Scovill's during World War I and then gone to work at the New England Clock Co. on South Main St. Hap's father was a member of the Lithuanian "103" Club, a predecessor of the present Lithuanian Club of Waterbury, and Hap served as its president. He has long been recognized as a leader of the Lithuanian community of Waterbury, serving as an alderman from the Brooklyn section from 1942 to 1951 and a member of the Waterbury Fire Commission. In his youth he went to St. Joseph's, the Lithuanian Church, but now goes to St. Patrick's, which was his wife's parish. He is still working as an electrical contractor.

These tensions were expressed in neighborhood rivalries that sometimes became violent.

Hap Lasky: Gangs used to come up from the other parts of town and pick on the boys here [in Brooklyn]. They'd come over and have a gang fight. Just fists. Maybe there'd be twenty-five, thirty, thirty-five come over.

Somebody tipped the crowd off there was a gang coming along by Plume and Atwood's. So they went around, somebody got up and called the cops. In those days there were horses. All of a sudden, you could hear the patrol wagon, ding ding ding ding! Then they ran one way and we ran the other way.

As we will see, these divisions were reinforced at the work place, where ethnicity was often the basis of favoritism and economic advancement. They were often passed on from generation to generation; many people could repeat a variation on the words of one Waterbury resident: "My mother taught me never to trust a _____." However, these divisions did not remain fixed; groups in conflict in one decade came to cooperate in the next.

Caroline Nardello: We could never go to St. Patrick's Church in those days because we were Italians, not Irish. They were very strict. You couldn't go to that church; they'd send you to your own church. "You don't belong here;

TABLE 4

Indications of Cultural Assimilation in Waterbury, 1900

Residency status	Number of foreign-born
Foreign-born (aggregate)	15,368
Less than 1 year in U.S.	489
1 year in U.S.	597
2 years in U.S.	529
3 years in U.S.	465
4 years in U.S.	583
5 years in U.S.	578
6–9 years in U.S.	2,142
10–14 years in U.S.	2,941
15–19 years in U.S.	2,003
20 or more years in U.S.	4,019
Foreign-born men over 21	6,943
English-speaking	6,419
Non-English-speaking	524
Naturalized	3,344
First papers filed	207

Source: Compiled from U.S. Census data by Peter Rachleff.

you're Italian." It was funny in those days; they didn't mingle in too much. Today, everybody mingles in.

3. Families: "At Night We'd Sit around with Our Feet in the Oven and We'd Share"

Over the past half-century, the family has become less and less of an economic unit. For workers in the nineteenth and early twentieth centuries, however, the family was not just a set of social relation-

ships, but a key to economic survival. In many families, not only the adult males, but also the older children worked in the factories. Younger children and married women often did "homework"— such as putting snaps on cards for the button companies.

In response to a talk by a Brass Workers History Project staff member, the Derby Senior Center set up a group interview with a number of its members who remember old times in the Valley.

Vincent Zak's parents came to America as teenagers from Czechoslovakia in the early part of this century. His father worked as a weaver at Blumenthal's. His mother worked there for some time as well, and then at the Allyn Corset Shop in Derby. He was born in 1910 in Shelton "by a midwife," and trained as a machinist at OK Tool where he worked for sixteen years. When OK moved away, he got a job as a machinist at Sponge Rubber. After twelve years "their machine shop went kerflop, and they got me a job at American Brass. At that time, ABC's machines were falling apart and they were looking for machinists. I worked as a millwright machinist, and then in the machine shop. It was hard work. There were big buggylugging machines, big wrenches. It was 'clang, clang, bang, bang' all the time. You wondered, how can you stand it? But we made it." Vincent retired from American Brass, then Anaconda, with seventeen years of service, in 1977.

Anne Zak's parents also came from Czechoslovakia. At age 16, her mother came to New York where she got a job as a domestic in the home of a wealthy family. She married Anne's father, who was working at the Driscoll Wire Mill in Shelton. They moved in with Anne's uncle in Derby. Anne was born there in 1918. When Anne was three, her mother got homesick. "She took me to

TABLE 5
Housing Conditions in Waterbury, 1890–1920

Housing type	1890	1900	1910	1920
Families (aggregate)	5,824	9,318	14,556	19,124
Dwellings (aggregate)	3,444	5,518	7,715	11,583
1 person/dwelling		57		
2 persons/dwelling		332		
3 persons/dwelling		523		
4 persons/dwelling		598		
5 persons/dwelling		617		
6 persons/dwelling		577		
7 persons/dwelling		477		
8 persons/dwelling		436		
9 persons/dwelling		359		
10 persons/dwelling		284		
11–15 persons/dwelling		716		
16–20 persons/dwelling		247		
21 or more persons/dwelling		295		
Homes (aggregate)	n.a.	9,204	n.a.	n.a.
Owned outright		687		
Encumbered		1,367		
Rented		6,973		

Source: Compiled from U.S. Census data by Peter Rachleff.

Czechoslovakia, and her plan was to settle there. When she got there she knew she wasn't staying. But she was pregnant with my sister, so we ended up staying a year. While we were gone, my father bought an eighteen-acre farm." Anne's father worked at Farrel's as a molder, and then in the tool crib, after he almost lost his hand. "It was cut off, but they sewed it back on and it grew back, a little crooked, but it grew back." Her mother and four sisters worked the farm. Anne met Vincent at a picnic in Shelton. In 1940 they were married. In 1941 the Zaks bought a thirty-three-acre farm in Shelton, where they raised three children. Anne worked twenty-five years as an LPN at the Griffin Hospital in Derby. After she retired, she started an arts and crafts store with two of her daughters. "That's how I keep busy," she says. Vincent and Anne still live on their farm, which is now planted with 6,000 trees.

Rowena Peck was born in Machias, Maine, in 1896. Her father was a railroad worker. She was trained as a nurse, and worked in the American Brass hospital during World War I.

Three of Bart Hennessey's grandparents came to America from Ireland in the 1840s and 1850s. Bart was born in Danbury, Connecticut, one of five children. His father worked for the railroad. The family moved to the Valley when Bart was small, living in Derby and then Ansonia. Bart graduated from Ansonia High School and attended Niagara University in New York, majoring in chemistry. He worked summers at American Brass while he was in college. In 1933, he went to work as a cost clerk in the mills. Until his retirement in 1975, he worked as a supervisor in various departments including the copper mill, the maintenance department, drawn copper, wire mill, metal storage, and the casting shop. Prior to the first strike in the early forties, the company put him "on a salaried basis." Bart recalls "I had nothing to do with the union, I was management all the way through." In 1942, Bart married Margaret Sullivan, and they raised two sons in Derby. One of his sons is presently a quality control manager at Anaconda. He has served on the boards of the Derby Neck Library, the Valley United Way, the Community Council, Catholic Family Services, the Knights of

Columbus, the American Legion, and the Parish Council of St. Mary's church. Today, in addition to serving as president of the Derby Neck Library and Catholic Family Services, he is active in senior citizens organizations, including the Derby Senior Center, the Western Region on Aging, and the Southern Connecticut Region on Aging. Of his extensive involvement, Bart says "somebody's got to do it."

Mary Poeltl's grandparents came from County Cork, Ireland. "We're 100 percent Irish," she says. Her father was a factory worker in Massachusetts, her mother a Connecticut native. Mary was born in the Brooklyn section of Waterbury in 1899. She went to work in the Box Shop when she was fourteen, and then at Ingersoll Watch when she was seventeen. In the late teens she met her husband, a ma-

chinist at American Brass. "He worked on the slitting machines, and many a time he took a guy's hand out of there." She got married in 1920, and remembers the turmoil of that period: "We stayed home all the time during the riots and the strikes. It was too dangerous. American Brass drove me crazy, going on strike all the time. I was glad when my husband finally left there and went to work for Mobil Oil." Mary raised two sons. She is now the grandmother of eleven, and the great-grandmother of one, a job she says is "full-time." She presently works as a volunteer at the Derby Senior Center three days a week.

Emil Antinarella was born in Italy in 1904. He came to America when he was nine years old. In 1922 he went to work as a laborer in the Wire Mill at American Brass. He subsequently worked

spooling wire, in the packing room, delivering, at the pickle tub, sweeping, and sticking. He was one of the first union supporters in his department, and served as a steward for many years. After the union came in he became a roller. He has four children, and lives in Ansonia with his wife, Lena.

Food production, drawing on agricultural skills brought from the old country, was important for many families.

Anne Zak: They baked their own bread. My mother had a store down in the cellar where she canned. My mother had a garden, and we canned everything. We had cows, chickens.

Bart Hennessey: Come this time of year, there was everything in that cellar to go right through till spring planting started. Eggs in a crock downstairs. That was for all your cooking and baking.

Zak: We didn't have a freezer way back then, so everything had to be canned or dried. Name it—she canned everything.

Rowena Peck: Remember the sauerkraut? I loved that. Big crocks of sauerkraut. And dill pickles.

Zak: We put our carrots in sand and our beets in sand. They'd last all winter. Potatoes. My mother even canned meat. You couldn't freeze meat, so she would cook it a long time and put it in jars.

Peck: The men made their wine. Don't forget that. Every time you'd go by certain districts, you could smell that wine.

Zak: One of our duties, when we were kids, was to get a pail of blackberries every day. My mother would make pies or cakes, and she would make wine out of it. She made dandelion wine. We made cider from apples.

Frank Keane: My father had a garden a mile and a half from our house. The garden was on the property of Scovill. That was for employees to use. He'd go down to Hopeville and plant a garden. My mother would can.

We're Irish, so my father would grow potatoes. He would grow tomatoes, and my mother would can tomatoes. My mother would also can a lot of pears. She always had brandied pears around, and these would come out on Sunday night. You'd have a big meal at noon; Sunday night was pretty much catch-as-catch-can, but you always pulled out the brandied pears.

Many families took in boarders.

Peter Kukanskis: My mother, where she lived, had a couple of boarders. Just to make ends meet. A couple of bucks this one would pay for room and board, another one, another one, and that's how they paid the rent and the food bill and got started. I imagine there was a shortage of places to stay anyhow.

Workers' homes on Livery St. in Waterbury before World War I. Courtesy Mattatuck Museum.

The majority of those who came here were single and in their late teens, and they had nobody; they came on their own. They'd double up, triple up in the apartments. A lot of guys would work night shift, another one day shift. He'd use the bedroom until the next one.

Daniel Zuraitis: The beds never got cold.

Josephine Tedesco's father came to America from the Campobasso region of Italy when he was nineteen years old. He worked as a laborer on the railroad. When he was twenty-one, he returned to Italy to marry Josephine's mother, and bring her back to Waterbury. They raised nine children on earnings from their family-run grocery store in Waterville. Born in 1906, Jose-

phine was their eighth child. As a young woman, she worked at the Pin Shop, putting pins on cards, and at the Clock Shop as a time-keeper. She married and had one child. Josephine returned to the work force in 1963 as the manager of the Pantry Shop at Waterbury Hospital, a job she held for ten years. She is presently the manager of the Elderly Nutrition Program at the Bergin Center. She says, "I am proud of the fact that at 75, I'm still working and able. I think I do a good job."

"I worked all my life, I'm still working." Born in 1898 in the Italian province of Forli, Sarah Cappella came to Waterbury with her mother and sisters when she was

seven years old. Her father worked in two Waterbury foundries before he opened a saloon and restaurant on Bank Street. At sixteen, Sarah went to work as a spooler at Hemingway and Sons Silk Mill. During her life she worked at American Brass, Scovill, and American Fastener. While she worked, "My mother-in-law took care of the kids, she was good to me." Sarah

retired from manufacturing work in 1961, but returned to work in the Elderly Nutrition Program and then as a Senior Aide at the Bergin Center, where she has worked for the last six years.

The following discussion took place during a group interview at the Bergin Center in Waterbury.

Josephine Tedesco: My mother kept boarders, besides having six children. She used to save all that money she got from the boarders in a cigar box. She said she saved $200, and that's how [my father] bought the first store.

[The boarders] were men who had come from Italy. They had no families.

Sarah Cappella: When the young fellows came, their mothers would write to my mother and father: My son is coming; please make him live with you. Watch over him.

My mother had as many as twenty-one. All people where we came from. One day she said, "Hey, what do you want to do, kill me?" My mother was a hard working woman.

We had to respect [the men living in the boarding houses], and if we didn't respect them, we'd get this [a smack]. We couldn't answer them back or anything. My mother used to make homemade macaroni for them, used to cook, and she used to charge them three dollars a week. Washed their clothes. As soon as she could put

an iron in my hand, she made me iron all their shirts.

We had eight rooms, and the men shared. Where two beds could fit, there were two beds. Where a twin bed and a full-sized bed would fit, [they would put them]. And they all slept together.

We didn't have a dining room, but we had a room with a big, big, big table. We had to have it— that's where we all ate.

One Saturday, my mother said to [the boarders], "Boys, you'd better go out, go downstairs, because I want to wash the floor." She told them once, she told them twice, she told them three times. They didn't move. She got a hot pan of water and she threw it— brrrooom! They moved.

Women in the family could be very powerful.

Peter Kukanskis: In those days, most of the women were the head of the family more or less when they came here. They raised the kids; they took care of the home; they took care of the money end of it. A lot of the guys used to come home, throw the paycheck on the table, and that was it. He'd maybe get a couple of dollars for his beer and tobacco, and that was about all.

A good woman—that's how a lot of [the immigrant families] made out. They worked like mules. Feed [the family], feed the boarder, feed the kids, dress them, clothe them, make their own clothes.

Frank Keane: My mother [was head of the family]. I think in a good many Irish families it was a matriarchal situation. Your father worked, and he worked like hell. He turned over his pay, at least to my mother. She did what she could with what he gave her. I have no statistics, but I wouldn't hesitate to say it was a matriarchal situation in at least half the Irish families. Not just your mother, but the girls in the family made the major decisions.

I'm sure if my father wanted to buy a team of horses, which he did, he would have to consult my mother. If he had to buy a wagon to go with that team, he had to consult my mother, because she took care of the finances. Did she have any education? No. But she had intelligence. He just worked like the devil, came home, ate, read the paper, and went out and did his second job. When he came home, he probably went to bed.

Women could also lead very restricted lives.

Caroline Nardello: My mother was very bashful. She came here at sixteen, but she never mingled. At seventeen she was married. She didn't even have a chance to go to school. At eighteen she had me.

My father spoke a little [English], but my mother was very shy to learn the English language.

My mother was always home with the children.

Josephine Tedesco: All the girls had to help. My brothers never did any housework. Never. It was a disgrace for men to do housework in those days. We [girls] didn't mind it; we accepted it. I felt that was the way it had to be.

Louise Lombardo's parents came from Italy. Her father worked until he retired at Scovill's to support his wife and six children. Louise was born in Waterbury in 1911. At

age fourteen, she went to work at Ingersoll Watch. At sixteen, she went to work at Scovill's. During her ten years there as a machine operator, she married and had three children. She worked at various shops afterwards in order to support her children, including Benrus for twenty-two years and Uniroyal for five. Since 1978, she has been the manager of the Elderly Nutrition Program at the Palladino Center.

The family was a place where values were inculcated.

Louise Lombardo: My mother taught us to be very good. In fact, she taught us to be so good that I resent it today. She always taught us that we should never answer our elders, and we always had to have respect for them, which I think was wrong. There were times when I felt as though I should have answered people, but I didn't do it, and I'm still that way today on account of it. You always had to be nice and have respect for people. People were pushing you all the time, and you knew they were pushing you, but you wanted to have respect for them. Today I look back and I say, "If they were doing it to me, I should have done it back to them." But I didn't. Today I tell my children different.

Rachel Piccochi Doolady was born in Waterbury in 1918. Her father worked at American Brass until he got silicosis of the lungs and was unable to work. "All he got from the company was a dollar a day for the rest of his life. We had to supply him with oxygen every day." One of eight children, Rachel had to leave high school at fifteen to help support the family. She went to work at U.S. Rubber, under her sister's name. "I was known as Florence down there. In those days they couldn't hire you until you were sixteen years of age."

After working as a group worker on a conveyer at U.S. Rubber, Rachel left to work at International Silver and Eyelet Specialty. During World War II she worked at American Brass, but had to give up her job to the returning veterans. She then went to work at Lux Time, where in the mid-fifties she became involved in organizing the union. In 1957 the Lux workers won their election. Rachel served on the negotiating committee, and remained active as a steward in the local until her retirement in 1981. She was one of the few women elected to union office in her local, UAW Amalgamated Local 1251, serving as treasurer for four years. She chaired the local's Community Services Committee for several years and served as Labor Representative on the board of the United Way in Waterbury. She has been active in local politics for many years, in campaigns and voter registration drives, and as an officer of the Waterbury Area CAP Council, UAW Region 9-A. "I like to think it was through the efforts of the labor movement that we got civil service here in Waterbury." Since June 1972, she has been the director of the Senior Community Service Employment Program, a Labor Department-funded program which employs poverty-level seniors in part-time positions at non-profit agencies in the Waterbury area. Rachel says of her program, "The community is a lot richer for having these seniors working in these agencies. The elderly have a lot to contribute to society and to the community as a whole. They bring their expertise to their jobs, and I know for a fact that a lot of agencies would not be able to operate without Senior Aides." Rachel has one son, Ron, who presently works as Vice-President for Economic Development at the Waterbury Chamber of Commerce.

The family was a place where people shared the pleasures as well as the demands of intimacy.

Rachel Doolady: I loved those days. I remember when I was a kid and we were seven girls and a boy in my family. Every Saturday my father would go out selling cheese. On payday he would come home with some cookies and stuff. At night we'd all sit around the fire with our feet in the oven in front of the stove and we'd share. My grandmother would tell a story; my mother would tell us stories. We were taught how to wash; we were taught how to bake bread. I can remember getting up at 3 o'clock in the morning and kneading that stupid bread that had gone over the top. And I remember washing clothes by washboard—no such thing as a washing machine. I remember washing wooden floors—no linoleum on the floor. Every week we got down on our hands and knees to do this.

At times, alcohol caused serious disruptions of family life.

Hap Lasky: It used to be pathetic at some times. Women used to meet their husbands at the gate of Booth and Hayden and try to take their pay away from them, so they wouldn't stop at the tavern. They'd say to them, "The kids need clothes. They're hungry. Take two dollars and have a drink, but give me the rest of it, so I can clothe the kids and buy food for them." A lot of them wouldn't bring home a penny.

Families had few public support systems.

Frank Keane: The only agencies that I knew were orphanages. They didn't apply to a kid with a parent. They did have poorhouses, where people went in their old age if they had no families. We had a place for indigent people, Brookside. For the winter, if they didn't have any place to go, they'd send them up there. The City of Waterbury ran Brookside.

4. Social Life: "You Knew Your Next-Door Neighbor"

Another key to survival for the immigrant groups were networks that extended beyond the family itself. These were often based on ties among those who came from the same region in the old country.

Daniel Zuraitis: My mother said that, basically, when the girls would get off the train in Waterbury, they'd be lost. But they'd just listen and all of a sudden hear somebody talking Lithuanian. So all they had to do was talk to them and mention the part of the country they were from. "Go see such-and-such." Automatically, you're with family.

The ethnic thing was the same as the Italians and the other ethnic groups. You're a Ponti, or you're a Neapolitan, or you're a Sicilian. For the Lithuanians, you're a Koniski from Konish; you're a Lukaviscus, or you live close to the German border. Each one had a district. Each had a little bit, not of a dialect, but of an accent for their wording.

The immigrants, generally cut off from the rest of city life by the language barrier, often developed an intense social life of their own.

Hap Lasky: In Brooklyn alone there were thirty-two saloons before Prohibition. This was along Bank Street. And then there were some up along South Leonard.

Women weren't allowed [in the saloons]. What they had to do, if they wanted a drink, was to go in with a bucket and get a bucket of beer and drink it at home.

In the morning [the saloons] used to open up at 6 o'clock. They used to go in there for their "eye-openers." At that time whiskey was five cents a glass. They used to have kegs. They had keg on top of keg.

Nearly every evening there was something going on here years ago. When they had a wedding, the wedding lasted one week. They'd get married over in the church and come over here and have drinks and something to eat. Most of them got married on Monday. It used to be for three days, rest on the Thursday, then they'd wind up Friday and Saturday.

Different women used to get the food out. It was all Lithuanian cooking. At that time there were a lot of women around who were tickled to death to do it. It was done voluntarily; I don't think they ever got paid. They used to help one another doing different things. Most of them came from the same part of Lithuania. They were like first cousins, second cousins; 90 percent of them, I think, were related to me.

They never had a doctor when

The Portugese Scovillites, a soccer team made up of Scovill employees, in the early 1920s. Courtesy Scovill Collection.

a baby was born. There was a woman by the name of Mrs. Rubis. She was at nearly 90 percent of the Lithuanian births. I remember her well. I remember when my sister was born. She came over and I said to her, "What are you doing here?" She said, "I'm up paying a visit to your mother. You'll find out after I go."

We used to play baseball. We used to go fishing out to Tracy's. We used to go berry picking. Up over the wall here, before they cut the hill down, there was a big blueberry patch; we used to go there and pick blueberries. Right where this club is now there was a big apple orchard. There were maybe ten or twelve [Lithuanians going to high school]. We used to all meet and walk up to Crosby.

Rachel Doolady: I remember when I was a kid. My mother used to have a beautiful voice. They used to get together Saturday nights with their friends. One Saturday night to Mary's house, the following Saturday to Anne's house. They used to sing—they used to sing duets. They used to have their own accompaniment, guitar players and that. It was like a great big party, Saturday night after Saturday night. They'd sit and they'd drink and they'd sing.

The whole community was involved, it seemed. You knew your next-door neighbor. If Mary was sick, you'd run over to take care of Mary. Today your next-door neighbors don't even want to know you,

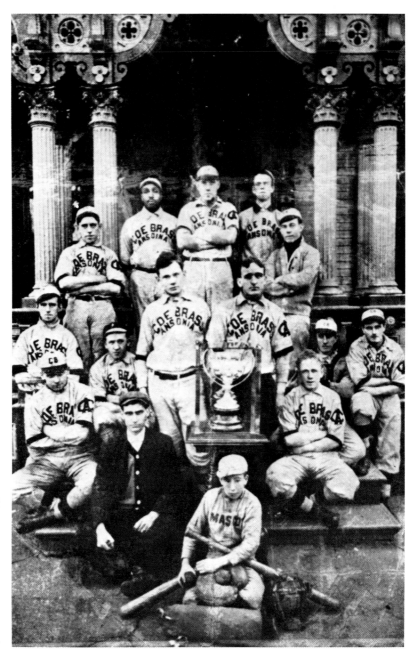

Coe Brass Co. baseball team, the Industrial League champs, in 1910. Courtesy Peter Hylwa.

Waterbury's North Square in 1913. Courtesy Waterbury Republican-American.

or good morning, hello, good-bye, and that's it.

They used to sing and dance, and when it got to be 1 o'clock in the morning, they'd cook spaghetti. They were up all hours of the night. Just neighbors and friends.

Mary Sabot's father was Austrian, her mother Czechoslovakian. They settled in Waterbury's North End, where her father worked as a carpenter. Born in 1910, Mary was the oldest of twelve children. Like other young girls, she went to work at an early age to help support the family. She was twelve

when she got her first job at the Waterbury Clock Shop, pinching wires and balancing wheels. "I said I was 18, but the boss found out. He said if I quit voluntarily, he would release my working papers, so I did." Mary worked minding kids and doing housework until she was sixteen, when she got a job

at Scovill's tinting wires. At 18, she got a job as a coremaker at the Waterbury Manufacturing Company. "It was the first time they had women in there. The men used to heckle you: 'It's a man's job, it's a man's job,' they'd say. I finally told them to stick the job, and quit. I was a real spitfire." Mary got married when she was nineteen and had one daughter. She worked at the Mattatuck Manufacturing Company, and then during the war she returned to Waterbury Manufacturing, to work in the Spring Room and the Dip Room for nineteen years. Later she worked for ten years at Wilby High School as a matron, until her retirement at age 67. "I got fidgety when I stayed home," so in 1979 she went back to work as a Senior Aide at the Palladino Center.

Catherine Ruggles' family was

from Waterbury. Her father worked at American Brass. One of nine children, Catherine was born in 1902. In 1926, she married and raised four children. She is a member of the Immaculate Conception Church, and is an active bridge player and bowler. Presently, she works as a Senior Aide at the Palladino Center.

Mary Sabot: If a neighbor said, "I'll tell your mother or your father," boy, you'd get it when you got home.

Catherine Ruggles: 'Cause if the neighbors said you did it, you did it. If we'd get a crack in school, we'd go home, we got another one.

Sabot: Neighbors helped one another with their kids. That's why we had to be good—or else.

Clubs, benefit societies, and coop-

eratives helped provide a degree of economic security and cheap commodities for workers with small and irregular paychecks. As early as the 1870s, a national workers' organization called the Sovereigns of Industry had 400 members and a cooperative store in Waterbury. As the Brass Valley became more multiethnic, such organizations came to be formed increasingly along ethnic lines.

Daniel Zuraitis: In the Lithuanian ethnic community, the clubs that were established, the 103 and the 48, had their own summer parks. They had Lymon Park down in Naugatuck for summer picnics and another up in Lakewood. Then they established cemetery associations of their own. They had insurance of their own. They had ethnic group stores and also cooperative stores.

Peter Kukanskis: The Lithuanian Merchandise Corp. was one of the meat markets. They all chipped in. It was a place they all went and bought. It got them a little cheaper price.

The clubs were important social centers for immigrant workers.

Louise Lombardo: My parents came from the old country. They were married here. My father came about 1904. From Italy. My father, the Italian people had clubs. They had picnics and they had dances. They tried to start a bank corporation at one time, which flopped.

The Sons of Lithuania, photographed in the Brooklyn section of Waterbury during World War I. Courtesy Daniel Zuraitis.

Just the paisans came to the dances. Everybody that came from the old country, all their families.

Often the clubs developed a political role, and at times this became a basis for rivalry between different groups.

Peter Kukanskis: There were two factions. This club had more fellows that were Catholics, that went to church. The other club was formed by people who weren't church members. There were quite a few of them. Eventually there were some [members of the other club] that were Communists, some that were nothing at all. Still, a lot of Catholics belonged to both clubs. I did myself and my father and a bunch of them.

I remember quite a few times there were remarks made like "You people belong up at the Communist club." It wasn't Communist any more than anything else. It just happened to be that maybe thirty or forty were members there. It was mostly something to do, a place to hang out. Their clique was there.

The two clubs started originally as social clubs for the people that came here, somewhere to hang around. Then little by little they got involved in politics. This was the Lithuanian Independent Political Club; the other was the Lithuanian Citizens Political Club. Two different factions. They were involved in politics. Many a time politicians would be down here looking for votes. The way the club swings—that's how they'd get elected.

5. The Church: Religious, Educational, Social

By the end of the nineteenth century, a majority of workers in the Valley were Catholics. For many immigrant groups, the church was the central embodiment of ethnic identity and group life. For many individuals it served as the principal source of values and understandings of the meaning of life and the nature of the world.

The following brief history of a Polish parish in Waterbury, St. Stanislaus Kostka, gives some sense of the core role of the church in the immigrant community and the sacrifices made to build and maintain it.

"[The first Polish immigrants came to Waterbury in 1880 and lived close together in the area of Pond St.]

"Within a year of their arrival, the Poles began to feel a need for their own church, priests and school. Having these things, they felt that, when their problems built up and their longing for their native land became too great, they would have a place where they could pray to their God in their

TABLE 6
Churches in Waterbury, 1890

Denomination	Number of edifices	Value of property ($)	Number of members
Churches (total)	18	708,000	16,041
Adventist	1	12,000	160
Regular Baptist	1	61,500	549
Catholic	4	180,000	11,800
Congregationalist	2	130,000	1,220
Jewish	1	n.a.	105
Methodist Episcopal	4	83,500	850
Colored Methodist	1	n.a.	111
Protestant Episcopal	2	220,000	1,135
Universalist	1	18,000	70

Source: Compiled from U.S. Census data by Peter Rachleff.

own tongue, they could go to their own priests for support and counsel and could have their children taught in their own schools and language; they could better their futures.

"In a few years after coming to that city, helped by the initiative of Jozef Wojdyl, they assembled in his home to confer together and organized the Society of St. Stanislaus Kostka. The goal of this Society was to help each other mutually and to group together all the Poles in Waterbury in one of the already existing parishes rather than to have them spread out and belonging to the separate parishes in the various parts of the city. Their desire was to stay together. The idea was a good and well-timed one, insuring them against scattering and being swallowed up by a society other than Polish.

"It was definitely decided that they should all join the German parish of St. Cecilia whose Irish pastor had a genuine liking for the Poles, who supported their causes and who was sincere enough in his friendship so that he even learned enough Polish to enable him to read the gospel to them in that language.

"This was the way matters stood until 1910, when the Poles decided that the time had come for them to appeal to the Bishop for permission to set up their own parish in Waterbury. The Bishop in fact gave his approval, advising them first to make up a list of the Polish population in that city and to set up a parish account.

"The parishioners worked hard to fulfill these two conditions. They organized numerous and varied fund-raising events in order to build up their parish funds. Services took place in a rented chapel in 'the Polish tradition.'

"The new pastor began his energetic work immediately by proceeding with the building of the church. The lower portion was completed within a year and was blessed as the St. Stanislaus Kostka Church. Father Zimmerman himself, on the other hand, continued to live in private homes for the first three years until finally a building was bought on Farm Street, which was to serve as the rectory.

"In 1920, the Bishop assigned a new pastor, Father Stanislaw Blazejewski. The years during which Father Blazejewski was pastor in Waterbury were years of great financial strain and sacrifice on the part of the parishioners, whose offerings made it possible to complete the upper level of the church by 1926, at a cost of $87,000. Not stopping to rest on his laurels, Father Blazejewski continued to gather funds, this time to purchase property on which to build a convent for the Sisters of the Immaculate Conception. In 1935 these Sisters came to the parish from New Britain.

"In 1940 the parish buildings were repaired, in 1941 furniture, which was badly needed, was purchased. In 1942 a church bell was bought, and in 1943 three altars were placed in the church. After 1945 a heating system was installed in the church, a parking lot was

built for the use of parishioners, the church building was repainted and the lighting modernized.

"Father Marian Karwacki arrived [in] 1959. With him he brought an atmosphere of love of Polish Liturgy and tradition and a force which drew the parishioners to enthusiastic participation in spiritual work.

"He did not forget, however, the numerous other matters which needed his attention. He enriched the parish fortune by buying three buildings on Locust Street, had the tax rate modified by breaking them up into smaller monthly rates rather than the previous larger yearly rates and he began a school where the Polish language, songs, dances and traditions were taught."*

The church served as a social and educational as well as a religious center in the immigrant communities.

Frank Keane: The Holy Name Society was the big thing in the Catholic church. Just about everybody in the church belonged. They would get together and plan things for the school and the church.

As soon as you had a church, the next big thing was to get a school. The people from the Holy

* Mieczyslaw Kierklo i Jan Wójcik, *Polonia w/in Connecticut* (Hartford: Wydawca, Komitet Obchodow Tysiaclecia Polski Chrzescijanskiej na Stan Connecticut, 1966), pp. 93–96.

Name Society were the ones who pushed the building of schools, maintenance of the church, just about anything that had to be done. That was the main purpose of the Holy Name Society. It was just men. Women had their sodalities.

If there was a parochial school, you went to the parochial school. A small minority went to the public schools. Just about all the Catholics went to the Catholic school, in which you learned the catechism—by rote; you memorized every single word in it.

The church served as a focus for other ethnic organizations as well. Father William Lawrence Wolkovich-Valkavicius, biographer of Waterbury's first Lithuanian priest, Joseph Zebris, describes the role of such groups in the St. Joseph's parish in the Brooklyn section of Waterbury, based on Zebris' report to his bishop in 1895:

"Mutual-aid fraternals, though not strictly parish organizations, functioned in harmony with the pastor, and under his supervision. The St. Casimir group listed in the parish report began in 1884, and registered at city hall in 1889. This corps was the more literate and articulate of Catholics who gave impetus to creating the parish.

"The St. George ensemble was a military unit which very much appealed to the priest. This Naugatuck contingent lent color to local parades, with their white gloves, ornamented walking sticks, braided shoulder decorations and military caps. On the more practical side, the men of St. George won Zebris' plaudits for fostering literacy. New members were admitted only if they could read or write Lithuanian. Those who joined prior to the insertion of this rule were asked to promise they would learn within six months so as to retain membership.

"Curiously the Gediminas Society, though labelled by the pastor as 'mostly non-Catholic,' appeared in the statement to the bishop. The group was a sign of a liberal, non-churchgoing wing of the Balt colony. Gediminas assisted new arrivals in rudiments of civics, staged social functions, and engaged in a variety of patriotic events. Because of its freethinker orientation, the lodge was denied full entry into the national alliance, being offered only a qualified membership. Here was one local body which Zebris could not supervise. Inclusion of Gediminas in the pastor's report suggests he had hoped to win them over to parishioner status, but subsequent episodes showed sharp difference of opinion between Zebris and this 'outside' group."*

*Father William Lawrence Wolkovich-Valkavicius, *Lithuanian Pioneer Priest of New England* (Brooklyn, N.Y.: Franciscan Press, 1980), pp. 69–70.

Sid Monti's parents came to New York from Italy. He was born in Brown Station, N.Y., in 1910. His father worked as a construction laborer. A Black mechanic took him under his wing, taught him the trade, and made a union man out of him. "My old man was probably the best union man I ever knew. Instead of saying grace, he would start each meal by saying, 'Bless the union.'" Sid worked as an insurance agent, where he helped unionize the agents. In the 1930s he went to work at Scovill and again became active in the union. He worked closely with Mine, Mill until the Scovill local joined the UAW. He soon emerged as president of the new UAW local. He became highly visible locally as the leader of the 1952 Scovill strike, and in its wake played a major role as a community leader in Waterbury. He was the first head of the UAW's Copper and Brass Council, and in the 1950s became a UAW International Representative. He has since retired to Cape Cod, but continues to serve as the head of the organization of retired UAW International Representatives in Region 9A.

Many immigrants, especially men, brought anticlerical sentiments along with their religion.

Sid Monti: My old man didn't have any use for priests. In the old country, in a small community where most of them came from, the priest actually ran it, and he was heavy-handed with the boys; he didn't mind slapping them around. They never forgot it. They said: If that's religion, I don't want any part of it. So they were anticlerical.

As we saw above, Catholics met serious hostility when they first came into the Valley. As the Irish rose in the social structure of Waterbury, discrimination on religious grounds declined. In Ansonia, however, where Yankee and English workers retained many of the skilled jobs, a generalized prejudice against Catholics—including the Irish—long persisted.

Charles R. Walker recorded in his diary how religious bigotry was expressed in Ansonia in 1920:

"Jim Buzwell on the 'damned Catholics':

"Jim is one of a perfectly ubiquitous Ansonia family, that has a relative in three quarters of the departments and offices of the mill. He seems old stick New England with a decided relish for argument and an inherited interest in theology.

"'The Case against the Catholics:

"'They run everything.'

"'They are a "poor class of people"; mostly Micks.'

"'They are priest-ridden.'

"'They are Irish, and the English have always hated the Irish.'

"'When in office a Catholic will never appoint a Protestant, but a Protestant often appoints a Catholic.'

"'They have shown this in local politics and in the public schools.'

"Theological and ecclesiastical objections.

"'They get the children young and compel them to be Catholics.'

"'The priests are celibates, which is unnatural and probably makes for lasciviousness.'

"'They believe in monks and nuns.'

"'They believe they can purchase salvation by giving money.'

"'They take sin lightly because they can secure swift and easy forgiveness by the priest.'

"What the Irish Catholics say about the Protestants:

"'They shout for England, and support her in her oppression of Ireland.'

"'In many places they keep Catholics out of jobs, schools and businesses, and exclude them from social clubs.'

"'They are stuck up, and think themselves better than other people.'

"'They constantly misrepresent the facts about the teachings and practices of the Church.'"

The church played an important role in shaping attitudes about politics and the labor movement. Father William Lawrence Wolkovich-Valkavicius describes a revealing incident:

"On the issue of labor, [Zebris] was typical of both native clergy and immigrant priests. Zebris regarded any campaign against the capitalistic system as disruptive of good public order. Instead, he constantly taught self-reliance through cooperatives and personal investments in real estate. But the immigrants must save and practice thrift within the economic system which welcomed them. To Zebris' conservative perspective, agitation among the working class was a display of ingratitude to those who provided a means of livelihood. A dispute at a brass factory furnishes an insight into Zebris' attitude. The West Brass Mills carried a large number of Lithuanians on the payroll. When one of the socialist-minded immigrants imprudently berated a foreman as nothing but a capitalist's tool, all the Lithuanians were discharged ar-

bitrarily. Zebris' informant, an unemployed laborer, told the pastor in an outpouring of expletives: 'Let me explain a bit and then you will understand what those stinking followers of Sliupas are doing to us Lithuanians, how they are blackening our name in the eyes of outsiders.' In response to the incident of the expulsions, Zebris cautioned readers that the 'best' factory has no longer been accepting Balts for work. Bemoaning the fatuity of biting the hand that offers food through employment, the pastor warned that 'If Lithuanians further listen to the apostles of darkness, other factories will likewise close their doors to them.'"*

6. Politics: "Workingman's Mayor" and "King of the Bolsheviks"

The society that workers entered presented two contradictory faces. On the one hand, compared to the places from which most of them had come, the U.S. was a land of freedom and economic opportunity. They could practice their own religions, speak their own languages, usually avoid the draft. Wages were above subsistence level, and no law prevented them or their children from rising to a higher social status.

On the other hand, it was also a land of poverty and industrial des-

*Ibid., pp. 94–95.

potism. The bosses on the job held absolute authority over life at work. Workers and their families had little or no recourse if they were maimed or killed on the job. The hours of work left little time or energy for any other life. Long periods of unemployment eroded whatever savings people were able to put away. While formally democratic, the Brass Valley's political life was often dominated by the small group of manufacturing families who controlled the Valley's wealth.

The framework into which workers moved was largely determined by the manufacturers. Much of the time, workers created institutions and lifestyles that would let them survive within that framework. But at a number of points, they attempted to alter that framework through collective action.

The first major collective action by workers in the Naugatuck Valley came in the 1880s with the organization of the Knights of Labor and the occurrence of strikes in the brass mills. It also appeared in the formation of workers' political parties and the election of union leaders and other workers to public office.

Recent immigrants were, of course, excluded from participation in the formal political process. As they became citizens, however, many became active within the established two-party framework.

The first Irish mayor was elected in Waterbury in 1894. Frank Keane describes some of the social underpinnings of the Irish role in politics.

Frank Keane: You had Irish ward bosses who took care of their people. If you needed a job, you went to this guy in the neighborhood who had great political influence. He didn't necessarily have a political job himself, but one way or another he contributed to the party. He might have been a saloon-keeper, or an insurance agent, or anything, whereby he managed to accumulate some money and would contribute to the party. Obviously, he was going to get something in return for this. In return he would get these favors. Jobs in the fire department, the police department, even use weight and get him a job in the mill.

More than that—he'll be at the boat when these people get off, and [without doubt] in six weeks they're going to be voting citizens. How they did it—you didn't ask any questions. The idea of voting was so important—everybody voted. It was like going to church, like blessing yourself. You voted, and in so doing, you got to control politically. This became part of their heritage; they became politicians.

In some cases, money and liquor were openly used to buy elections.

Caroline Nardello: In those days [before World War I], the people didn't know much, and the Re-

publicans would pay them to be in politics. They would pay the Italians to belong. (I don't think they had Democrats much in those days.) They would pay them to go down to vote. They paid them to vote Republican.

Hap Lasky: My father and ex-Governor Lilly were very good friends. When I was a kid, up came this man with his horses. What little we had in those days my mother put on the table. He was campaigning. I remember him giving my father some money and telling him, "Get some beer and get some whiskey and tell them to vote for me." So he did. That's the first I remember of politics.

Many of the ethnic groups became polarized between Republicans and Democrats.

Peter Kukanskis: For local politics, this was always Democratic around here. There was no other party, as far as anybody was concerned. These taverns—if somebody went in and mentioned Republican, I guess he'd get kicked out. They all were that years back. Like the old saying, the Republican Party's only millionaires. They had nothing to do with them.

Hap Lasky: My father was a Republican voter. I suppose [he became a Republican] through the factory. A lot [of the officials] were Republicans; they talked him into it. He was quite an orator; he used to go and make speeches and you could hear a pin drop, people tell me. They used to come over to my house; my father would tell them about the different political parties.

Workers also supported specifically working-class candidates for public office. In 1885/86, the Knights of Labor in Connecticut elected thirty-seven members to the state legislature and controlled the local city government in Naugatuck, just south of Waterbury. In 1901, Ansonia elected Stephen Charters mayor. Charters, an Irish-born carpenter, filled the appointed offices in the Ansonia city government with fellow unionists and union sympathizers.

Jack Meade was elected as a "workingman's mayor" in Ansonia in 1920. Charles R. Walker recorded some of the discussion of his role:

"Great satisfaction expressed throughout the shop at the election of 'Jack Meade,' as Mayor.

"People for him. Most of the men in the mill; (except the strong Republicans) the Catholic and Irish.

"People against him. The elite and strong middle class Republicans . . . .

"Arguments advanced in favor of Mr. Meade.

"'He bought us coal last winter.'

"'He kept them from raising the water rates on us.'

"'He settled the first strike in our favor.'

"'He's a working man himself.'

"'He's an Irishman.'

"'He's a Catholic.'

"'He's a Democrat.'

"Arguments advanced against Mr. Meade:

"'He can hardly speak English.'

"'Look at him!'

"'His sister used to keep a saloon.'

"'He peddles barrels?'

"'He's a Mick.'

"'He's a Catholic.'

"'He's always playing to the gallery; he bought coal for the laboring people, he mixed up in the water rates scrap; he double crossed the company in the strike.'

"'He's a Democrat.'"

John Driscoll is undoubtedly the best-known product of the brass industry labor movement. He says of his origins: "Both my father and mother came from Ireland, from the same area, County Kerry, the town of Tralee. My father came to Connecticut and Waterbury in the 1890s; my mother in the early 1900s. She did housework in the homes of some of the major brass families, like Irving Chase. My father was a retail clerk. He worked for the Reid and Hughes Department Store. His only background in anything close to unionism was his activity in organizing what was called the Clerks' League for Uniform Closing, an attempt to get the stores all to shut at the same hour weeknights. He was also active in the Ancient Order of Hibernians. This was in the teens. In the early 1920s, my father developed tuberculosis. My mother went back to doing housework. I was born in Waterbury, on West Liberty, on the Abrigador, which at that time was an Irish enclave, as it's now, I guess, a Puerto Rican enclave." John Driscoll was an excellent student who graduated from Wesleyan University, did graduate work in English at Wesleyan and philosophy at Brown, and briefly attended Harvard Law School. "I was all for the ideals of social justice and reform." He left law school and returned to Waterbury to work in a factory and immediately became active in the early

CIO campaign. He emerged as the most prominent local leader. In 1941, he came into conflict with the national leadership of Mine, Mill over the issue of Communist influence in union affairs, and became the leader of the opposition group which ultimately seceded from Mine, Mill (see pages 172–76). Those locals later affiliated with the UAW. In 1950, he became subregional director of the UAW in the Naugatuck Valley. He is currently head of the Connecticut State Labor Council, AFL-CIO.

Because so many of those who came to work in the brass plants came from countries with oppressive political and social conditions, many identified with revolutionary and nationalist movements in their homelands.

John Driscoll: [The Ancient Order of Hibernians] grew from the organization of Irish immigrants who fought in the Civil War and afterwards formed an abortive expeditionary force to try to take over Canada. My father was a member of the "Hibernian Rifles," a drill team of the Order. He had a lot of books on Irish history. He was a very strong nationalist.

After 1916 there was a lot of activity in Waterbury, selling bonds for the Irish cause, which were really contributions. Both my father and mother were active in that.

World War I and the international revolutionary upheavals that followed it gave great impetus to the radical impulse. The following account is from Charles R. Walker's diary:

"A talk with a little Italian who is apparently a Bolshevik in the rough. I said, 'Big strikes in Italy, eh.' 'Oh yes,' he said, 'they win!' 'Who win?' I asked. 'The Bolsheviki,' he replied. 'Rich man same as poor man.'

"'What English working man get out of war?' he said. 'Damn little,' said I. 'What French working man get out of war?' he queried. I made the same answer. 'Yes, what American, what Italian working man get out of war.' 'Well,' I said, 'we win the war.' 'Say,' he said, 'you poor man?' 'Yes,' I countered rapidly. 'So'm I, war no good,' he said.

"'You work for somebody here!' he said. I admitted it. 'Over there,' he said, 'I work for myself, you work for yourself. Rich men, poor men same. All right, eh?'"

Such sentiments were not unusual in the mills. Walker was told by Mitchell Wallace, a top executive, that there was "a school, called the Automobile School, where 300 Bolsheviks meet once or twice a week in Ansonia." He recorded:

"Talk at the supper table tonight about Reds. Mr. Brownell informs me that there are considerable numbers of what he terms 'Bolsheviks' in the mill. They are Rus-

sians, he says, and accept the term. They are known to all and hold meetings every noon, when one of their number reads to them from a Russian newspaper."

But working-class radicalism grew primarily from the conditions workers faced in everyday life. Walker:

"The King of the Bolsheviks who works on the electric rolls tried to persuade me in Anglo-Russian to the Bolshevik faith today. It was my first experience with direct propaganda in the mills. The moment chosen had interesting psychological significance. I was pulling a very heavy truck load of 30 bars past his rolls, when he rushed out and took me by the arm. 'Pretty soon you be Bolshevik,' he said. 'You work like hell.' 'Oh, no,' I answered and went past with the metal. On my return, he remarked:

"'You working man.'

"'Oh, yes,' I said.

"'You work like hell.'

"I assented.

"'You Bolshevist then,' he proceeded, 'you work like hell.'

"'No,' I said.

"'What ze matter,' he queried. 'You capitalist?'"

The son of a Russian father and a Polish mother, Mike Laban was born in Ansonia in 1916. As a youth in the early Depression, Mike Laban used to take the trolley to New Haven to spend his days in the warmth of Yale Univer-

sity's Sterling Library. Multilingual, he remains an omnivorous reader to this day, and still visits the Sterling regularly to keep up with dozens of publications from around the world. As a young man, in the mid-thirties, he worked for U.S. Steel in Gary, Indiana, where he became active in the CIO's Steel Workers Organizing Committee, and traveled to Birmingham, Alabama, and other steel industry towns helping to organize the union. He returned to Ansonia in the late thirties and opened a restaurant which became a hangout for union organizers. When the family decided that the restaurant business involved them in too much drinking with the customers, Mike went to work at American Brass in 1938. In his thirty-six years at ABC, he worked at a variety of jobs in the casting shop, the drawn copper department, the boilerhouse, the powerhouse, and the office. He was a roller, a saw operator, a wire drawer, and an inspector, among other positions. From the early organizing days, Mike played an active role in the union, serving as steward, zone steward, recording secretary, trustee, building fund trustee, and editor of the local's newsletter, *The Brasscaster*. During World War II, because of his fluency in Russian and Polish, he was attached to the Allied Control Commission and assigned to hunting down Nazi war criminals "from Budapest to Bucharest." He carried gold fillings from the concentration camps to Nuremburg as evidence for the Nazi war crimes trials. He lives in Ansonia with his wife, Mary, who is a garment worker.

Much of this radicalism was met with severe repression—blacklisting, raids, arrests, and even deportations. It has nearly been forgotten. Even Mike Laban, who represents the radicalism of the 1930s, knew little about the earlier radicalism.

Mike Laban: I don't know about this because right after that were the Palmer Raids. A lot of these people were deported. [U.S. Justice Department agents] came right into the shops, right into the American Brass, and deported them illegally.

A woman told me that her husband was deported to Russia because he was reading a Bible which was written in Russian. They came in: "It's subversive literature." They grabbed ahold of him and deported him.

THE WORK

7. The Brass Production Process: From Casting Shop to Widget

ORIGINS

Bronze—the alloy of copper and tin—was the first useful metal discovered by humans. Thus, the period of early civilization in India, China, Japan, Egypt, Nineveh, and Babylon is called the Bronze Age.

Brass—the alloy of copper and zinc—was produced in Rome before the birth of Christ. The process of brass casting remained extraordinarily stable from the Middle Ages until the early twentieth century. The industry was well established before 1700 in Birmingham, England, whence it was transplanted to the Naugatuck Valley.

BASIC PHASES OF PRODUCTION

The brass industry, as it developed in the Naugatuck Valley, involved the following basic processes:

A seventeenth-century French casting shop. It differed from those in the nineteenth-century Naugatuck Valley primarily in its lack of a chimney. Courtesy Bridgeport Brass Co.

The casting shop of Benedict and Burnham Mfg. Co. in Waterbury in 1880. Courtesy Scientific American.

The rolling mill at Benedict and Burnham in 1880. Courtesy Scientific American.

Casting

The first stage of brass production was casting. Raw materials—copper, zinc, and/or other metals—were melted down together to form an alloy. Until World War I, this was done in ceramic pots called crucibles; these were later replaced by electric furnaces.

When the melted metal reached the proper stage, it was poured into a mold. In the early days, this mold might form the actual shape of the final product—a button or a bell, for instance. By the 1830s, however, most Naugatuck Valley casting produced flat bars called "ingots" for subsequent rolling.

Rolling

In the rolling mill, the brass bar from the casting shop is squeezed between two heavy rolls to change its shape. To produce flat sheets of brass, for example, an ingot was passed several times through "breaking-down rolls," then, again, through lighter "finishing rolls."

As it is compressed by the rolls, brass tends to become hard. So after a certain number of passes through the rolls, the sheets have to be softened by heating in an annealing furnace, or "muffles."

In order to create a smooth surface, the sheet, at times, is run through a "scalping machine," which scrapes it. To remove surface impurities, it may be given a chemical bath in the "pickle tub." Finally, it may be cut into the desired widths in a machine called a "slitter."

Wire, Rod, and Tube

A variety of processes were used to make wire, rod, and tube from copper and its alloys. Most often it was done by some combination of rolling the brass to a given thickness, cutting it into thin strips, and then drawing the strips through a series of progressively smaller dies until the final size and shape was achieved.

Manufacturing

Sheet, wire, rod, and tube were the basic products of the brass mills proper. However, many of the brass companies worked up their mill products into manufactured goods of many kinds. The techniques used were not unique to the brass industry, but were common to metalworking industries of all kinds. Processes included:

—*casting* shapes by remelting the metal and pouring it into molds;

—*forging* shapes by power-driven hammer blows;

—*stamping* shapes into metal by striking it between two dies in a press;

—*standard metalshop processes*, such as lathing, milling, drilling, and planing;

—*special automatic machine processes*, using equipment such as eyelet machines and screw machines, designed to turn out large quantities of a particular product

Annealing furnaces, known also as muffles, at Benedict and Burnham in 1880. Courtesy Scientific American.

The wire mill at Benedict and Burnham in 1880. Courtesy Scientific American.

The button rooms of Scovill in 1879. Courtesy Scovill Collection.

by automatically combining a variety of particular operations.

The brass industry and its parent in residence, the button industry, quickly moved from a household to a factory basis. Many of the processes just described were already in use in the 1830s. A visitor described the Scovill button shop of 1836, when the company boasted more than fifty employees:

"I witnessed most of the numerous processes in making buttons. The melted red-hot liquid is turned into molds, making narrow plates say 15 or 18 inches long, 4 to 5 inches wide and half or ¾ of an inch in thickness. These plates are then rolled down to the proper thickness for buttons between cylinders which are nearly a foot in diameter. Then the buttons are cut out. Then the buttons are stamped in a mold. The mold gives the figures, letters, or whatever is desired for the outside of the buttons, and gives them the flat, convex or concave shape. . . . The eyes cut from wire are then applied to their place and fastened there; the solder is then placed around the eye, and being laid on a plate, the buttons are heated, so as to appear red-hot. They then undergo various processes—fixing round the eye—fixing the edge, making the sides smooth, encasing on the outside of figured buttons, etc. They are then gilded by dipping them in an amalgam of gold and mercury or quicksilver and then made smooth and bright. Everything is done by machinery. Every process upon the buttons is done in an instant, as it were."*

In his 1920 diary and unpublished autobiography, Charles R. Walker gives us a detailed description of work and workers in a fully developed brass factory, the Coe copper and brass rolling mill of the American Brass Co. in Ansonia in 1920:

"At one end of the mill were large rectangular furnaces, heating copper ingots for hot rolling; then many pairs of rolls with grooves in them, which from where I stood and worked in the other end of the mill seemed to be turning the hot ingots into red snakes. (They were grooving them down into copper wire.)

"All of this, as I remember it, absorbed less than half of the mill floor; the larger area where I worked consisted of batteries of cold rolls which ate up metal from an endless pile of flat coils of copper, squeezing and shaping them with precision. The 'rolls' themselves were hardened steel cylinders, weighing several hundred pounds, set pair by pair in massive iron stanchions. On either side of the stanchions were spanners, sticking out like arms. The roller used them to raise and lower the huge cylindrical rolls thus altering by a few thousanths of an inch the space or 'bite' between the cylinders. It was into this bite that the copper coils were fed.

"A team, or crew, of five

*Kenneth T. Howell, "History of Abel Porter and Co.," unpublished manuscript, Scovill collection, Baker Library, p. 16.

A "sticker" inserting a sheet of brass into a straightening rolls at Scovill in 1919. Courtesy Scovill Collection.

manned each pair of rolls. The roller, who was boss, 'set' the rolls for an order, a sticker's helper mounted a hundred pound coil on a jigger, a giant spool, the sticker (my job) introduced the end or tongue of the coil into the bite and oiled the flowing copper, top side, bottom side as it went through; the blocker caught the moving coil on the other side, mounted it on a whirling wooden core where it rapidly rolled itself like tape around a spool; the blocker's helper, at the right moment, removed the finished coil. That briefly is what a visitor going through the mill would see. . . .

"Surveyed pretty nearly the whole Coe mill; watching first the hot rolls men, taking the red hot bar from the fires in a little truck, and dropping it into the rolls, where with steam and flame it shoots through. After a half dozen passes, it comes out a fiery snake, and is carried to the coiling machine. I then watched the 'big breakers' and the 'little breakers,' where the metal receives its first pinching after the hot rolls. I watched the big finishing rolls and the little ones; talking with the thin little roller who wears glasses, and who has epileptic fits I am told. Someday, he will have one near a pair of rolls and come through the other side pinched down to .020. Then I watched a variety of processes, like the circle cutting machine, which is simply a lathe, which revolves a square piece of copper against a cutting edge.

"In the middle of the afternoon my helper got the end of the coil twisted, and I straightened it out in a hurry before it came to the rolls. Somebody noticed my gyrations, and mentioned them to Seabury as he walked by, so he came on with a warning not to lose a hand, because it might be useful to me. There wasn't much need of the caution, for I had been thinking about it all day. He showed me some ground off fingers of his own to reinforce the remark.

"November 11: Characteristics of the job of sticker I should say were that it was light work, comparatively clean, monotonous, but not seriously so, requires almost no brains, but a certain modicum of judgement and in order to be a head roller, long experience, say three years. The necessity for this length of time is not due to the depth or extent of the learning required, but simply that a period of that length would pass before all types of job had happened to fall to your lot.

"November 27: Charlie Gelhert's rolls were taken down today. They were rough and grooved, one was broken and the brasses were worn.

"Wrestled today with my roller who felt in playful mood, and managed two falls, much to the delight of his helpers.

"A very considerable degree of skill is required to bring the bars through straight and at a proper gauge. Harry stood on the end of the blocker's plank and watched closely as the bar started through the rolls to see which direction it would turn; whether to 'Derby' which meant to the left, or to 'Seymour' which was always the way of saying right. Having noticed the direction, he would change the set to correct for it."

8. The Brass Business: "A Visible Employer"

In 1822 there was one company producing rolled brass buttons in the Valley; its total output was only about twenty gross per day. By 1843 there were three factories rolling brass in Waterbury, employing about 600 workers and using 250 tons of copper yearly. By 1855 the industry, which had spread to Torrington and Ansonia, used about 2,000 tons of copper per year. By 1880 the largest brass mill employed 600 workers.

This growth can be seen in the number of employees at the Scovill Manufacturing Co.:

1850	190	1900	2,000
1860	193	1910	4,000
1870	538	1920	7,000
1880	339	1925	7,500*
1890	1,200		

At its peak during World War I, Scovill employed 15,000 workers.

Companies in the Naugatuck Valley gradually expanded the range

*William G. Lathrop, *The Brass Industry in the United States* (Mount Carmel, Conn., 1926), p. 102.

The Scovill Mfg. Co.'s button shop. Built around 1835 and shown in a photo taken in the late 1800s, it was one of the company's earliest buildings. Courtesy Scovill Collection.

of copper alloy products they produced. Some of this expansion involved the processing of new materials, such as copper, copper plated with silver for photographic plates, and nickel added to brass to make "nickel silver."

Other expansion involved reworking the product. To rolling the companies added wire and tube making. After 1830 the capacity of Waterbury sheet and wire

Rose Hill, the Waterbury "cottage" of Augustus S. Chase, a Waterbury industrialist, banker, and entrepreneur. Courtesy Mattatuck Museum.

mills exceeded the market. Hence, Waterbury companies began to re-manufacture their own brass sheet and wire, producing hooks and eyes, butts made from rolled brass, lamps and burners for kerosene lamps, and copper for electrical use. By 1890 the Naugatuck Valley was producing 75 percent of all ammunition cases made in the U.S. It has been estimated that in the years from 1865 to 1925, an

TABLE 7

The Growth of Brass Manufacturing in Connecticut, 1880–1910

Product	Number of estab-lishments	Men*	Women*	Children	Total	Capital expendi-tures ($)	Value of products ($)	Value added by manufacturing ($)
All brass and bronze products								
1899	62				12,747	25,582,000	49,059,000	12,456,000
1904	64				15,382	40,571,000	53,916,000	16,003,000
1909	80				16,817	47,873,000	66,933,000	19,069,000
Brass and copper, rolled								
1880	15	3,302	673	251	4,226	6,712,000	10,985,000	
1900	11	4,980	312	16	5,308	11,900,00	29,787,000	
Brass castings								
1880	17	484	172	12	668	337,600	1,078,000	
1900	26	3,492	686	43	4,221	7,164,000	9,470,000	
Brassware								
1880	10	501	301	129	931	479,782	1,135,000	
1900	21	2,319	699	105	3,123	6,210,000	9,269,000	
Buttons								
1880	26	471	651	115	1,237	512,500	1,111,000	
1900	11	305	460	35	800	532,000	1,087,000	
Watch and clock materials								
1880	9	85	4	4	93	65,050	161,926	
1900	5	22	5	0	27	44,284	50,984	

*Over 16 years old.

Source: Compiled from U.S. Census data by Peter Rachleff.

TABLE 8
Connecticut Domination of Brass Manufacturing, 1920

Location	Number of wage-earners	Value of products ($)	Value added by manufacturing ($)
U.S.	75,051	482,313,000	177,489,000
Connecticut	29,580	169,550,000	59,312,000

Source: Compiled from U.S. Census data by Peter Rachleff.

TABLE 9
Connecticut Domination of Brass Manufacturing, by Product, 1920

Product	U.S. (lbs.)	Conn. (lbs.)
Ingots and bars	121,790,427	82,286,972
Plates and sheets	283,109,614	173,440,123
Rods	118,412,135	69,995,697
Tubing, seamless	66,076,897	28,359,308
Tubing, brazed	11,859,631	5,694,941
Wire	43,648,993	37,148,909

Source: Compiled from U.S. Census data by Peter Rachleff.

TABLE 10
Corporate Domination of Brass Manufacturing in Connecticut, 1919

Ownership	Number of establishments	Number of wage-earners	Value of products ($)
Individual	20	353	1,778,516
Corporate	48	29,170	166,575,164

Source: Compiled from U.S. Census data by Peter Rachleff.

average of 100 new articles were added each year to the output of the Scovill manufacturing department alone.

A half-dozen entrepreneurs played crucial roles in establishing the brass industry. The Scovill brothers, Aaron Benedict, and Israel Holmes were all natives of Waterbury; Israel Coe came from nearby Goshen; Anson Phelps was a major copper and brass importer from New York. These men were active organizers and partners in the eight large companies which, in 1884, produced 85 percent of the brass in the Valley—which was 85 percent of the total U.S. brass production.

According to industry historian William G. Lathrop:

"If one had after 1870 attended the stockholders' meetings of the various brass companies, of the subordinate concerns as well as of the rolling mills, he would have met in general the same group of men. For example, Mr. J. S. Elton at one time had large investments in four of the largest mills, as well as in many subordinate enterprises; and Mr. G. W. Burnham was a large holder of the stock of at least three of the most important plants. This list might be indefinitely extended."*

Historian Cecelia Bucki details the interlocking directorates of the late nineteenth century:

*Ibid., pp. 122–23.

"Gordon Burnham, Sr. had been president of both Benedict & Burnham and of Holmes, Booth & Hayden at the same time and had large holdings of the Waterbury Brass Company. Frederick J. Kingsbury, a founder of two of Waterbury's earliest banks, was both president of Scovill and director of Waterbury Brass. New Britain hardware interests held directorships of both Coe Brass and Waterbury Brass. James S. Elton, president of Waterbury Brass, was also a director of Coe Brass. E. C. Lewis, president of Farrel Foundry and considered the wealthiest man in Waterbury, held stock in all these concerns."*

As early as 1851, some kind of trade agreement was in effect, and a copy exists of an agreement setting prices as of February 10, 1853, signed by the owners of every brass mill in the Valley—one of the earliest such agreements on record. The pool functioned, though with periods of disorganization, down to 1900. In 1899/1900 most of the major brass-producing companies were merged to form the American Brass Co. When founded, it produced two-thirds of all brass in the U.S. It was also the world's largest roller of copper and a major producer of nickel silver and other alloys. The

*Cecelia Bucki et al., *Metal, Minds and Machines: Waterbury at Work* (Waterbury, Conn.: Mattatuck Historical Society, 1980), p. 24.

TABLE 11
Industrial Concentration in Waterbury Brass Manufacturing, 1920

Value of products	Number of establishments	Number of wage-earners	% of all wage-earners
Less than $5,000	50	22	.1
$5,000–20,000	69	168	.6
$20,000–100,000	62	564	1.9
$100,000–500,000	37	1,800	6.1
$500,000–1,000,000	13	2,379	7.8
$1,000,000 and over	22	25,329	83.5

Source: Compiled from U.S. Census data by Peter Rachleff.

TABLE 12
Ownership of Industrial Enterprises in Waterbury, 1914 and 1919

Ownership	No. of establishments 1914	No. of establishments 1919	No. of wage-earners 1914	No. of wage-earners 1919
Individual	77	94	208	220
Corporate	93	127	19,893 (98.5%)	30,044 (99.1%)

Source: Compiled from U.S. Census data by Peter Rachleff.

separate companies were gradually liquidated, and production became specialized in the various branches. While such mergers were common at that time, this one was unusual in that it was conducted by local companies and financiers, rather than by the major New York investment bankers.

The brass masters' families retained control of production well into the twentieth century.

Frank Keane: You could be working in the mill and you could see the owners—the big families, the Gosses and the Sperries and the others—walking right through the mill. They'd stop and watch the operations. They'd work there. Their children would start in by learning the operations. You knew they weren't going to stay there. But they'd come out of Yale and go in there and learn the operations in the different mills, and then they'd step in and kind of take

(Above) *Members of the Chase family playing backgammon in their home, Rose Hill, around 1910. Courtesy Mattatuck Museum.*
(Right) *Benedict and Burnham Mfg. Co. in the 1880s, before it became part of the American Brass Co. Courtesy Mattatuck Museum.*

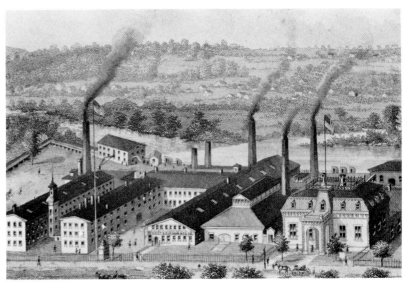

over. I don't think you see that much any more. There was a visible employer.

9. The Laborers: Bull Work and Buggy Lugging, Cramping and Charging

During the century from 1820 to 1920, the brass industry, like other American industries, was marked by a sharp division between skilled and unskilled workers. The skilled workers were crucial to the production process itself and, therefore, crucial to a company's success. They often held favored positions; in many ways they were positions close to what we, today, would call managerial.

The unskilled, "common labor," faced quite a different situation.

The men were primarily involved, not with direct production, but with moving materials from place to place by human musclepower. The women were predominantly engaged in repetitive jobs, producing or assembling manufactured products. In general, employers treated laborers as interchangeable and easily replaced.

MEN

Initially, unskilled workers were recruited largely from the surrounding farms. The factory system had not advanced to the point where most of the employees were exclusively industrial workers. Indeed, they were sometimes used on the employers' farms. As late as 1838, an order was delayed at Scovill because a factory manager and his gang were harvesting: "If

Buckingham gets through with his hay this week as he intends we shall begin to push the Buttons next week."

The early mills interacted economically with a substantial rural hinterland and required a large labor force of wood cutters, carters, and others who worked outside the mill itself. This continued long enough to be remembered by a group of brass workers and their wives, who met at the Derby Senior Center.

Bart Hennessey: [American Brass] owned land all around the countryside here. They used to cut the wood and bring it in. Stored it on the west side in what they called the Wood Lot.

Vincent Zak: Across the street from where my father's farm was,

(Left) *Women doing primitive benchwork at Ansonia Brass and Copper Co.'s shoe hardware division in 1899. Courtesy Anaconda Industries.* (Above) *S. M. Buckingham, a Scovill relative and executive. Courtesy Scovill Collection.*

they cut the woods down for American Brass.

Hennessey: All through Oxford and Southbury, they would haul it in every day. They had thousands and thousands of cords of wood stacked. They owned most of the land.

Zak: Or they'd buy the land and sell it back. The wood was their means of heat for the furnaces. Metal annealing. Melting metal.

From the 1840s on, immigrant men, in successive waves, began to replace local farmers as unskilled laborers. They were generally hired by the day or week and had no job security whatsoever.

Sam Kwochka: In the olden days, when the people were hired there, they used to have a wire cage on the outside. The people would meet in the wire cage. When the foreman needed somebody for a particular job, he went down and said, "I want you for an hour." Then you went back to that wire cage and hoped the foreman would call you again. That must have been when my father went to work there.

The following account from Charles R. Walker's diary of gang labor in one department gives a sense of the large role that human musclepower played in the brass industry:

"Started work in the Copper Refinery, working on the floor gang; all Spaniards. The furnaces and other arrangements impress me as primitive in comparison with the facilities in the way of crane service, charging machines, etc., in a steel mill. Furnaces are charged by hand, and require ten men for their care. Pouring, by hand from a large spoon. All moulds and ingots hand trucked. Program of day was as follows:

"(1) Gang brings up moulds in trucks and places them around furnace convenient for pouring. Each man brings up an empty mould in his truck, and returns with one filled with an ingot.

"(2) Pulling ingots from moulds. Done by means of tongs. The ingots that stick are pounded out with a crow bar.

"(3) Piling ingots. One man loads them on the trucks of the rest of the gang. They truck them to man with tongs who lifts them into piles.

"(4) Cleaning moulds. Each

TABLE 13
The Metal-working Labor Force in Connecticut, by Occupation and Ethnic Background, 1920

Occupation	Native-born white, native parents	Native-born white, foreign parents	Foreign-born white	Black	Total
Men, all manufacturing and mining (aggregate)	62,146	66,752	125,241	3,687	257,856*
Women, all manufacturing (aggregate)	12,928	27,705	19,089	622	60,350*
Blacksmiths	439	401	1,230	17	2,087
Brass molders	193	224	965	59	1,441
Buffers and polishers	643	1,224	3,087	11	4,965
Filers	142	151	466	4	763
Forgemen	247	269	430	12	958
Furnacemen	37	62	230	13	342
Grinders	328	322	869	8	1,527
Iron molders	321	455	2,585	36	3,397
Iron and steel laborers	1,298	1,892	10.293	459	14,018*
Brass mill laborers	422	835	6,343	313	7,933*
Clock and watch laborers	162	221	449	2	834
Machinists	6,890	7,070	8,571	101	22,634*
Millwrights	372	348	514	1	1,235
Rollers and roll hands	200	167	710	27	1,104
Iron and steel workers, semi-skilled	4,319	5,446	10,524	143	20,558*
Brass workers, semi-skilled	693	1,033	3,148	66	4,940
Watch and clock workers, semi-skilled	655	933	925	0	2,513
Toolmakers	1,921	2,373	1,808	4	6,106
Female laborers, brass	48	185	224	0	457
Female laborers, watch and clock	67	167	59	1	294
Female laborers, iron and steel	221	573	643	14	1,451
Female brass workers, semi-skilled	381	1,050	836	3	2,270
Female watch and clock workers, semi-skilled	546	1,294	473	0	2,313
Female iron and steel workers, semi-skilled	1,480	3,421	2,595	26	7,522

*Census figures do not add up.
Source: Compiled from U.S. Census data by Peter Rachleff.

Workers moving brass sheets by hand at the Ansonia Brass and Copper Co. in 1899. Courtesy Anaconda Industries.

mould is brushed out, with a long handled brush, and the end cleaned. The workman then knocks it down, and stands it on the other end, brushing it off again.

"(5) Assembling moulds. Moulds are trucked to one place and arranged in rows. In order to have room to knock them down and draw the ingot, they have been sectioned over a wide area. They are now collected, and covered with sheets of copper to prevent dust from entering.

"(6) Piling large ingots. By this time the pourers have made a dozen or two large ingots. They are now trucked and piled by the floor gang. One or two men lift the ingots with tongs to the truck, and two men make the piling with tongs, when the ingots have been trucked to the proper position.

"By this time it is nearly noon, although there may be time to truck a few loads of scrap for the furnaces before 12.

"Afternoon.

"(7) Trucking scrap in bundles. Scrap arrives in the mill in trucks, and consists for the most part of tangled bunches of wire of all sizes, weighing from 100 to 125 lbs each. These are piled on a four-wheel truck and dumped beside the furnace. 'Scalpings' arrive in barrels, and are hand trucked and dumped beside the furnace.

"Other afternoon duties: shovelling, sorting scrap from dirt. Trucking scrap pounded from ladle."

Workers had to have a certain knack to perform even "bull work" well and safely, as Walker indicates:

"Got the knack today of taking a mould or an ingot on a truck, so as to avoid over reaching and putting strain on my back. Also have pretty well memorized the holes and broken plates of the floor so as to avoid spills. Know how an ingot should sit on a truck to give least weight; and the best trucks.

"Most crude labor has its technique. When taking a 200 lb mould on the truck, shove edge of truck at least half way under raised end of mould, pressing it in with foot on lower rung of truck, place foot on 3rd rung, and press down handles of truck, to seat mould; be sure mould lies flat; otherwise weight will be too far forward, and double the difficulty of pushing the truck."

WOMEN

As we have seen, many families were dependent on the wages of women and children. Before World War I, the women usually stopped working outside the home when they got married. Many women, however—notably many Irish immigrants—did not marry and continued to work in the plants all their lives.

Women were only rarely considered "skilled" workers. A number of factors contributed to their exclusion from the better jobs in the industry:

In many cases, the work women did required just as much skill as the "skilled" jobs held by men. In many industries, jobs were defined as "unskilled" simply by virtue of the fact that they were generally held by women.

Many assumptions about what was and should be "women's work" were shared by men and women, employers and workers alike. Until the last few decades, few questioned the belief that the heaviest physical labor in the brass mills was "by nature" for men— that women were not physically capable of performing it. It was also generally assumed that the brass mills were socially inappropriate places for women—that women and their families would be contaminated somehow by their contact with such an environment. Such assumptions were largely arbitrary; when employers' labor requirements changed, the conventions about what were, or were not, "acceptable" jobs for women changed rapidly, too.

In many instances, male solidarity functioned to define "woman's place" and preserve male prerogatives. Many men preferred that their wives work only occasionally or not at all, because they wanted to retain their services in the home and limit their independence. The work groups in such male preserves as the casting shop would, no doubt, have met any proposal to introduce women as their co-workers with scorn. Al-

A wire mill worker at Ansonia Brass and Copper Co. in 1899. Courtesy Anaconda Industries.

though tool and die making requires little strength and demands the manual dexterity at which women are supposed to excel, women were excluded from this highly skilled occupation in the industry until World War II.

Despite the fact that many women in this period—particularly single women—spent their whole lives from their early teens in the industrial work force, employers tended to assume that women were not permanent workers, that they would move in and out of jobs. This was complemented by the assumption that they were not family breadwinners

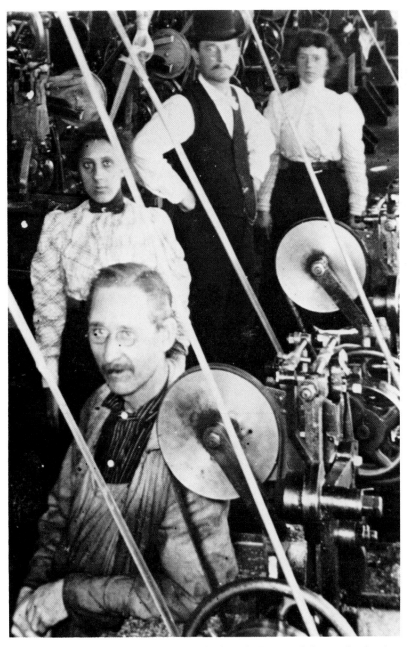

Workers in the shoe hardware division of the Ansonia Brass and Copper Co. in 1899. Courtesy Anaconda Industries.

and, therefore, did not work out of economic necessity. Because of these assumptions, employers often limited women to jobs that did not require long experience to master skills. This exclusion of women from skilled jobs, in turn, encouraged women to limit their attachment to any particular job. To make matters worse, there were no provisions for maternity leave or seniority protection. If a woman left the work force to have children, she had to look for a new job when she returned.

The rapid expansion and contraction of the brass industry, especially in wartime, required a body of workers that could be called into service when needed, workers who would neither revolt nor migrate out when jobs were not available. The definition of women as people whose basic responsibilities were in the home, but who were available as temporary workers when needed, created such a "reserve army."

The sexual division of labor dated from the household era of the brass industry and was perpetuated by tradition except in times of labor shortage. If it had been a "man's job," it generally stayed a "man's job." Where formal apprenticeship arrangements prevailed, women were not apprenticed to male jobs. By these means, the exclusion of women from skilled jobs became self-perpetuating. The sex line was drawn and rarely questioned.

"A group of good-looking press room girls in their new uniforms." The Scovill Bulletin *published this picture with that caption in 1919. Courtesy Scovill Collection.*

Rolling and wire mills were, from the beginning, male preserves. In manufacturing departments, however, women played a major role. For example, thirty-three of the fifty-two employees at Scovill in 1831 were women. According to Scovill historian P. W. Bishop, "More than half of the women were engaged on 'cramping and charging' for which they were paid 3 cents a gross. This operation, which was to be carried on in substantially the same way until the first decade of this century, attached the wire-eye to solid buttons. Cramping consisted of centering the wire on the button-back and securing it in position with a heavy wire cramp. In charging, the necessary amount of flux was ap-

(Right and above) Women at the Chase Brass Co. Many women were employed in jobs formerly held by men during World War I. Courtesy Connecticut State Library.

plied with a small brush to the points of contact between the button and the eye. The buttons would then be ready for soldering by the application of heat in a small furnace."*

Women served as a kind of labor reserve, drawn into the brass plants when labor was needed.

Hap Lasky: In those days none of the [Lithuanian] women worked. Married women didn't start working until before World War I. They were short of help at that time, and they brought in the women. During the war I worked out in Scovill's, and there were a lot of married women working out there that I knew.

Rowena Peck and Sarah Cappella recall the World War I era.

Rowena Peck: They were glad to get women because so many of the men had gone into the service. They had no trouble getting the women. Anyone who wanted to work. They advertised in the local papers.

Sarah Cappella: I came from Italy when I was seven years old. I went to school here. I grew up, got married, and I worked all my life.

The First World War I worked in Scovill's. I worked on drill presses, on some kind of a bullet. I worked there till after the war, then we all got laid off.

*Bishop, "History of Scovill Mfg. Co.," pp. 182–83.

Then I went home and I had a baby. I went back to work in the American Brass. I worked on draw benches. We stretched tubes. I worked there eleven years.

Then I worked in the American Fastener on power presses. I also went back to Scovill's in later years and worked on power presses.

I was twenty-one [when I went to work at Scovill's]. I loved that job. I was looking for work. I went in and that's what they gave me. There were a lot [of women working there]; a whole lineful. There was a line that was all drill presses, but then there was other kinds of work, which I didn't work on.

A drill press is a machine that has a wheel and moving parts and a handle. We'd pull it down, and it came down on our piece of work. Drilled holes, anything.

We had to work and then they paid us and that was it. No special allowance for anybody. No coffee time like today. At that time we worked nine hours a day.

CHILDREN

Because of low wages, many families found it necessary to send their children to work as soon as they legally could, or even before. Children's earnings were normally turned over to the parents and became an important part of the family income.

Employers regarded children as "nimble and light on their feet." They often hired the children of their current employees, both as a

Scovill employees included children in the late 1880s, when this picture was taken. Courtesy Scovill Collection.

paternalistic gesture and as a means of recruiting workers whose families would help enforce their work discipline. Like women, children also provided a "reserve army" which could be employed when more workers were needed but who could be let go with little cost when they were not.

Industrial work provided the primary job opportunities for the children of most immigrants. Because jobs requiring education were rarely available, working-class families did not place the same stress on education that they did later.

Joe Sciaretta's father worked as a railroad man in Italy before he and his family came to America in 1915. His first job in America was placing ties for the railroad. About 1920, he went to work at Chase's as a boilerman. Joe's mother returned to Italy soon after they arrived in America, but came back to Waterbury in 1920. Of her four children, Joe, born in 1921, was the first to be born in America.

His mother died when he was ten. He was raised by his older sister, who worked at Debner's Textiles, and his older brother, a metal forger at Chase's. Joe's father returned to his home in Italy for many visits. Joe graduated from grammar school and high school, the only one in his family to do so. He is married to the former Angelina Cariello, and is the father of three sons. He worked at Uniroyal, Inc., in Naugatuck for thirty-nine years. He has been the union time study man (United Rubber Work-

Many children worked at Ansonia Brass and Copper Co. in 1899. Courtesy Anaconda Industries.

A teenage worker at Ansonia Brass and Copper Co.'s wire mill in 1899. Courtesy Anaconda Industries.

ers, Local 45) for the past twelve years.

Joe Sciaretta: They didn't believe in schooling in those days. When you got a certain age, you went to work. They figured, as long as they could bring home a day's pay, that's all they were interested in. In those days [education] wasn't as important as it is today.

Hap Lasky: My first job was for A. H. Wells. I was on vacation. That was in 1910; I was only twelve years old. On the draw bench pulling tubes. There was a lad who put some goo on it. He put it through a die. With a pair of pliers, we'd grab it. They had a chain that would carry the pliers through. When it came to the end, we'd pick it up and throw it over on the bed.

The next vacation I went to

work for my father. He was a brazed tuber at American Brass. He used to put a goo, a sort of a paste, on the seam. It would go through a lot of heat. That would melt it and weld it in there. Then they'd run it through machines to smooth that weld off. That was 1913.

Russell Hunter worked as a blocker in the slitting department of American Brass; his father worked there before him. Although Hunter is Black, he grew up in predominantly white neighborhoods. He describes many aspects of local life and work in detail, but he seems to become really alive when he describes the good times he had growing up in Waterbury. He does not care for recent changes in the city. Pointing out his window, he said: "North

Main Street out here used to be a beautiful street. People by the thousands during the war used to work in the factories. The way I look at life, when they chopped down all the trees and shrubberies, they cut down the life of the city. Now it's all bare. What do you see out there?" (Russell Hunter is the uncle of William Freeman, who is introduced on page 196.)

Russell Hunter: In those days kids who went to grammar school could come out in the summertime and go into Scovill's. I had jobs in there. Like plating things and putting them on a board. Kick them around in a solution. Nickel plate them.

You see these old-time Fords have a kind of square hubcap on them? We'd put them on a board or a rack and dip them down in whatever color they wanted. Afterwards we'd bring it out, soap it up, and wash it off.

HOMEWORK

Many families did production work in their homes. The most frequent homework was the attaching of brass snap fasteners to the cards on which they were sold. Scovill, Risdon, and the American Fastener Co. employed such homeworkers.

Evelyn Cambigue was born in Waterbury in 1912. Her father worked at American Brass until his retirement. Evelyn went to work at age fourteen as an usherette and cashier in a local movie theater. At sixteen, a friend of hers got her a job as a file clerk at American Brass. "I never knew too much about what was going on inside the factories." Evelyn married when she was nineteen, and raised six children. She didn't work outside the home after her marriage. "I thought that was it—you're married, that's it."

Mary Cocca's parents came from Italy to Allentown, Pennsylvania, where her parents kept a store. Mary was born there in 1903, one of five children. She came to Waterbury with her husband and got a job in the lacquer room at Chase's spraying hubcaps. Her husband also worked at Chase's in the buff room for thirty-six years.

After she had her second child, she quit Chase's because she couldn't find anybody to take care of her children. Later on, she worked at a concession at the YMCA for twenty years. She has been a Senior Aide for the past fourteen years, the majority of that time at the Bergin Center.

Evelyn Cambigue: I remember when we were little kids, my mother worked for a while because it was tough times. She worked down in the pin shop. She used to come home with these pins and snaps.

Mary Cocca: I remember doing them, too.

Sarah Cappella: Everybody.

Cambigue: My mother would bring it home [from the Oakville Pin Shop].

Cappella: I was married when I started putting them on. I couldn't go to work. The kids were small. We used to go get them at the fastener shop. We used to get big bunches. My brother-in-law made square pieces of wood and carved them the same shape as the fastener. We'd only have to put the fastener, put the card on top, and put the other piece, and we'd do fast.

They gave us about two cents a card. That's all. We made enough because we were a bunch in the house. Everybody was putting them on.

Josephine Tedesco: We didn't do them, but we did the safety pins.

My brother Henry used to take my father's horse and wagon in the morning and go around collecting the baskets from five or six families and bring them to the shop. He'd have to sit in line till they checked him in and gave him more pins to bring back to the people. We did it, and my mother used to buy our clothes with that money.

Homework continued legally until 1929, when it was outlawed by the Connecticut General Assembly. To a small extent, it continues today on an "under the table" basis.

10. The Skilled Workers: "The Shop Would Have to Stop without Them"

Although English workers continued to play important roles in some plants well into the 1930s, by 1850 American men had come to form a large part of the skilled work force. They predominated until around 1870, when Irish men began to take over. The Irish were followed by subsequent immigrants.

Industry historian William Lathrop, writing in 1926, describes the evolution of a system that, at one time, tied skilled brass workers close to their employers:

"As early as 1835, as it was found that the kettlemen at Wolcottville were unwilling to train apprentices, the system was adopted of regulating their pay by the pound of product. Under this stimulus they were persuaded to employ American helpers. This system of paying a skilled mechanic a fixed price per unit of production once generally prevailed. The mechanic then hired his own helpers, using machinery furnished by the proprietors. This

Skilled workers and foremen from a variety of departments at Scovill in 1884. Courtesy Scovill Collection.

system, together with the fact that individual skill plays such a large part in the value of some workmen, has made a uniform wage scale impracticable.

"The policy generally adopted by the mills has been to pay skilled laborers high wages. The result has been to attach these closely to the plant in which they were employed. Many own their homes and are in very comfortable circumstances." *

As Lathrop points out, "The system adopted tended to the development of specialization and unusual skill in the head mechanics. Formerly the men having in hand some special line of work were reluctant or absolutely refused to impart their special skill to others." † Charles R. Walker found remnants of such craft traditions in Ansonia in 1920:

"A very interesting case of craft secrecy turned up today in conversation with 'George' the clerk. Asked me if I'd ever seen the refiners [perform a particular process]. Said he never had, though he'd been in the refinery 18 years. 'The refiners keep those things to themselves,' he said. This is like the mysterious ingredient the old casters used to use, in their pots of metal.

"The two refiners here have a very good case for secrecy; they

are the only ones in Ansonia, and the shop would have to stop without them; they can command the situation. For years until Gervin came they had matters to suit themselves since none of the foremen knew any metallurgy."

The skilled workers played an important part in the ferment that would keep the Naugatuck Valley at the forefront of the Industrial Revolution in America, but they rarely reaped the benefits or gained any credit for it.

Hap Lasky: My father had a lot of patents. But they'd bring him in there and give him a few drinks and that was it: Sign here. He'd sign the patents over to Booth and Hayden's.

THE MACHINISTS

In the latter part of the nineteenth century, when the brass companies were producing an increasing number of finished products, there was a great expansion in the role of machinists. By 1874 Scovill had organized its machine room as a separate department. According to the International Association of Machinists, by 1901 there were 800 machinists in Waterbury, most of them in brass plants. In 1910 Scovill employed 300 machinists and tool- and diemakers to prepare machines and tools. In 1915 it was 500; by 1920 the number had grown to 850.

In the nineteenth century, ma-

chinists' skill levels were already being reduced. Bishop indicates that between 1850 and 1892, "the relative sophistication of the machine tools was evidently already permitting the employment of lower paid workers to supplement the skills of the tool men." ‡

John "Jack" Hollingworth was born in 1890 in Sheffield, England, the home of the British cutlery industry. His family had been skilled

workers for two generations before him, and at the age of fifteen he entered a toolmaking apprenticeship. In 1908, he became a charter member of the Boy Scouts. He and his friend, Harry Holmes, organized fourteen troops in two years in the Sheffield area. The woman Jack married, Lily Bunting, was

*Lathrop, *The Brass Industry*, p. 96.
†Ibid., pp. 96–97.

‡Bishop, "History of Scovill Mfg. Co.," p. 197.

born in Waterbury to English parents. She met Jack on a trip to Sheffield with her ailing father. In 1913, Jack and Lily left for America as husband and wife. After working for two years in Philadelphia, he moved to Waterbury, where he was employed as a toolmaker by various brass plants including Scovill, Plume and Atwood, and American Brass, from which he retired in 1958. He continued to work at various part-time jobs in the brass industry until 1975. He lives at Robin Ridge, an elderly apartment complex in Waterbury, where he still puts his skills to good use preparing materials for various arts and crafts projects.

John Hollingworth: Scovill had an apprentice system; they made specialized mechanics out of them. Where I came from, you had to learn all the machines; it took six years.

I came from a mechanical family. It was just the age when things were being manufactured of metal. I happened to be born in a family like that.

To start out [the toolmakers in Waterbury] were mostly German, Swedish, and English. Then the Italians got into it. The first ones that came over were construction men. Then their sons went to school, got smart, and learned the trade.

[I worked with my first Italian toolmaker] around the 1940s.

[The companies did not push the toolmakers] in England; you had pride in your production. They tried to push here. The answer used to be: I've only got one pair of hands. I resented all that stuff. If the boss told me they wanted a job, I'd say, "I'll do the best I can."

11. De-skilling: The Story of the Casters

The actual production of brass was entirely dependent on the skill and knowledge of the caster. The basic decisions, including the mixture of metals to be used, when to introduce the spelter, and when to pour, all rested on his judgment.

The power of the casters was extraordinary. In 1899 C. P. Goss, Jr., son of a top Scovill manager, paid a fifty-dollar fee and was apprenticed to a caster to learn the mysteries of the art. He recalled that "under the old system the caster . . . worked things out according to his own ideas. Everybody was happy and everybody made top wages. If the caster had trouble with the office, he walked over to another shop and hired out there. He sent for his crew and the offending mill simply shut down a fire until some other caster got mad or they could entice the old man back." *

*Ibid., p. 214.

Management was loath to tamper with the casters' prerogatives. P. W. Bishop relates this story about the casting shop under the reign of "Chan" Goss:

"One day an efficiency expert checking up on the casting shop at the East Mill discovered that the casting crews went across the way for beer after pouring a heat. Without consulting 'Chan,' the bright lad posted a notice forbidding any beer during working hours. A fireman smeared soot over that . . . notice and thought no more of it. The next move by the efficiency man was to have the main gate locked. When the casters ran out for their beer, the gates were closed tight and they ran into 'Chan's' office instead. Looking up from his mail, the brass master listened to the story, picked up his hat and went across the way with his men and ordered 'free beer for a week.' The efficiency man vanished." †

The casting shop was recognized as a bottleneck in which "the Company was at the mercy of the casters." In 1889 (two years after a strike in the casting shop), Scovill began to try operating the casting shop furnaces with oil. When this failed, company officials introduced the contract system. They signed a contract with a boss caster, agreeing to pay a fixed price per pound for "good" metal. The

†Ibid., p. 215.

The crew of Scovill's east casting shop in 1919. Courtesy Scovill Collection.

caster would employ his own help. The immediate result was that labor costs were cut by 50 percent, and the system became standard.

Nonetheless, technical control of the production process remained in the hands of the boss caster, who could always improve his chance of meeting quality standards by substituting expensive virgin copper for cheap scrap. To combat this, management at-tempted to assert control over the mixture. In 1899 Scovill hired an expert from Yale to draw up directions for the weighing-up crew, thus determining the proportions of the various ingredients. The innovation was opposed by the casters, but without effect.

Around 1910 the brass companies began intensive efforts to eliminate caster control. At Scovill, "the erection of two buildings, equipped with a total of 72 additional oil furnaces, was authorized at a cost of over $1,000,000."

The old casters "felt no inclination to work under new and untried conditions at a reduced rate of pay" and were "more hindrance than help when induced to assist with the new furnaces." A new casting shop labor force was recruited from the unskilled, consisting, at Scovill, of "a baker, a drug clerk, an undertaker's assistant, a hat-maker, a core-maker, a plasterer, and a mining engineer from Mexico!"* As each company introduced the new furnaces, most of the casters left to seek work in the remaining traditional casting shops.

By 1917 the Bridgeport Brass Co. had introduced electric brass furnaces on a commercial scale. They represented a far greater technical advance than the oil furnace. They were publicly proclaimed as the way to end company dependence on the skills of the casters.

When George Chapman, who started working at Plume and Atwood in Thomaston in 1890, was interviewed by the Works Progress Administration in 1939 he spoke of the impact of the electric casting furnace: "No, with these new electric furnaces, it isn't like it used to be. One man can pour, where they needed four or five. Of course they laid off casters when they put 'em in. That's the main reason they got 'em."†

At Seymour Mfg. Co. the older brass-casting techniques lasted longer than in the larger companies. Sam Kwochka, John Chubat, Joe Yrchik, and Frank Pochron describe the older system and how it changed.

*Ibid., p. 216.

†Works Progress Administration, Interview of George Chapman, March 6, 1939; record at Connecticut State Library.

Sam Kwochka: With the coal fires, the caster was boss. He got money for the amount of metal that was produced. He would hire a fireman. That man would come in about 1 or 2 o'clock in the morning. Then you had a wheelbarrow man; he was handy. You had a pot puller. And the caster himself.

He'd get the alloys that were listed on the ticket, and he'd pour so many bars for that particular day.

If the fireman came in at 1 o'clock, at 3 o'clock the fire was hot enough to melt metal. So then came along the caster and his assistant. He would set the pots up. If they were fortunate and everything went right, by 12 o'clock they'd have the pouring done and they went home.

John Chubat: They also had a man to grease the molds, because you

(Above) *Weighing up a charge of metal before melting it at Scovill in 1919. Courtesy Scovill Collection.*
(Below) *A caster and his helper checking the casting shop furnaces at Scovill in 1919. Courtesy Scovill Collection.*

cannot pour the metal in the mold until it is greased. Then ream it out with a chisel.

Joe Yrchik: These molds were down in the pits. They'd pour these molds. By the time they got around, two guys would break the molds. They were taking these red hot bars with a pair of pliers, one at each end, picking it up, and throwing it on the wagon while it was still red hot. Then they'd have to start all over by greasing the molds.

Frank Pochron: Years ago they only hired the caster and paid him the money. He'd try to get as much money as he could for his own pocket.

Chubat: The casters mostly were Irish. Our people would just grease the molds.

Kwochka: There is no longer a caster, there is an operator. He sees to it that the furnaces are charged; all the setups and all that are arranged prior to the melt by the supervisor. The supervisor really has to spend a little effort at the beginning of the week to see that everything is lined up. The rest of it is just operations.

Pochron: You've got to have certain ingredients. That's controlled by the laboratory. Before, they had to dress the molds. The molds had to be just so; they had to do it just right.

Russell Sobin, the son of a Russian immigrant who worked at American Brass, was born at home in Ansonia in 1911. He followed his father into the plant in 1929, was laid off during the Depression, and returned in 1935 to work until his retirement in 1975. In his forty years at ABC, he worked as a shear operator, roller, annealer, packer, and clerical worker. He was one of the first two union supporters in his department when organizing began in 1937. "You had to have a lot of guts because at that time a lot of them would say, oh, if you're going to be a union man, they're going to fire you. You couldn't be a roller at that time. After we got the union in, that's when we broke the barrier. I became a roller. We had a Russian roller, a Polish roller. I think I was about the first one." In the early days, he served as a union steward but his wife

Stella made him quit because "he was never home." He and Stella have two children and seven grandchildren. He is an active member of the Derby Senior Center, the Russian American Club in Shelton, and the Lemko Club in Ansonia.

The casting shop remained a notoriously dangerous and unhealthy place to work.

Russell Sobin: You just went through, you'd come out, and you'd be black. I would never work there. That was a tough job. That's why those guys would knock off a pint or a quart of whiskey a day, to clean that dust out. Just like the coal mines where you get the black lung. For a while there, almost every week somebody would drop dead of a heart attack. It was hot; in the winter it was cold. There were no windows; all the gasses had to go out. To keep warm, they had an old oil drum. Fill it up with wood and put some coal on it—that was their heat. Mostly Lithuanian, Polish, Russian, Italian, Blacks, worked in the casting shop in the old days.

Years ago more than one man would get scalded with hot metal. If your molds were a little damp or something and you poured that metal in, it would blow up and you would be cooked.

Now they've got asbestos clothes on: gloves, shoes, leggings—otherwise they would burn up.

Workers pouring a heat in the Scovill casting shop in 1919. Courtesy Scovill Collection.

12. Working Conditions: Maimed Hands and Spelter Shakes

HIRING

In the early brass mills, the owners themselves directed the skilled workers, who in turn bossed their helpers and the unskilled laborers. As the companies grew larger, room foremen who were given the power to hire and fire managed the work force. They set the hours of labor and even negotiated wage rates with the individuals under them. In 1887 M. L. Sperry at Scovill wrote:

"We have never had any shop rules printed. There is a general understanding that ten hours constitute a day's work and that the hands are expected to do a day's work if they get a day's pay. Each department is under the direction of a foreman, in whom we trust and who sees that the hands are industrious and attend to their business. If they do not do it, he sends them off and gets others. The managers do not deal directly with the hands. They simply deal with the foremen and if they do not like the way the hands under a foreman work, they bounce the foreman and get another.

"We do not think printed rules amount to anything unless there is somebody around constantly to enforce them and if such person is around printed forms can be dispensed with."*

As P. W. Bishop wrote, hiring was done "largely through personal acquaintance between the men and the foreman who would know where to find an individual if he wanted him, usually in a neighboring saloon, the workers' 'club' of the time. Even as late as 1922, we hear of a foreman of the rolling mill seeking out some of his striking workers in a saloon and bringing them back to work!"†

Born in Waterbury in 1897, Jim Cusack went to work at the Scovill Mfg. Co. in 1918 as a clerk. He spent thirteen years in the general manufacturing department, serving in various departments, particularly the planning department. During this time he undertook related courses of study and gained a broad knowledge of production engineering. In 1930, he went into the mills department to study methods, standards of quality, and so forth then in use, looking toward possible improvement. He and others determined that, for the most part, the equipment was badly antiquated. To be competitive in the industry, Scovill decided to undergo a total modernization. He was closely involved with the changes which brought about modernization. When he retired in 1963, he was the Works Manager of the Mills Division. Frank Keane, introduced on page 7, is his brother-in-law.

Ethnicity was of great significance in the selection of foremen.

Jim Cusack: [The old foremen] were a very fine type of man. They were a little bit above the average in intelligence and in drive. Almost all manufacturing department foremen were former toolmakers, because they had an intimate knowledge of the equipment and the tools. They were either Anglo-Saxon or German, or some Swiss.

When you got into the rougher parts, then you found the Irishmen. The foremen in the mills were mostly Irish who had come up through the ranks. They were not toolmakers or other types of mechanics, but they were skilled in what was being done in the mill department in which they were working. They would have come up from a roller's helper to a roller to an assistant foreman to a foreman. Hopefully, [they might go on to be] a general foreman or a mill superintendent.

Hiring was often done on the basis of "pull." Charles R. Walker writes:

"That nepotism was the rule in old times is evident from the very strong persistence of it today. A well-known baron not long ago sent up a lad to the employment office, just arrived from England. He expected to slip him in at once, despite the fact that there was a waiting list of several hundred old hands, who had awaited a job from one to six months."

The outright selling of jobs was also a continuing abuse. The following story, whose truth it would be impossible to verify, indicates the resentment with which this practice was regarded by workers.

Mike Laban: A Lithuanian guy came in [to a tavern], grabbed hold of his foreman, bought him a beer, and told him, "Hey, I've got a nephew who just got off the boat, he'd like to have a job." He slipped him twenty dollars. Twenty dollars in those days was a lot of money.

This nephew worked for quite a number of weeks. When the bottom fell out and we had some hard times, the foreman came over and said, "John, you're all through today."

This guy wasn't that stupid. He said, "I've just got on my feet. Everything is working pretty good." So Monday morning he shows up with a big wrench [and starts to disassemble his machine]. He's working away at a bolt and loosening it. Right away one of the guys says, "You can't do that." "That's

*Bishop, "History of Scovill Mfg. Co.," p. 205.
†Ibid., p. 209.

my machine. The boss told me when I was hired: that's my machine. I want to take my machine home."

He knew he couldn't take it home, but he figured, "I'll get this sonofagun." A big 6'4" guy who weighed around 240 with a big wrench—you'd be crazy to tackle him. So the guy goes right away to get the foreman. "My machine—I take my machine home." Right away there's a commotion, and one of the big shots from the office comes by. He said, "I pay that sonofabitch twenty dollars for this job. He tell me this my machine, this my job. No more job, and I want to take machine home." The guy was repaid the twenty dollars, and the foreman was let go.

WAGES

It is difficult to construct a reliable account of the incomes of various types of workers. Because there were no standard pay rates before collective bargaining was established in the 1940s, wages differed from individual to individual. Methods of payment—piece- and day-rate systems, incentives, contracting, salaries, and the like—were complex and changed drastically over time. Prices fluctuated, changing the real value of wages. Wage information for Scovill in 1850, 1874, and 1892 has been compiled by P. W. Bishop and appears in Table 15.

Skilled jobs were considered relatively well paid. Charles R. Walker describes a roller's income level in 1920:

"Bill says he can save $10 out of a $30 pay envelope. His wife and kids live at his mother-in-law's so he hasn't that to figure on. He is paying off some big debts, he tells me. When he finished buying things after getting married, he owed the furniture man over $800; this is down to $40 now. He has run other debts; all of which he would be free from, he tells me, had he worked steadily."

When asked about unskilled work of the early days, most people remembered the low pay.

Joe Sciaretta: My father worked twelve hours a day, six days a week at Chase's. He came home with about eleven or twelve dollars a week, twelve, fourteen dollars. He used to shovel coal into the furnaces. He worked hard. There was no incentive at that time. There was no pension either.

ACCIDENTS

Accident rates in the brass mills were high. In 1916 the Scovill hospital recorded 16,000 accidents; 11,287 casualties; and 60,000 surgical dressings given to its workers.

Memories of such accidents are widespread among brass workers. Daniel Loffredo, who started working in the brass mills in Waterbury in 1920, recalls that one time he saw everyone running—someone had had his arm pulled into a machine. They pulled him

TABLE 14
The Workweek in the Era of World War I, 1914 and 1919

Length of workweek	No. of wage-earners (Waterbury)		No. of brass workers (Conn.)	
	1914	1919	1914	1919
Workers (total)	20,189	30,030	16,781	27,806
48 hours	484	394	64	300
48–54 hours	4,744	11,829	4,143	8,300
54 hours	3,440	2,324	358	255
54–60 hours	7,671	15,227	9,328	18,942
60 hours	3,691	50	2,888	9
Over 60 hours	159	206	n.a.	n.a.

Source: Compiled from U.S. Census data by Peter Rachleff.

TABLE 15
Daily Wage Scales, Scovill Mfg. Co., 1850, 1874, 1892

1913 Scale Daily Rate	Equivalence in 1948* Prices Daily Rate	1850 Males	1850 Females	1874 Males	1874 Females	1892 Males	1892 Females
$5 Plus	$10 Plus			2 .8%		41 5.4%	
4.00–4.99	8.00–9.99			5 2.0%		68 9.0%	
3.00–3.99	6.00–7.99	3 2.2%		17 6.8%		90 11.9%	
2.00–2.99	4.00–5.99	34 25.0%		53 21.5%		52 6.9%	5 1.2%
1.00–1.99	2.00–3.99	42 30.9%	1 1.1%	129 52.3%	3 4.5%	476 63.2%	60 15.0%
.50– .99	1.00–1.99	57 41.9%	67 77.9%	33 13.4%	39 58.2%	7 .9%	118 29.5%
Less Than .50¢	Less Than $1	—	—	5 2.0%	—	—	—
Pieceworkers			18 21.0%	3 1.2%	25 37.3%	20 2.7%	218 54.3%
		136 61.2%	86 38.8%	247 78.5%	67 21.5%	754 65.3%	401 34.7%
Total Workers		222		314		1,155	

*Based on an extrapolation of the Hansen index to 1948 by linking with the Bureau of Labor Statistics Cost of Living Index. The index for 1948 (monthly average) was, on this basis, 214. It has been taken as 200 to simplify the comparisons.
Source: P. W. Bishop, "History of Scovill Manufacturing Company," manuscript in Scovill collection, Baker Library, p. 196.

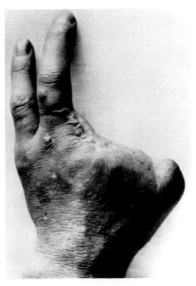

"Injured hand." This photo, taken around 1919, was deposited in Scovill's archives. Courtesy Scovill Collection.

out and rushed him off to the hospital. A few months later, he came back to work with his arm cut off at the shoulder. The company found a job for him—"they had to." Another time he saw someone get four fingers cut off all at once.

Charles R. Walker describes some of the occupational health problems at the Ansonia plant:

"Are there any bad physical effects of working around pickle tubs? Men complain about job, and turnover is high.

"In case of hand getting caught in rolls, no way of shutting off except by going to motor, in case of electric rolls, and stopping engine which drives entire mill, in case of engine run rolls. Engine 10 to 50 feet from rolls.

"Other accidents: Loss of hands on rolls, and fingers under metal on block. Rolls likely to cut hand off at wrist, and not go up to shoulder, as on rubber calendars."

SPELTER SHAKES

In the casting shops, the characteristic occupational disease was metal fume fever, known as "spelter shakes," "spelter bends," or "brass founders' ague." The disease was caused by inhaling metal

A Scovill worker cleaning the rolls with a piece of waste in 1919. Workers often caught their hands between the rolls and were injured. Courtesy Scovill Collection.

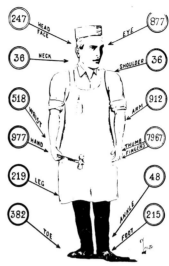

A chart showing how many accidents occurred to each part of the body at Scovill in 1916, published by Scovill Mfg. Co. Courtesy Scovill Collection.

oxide, particularly zinc, fumes. Resistance developed from steady exposure, but a new worker or even an experienced worker who had been away from the job was vulnerable to attack.

Stella Horoshak's parents came from Salonica, Greece, in 1920. "The Turks were having a fight; they got away from it and came here." Her father kept a restaurant. She started working at Seymour Products Co. in Seymour when she was still in high school. During World War II, she worked at the Seymour Mfg. Co., now Bridgeport Brass. She got married in 1946, "But I still worked. My husband worked days, and I

worked nights. We had an hour babysitter in between." After the war she worked at Seymour Products Co. for twenty-eight years, until it closed down. For the past nine years, she has worked as a jitney driver at the Bridgeport Brass plant in Seymour. She has served on the union negotiating committee and as trustee and steward. She and her husband have two children and five grandchildren.

Stella Horoshak: I was married one year. One night my husband was shaking. I didn't know what happened. I said, "I'm going to call a doctor." He said, "No. Just get me a lot of blankets." Their body gets to a certain temperature, and they

Hand casting at Scovill before World War I. It involved inhaling fumes from the hot metal, which led to spelter shakes. Courtesy Scovill Collection.

start shaking. Like a malaria. He told me after about four hours he was all right. In the thirty-three years I was married, it happened four times to him. They don't have that anymore, because in the casting shop they have a baghouse that draws all the smoke.

The casters had numerous home remedies for this condition. According to Walker: "The Negro Al Dolson . . . who files test bars for the lab, and assists at labor, worked for seven years in the casting shop. Says the best thing for 'spelter shakes is hot cider and pepper.' An 'old-timer' told him, and it works, says Al."

Sam Kwochka: Oatmeal and water was what they used to suck. You got home, warm milk and butter.

13. Early Worker Organization: The Knights of Labor and the Lady Brass Workers of Waterbury

According to the only published history of the brass industry, "No labor union or other combination of the skilled labor in the industry has ever been effected. . . . There has been in the entire period of nearly a century and a quarter only one strike." * The reality is rather different.

*Lathrop, *The Brass Industry*, pp. 94–95.

THE KNIGHTS OF LABOR

As early as the 1880s, workers in the Brass Valley were organizing unions. The earliest union in the brass industry was probably a local of the Knights of Labor, organized in Waterbury between 1882 and 1884. The Knights were a rapidly growing national organization which tried to unify all workers, skilled and unskilled, men and women, into one united force. The organization came to play a major role in both local and state politics. By July 1886, there were local assemblies of the Knights in all the Brass Valley towns, including Waterbury, Watertown, Winsted, Torrington, Thomaston, Derby, Birmingham, Ansonia, and Naugatuck.

In Naugatuck, a center of Knights of Labor strength, a labor newspaper was published and a labor ticket was elected to local government. In Waterbury, eleven Knights of Labor lodges were chartered between 1883 and 1893. Six local assemblies were formed during the upsurge of 1886—four trade assemblies of metal workers, one assembly of women from different industries, one assembly of building workers.

Internal fights and the defeat of strikes caused the national Knights of Labor to splinter apart. Brass workers were divided among three different national unions. According to Cecelia Bucki:

"The depression in 1893 caused the small unions to merge together and by 1896 most brass workers were part of a newly-formed union, the Metal Polishers, Buffers, Platers and Brass Workers International Union (affiliated to the AFL). Bickering continued, however, as the International Molders Union (composed mostly of iron molders, but fearful that brass molders could take over their jobs) claimed jurisdiction over brass molders. This dispute was only settled in 1911 when the Polishers union agreed to give up jurisdiction over brass molders." *

The Connecticut Bureau of Labor Statistics reported:

"Metal Polishers Union, No. 37, of Waterbury, was organized in September 1895, and by 1902 claimed 620 members.

"The union provides for a death benefit of $50, when members have been in good standing for over a year and $100 for two years or over. The principles of the organization are: '(1) Reduction of hours of workday; (2) Government ownership of national monopolies; (3) Municipal ownership of all public utilities; (4) Election of all public officials by popular vote; (5) Abolition of government by injunctions in controversies between capital and labor.'" †

THE LADY BRASS WORKERS OF WATERBURY

Women, as well as men, were organized. The Lady Brass Workers of Waterbury, organized in 1901, had 200 members. Marie Smith made the following report to the Connecticut State Branch, American Federation of Labor:

"Greetings. I am pleased to report for the Lady Brass Workers of Waterbury, that, although our organization is young we are growing in membership. You are aware of the fact that labor organizations among our sex, especially in the East, are very rare, but I am pleased to note that the time has come when the various labor organizations realize that if they want to perfect the labor movement it is necessary to assist in organizing the women wage-earners of this country. This being done as thoroughly as in the male line, I believe the organized labor problem will be solved. If it is necessary to have the ladies in every other reform movement, why is it not more necessary to enlist every woman wage-earner in the country in the ranks of organized labor? And if the organizers spend a share of their time, you can rest assured that the ladies will do the rest." ‡

*Cecelia Bucki, "Waterbury Industrial History, 1820–1920," unpublished manuscript, p. 6n.
†Connecticut, Bureau of Labor Statistics, *Eighteenth Annual Report of the Bureau of*

Labor Statistics, for the Year Ended November 30, 1902 (Meriden, Connecticut, 1902), p. 482.
‡Ibid., p. 480.

EARLY STRIKES

Connecticut Department of Labor records indicate a substantial number of early strikes in the industry. At least one strike occurred among metal spinners in a Waterbury brass works as early as 1882. Between April and June 1886, separate strikes occurred among trimmers, buffers, stampers, and tenders in Waterbury brass works.

There may well have been other strikes that are now virtually untraceable. For example, twenty-five "female employees in the casting department" struck at Scovill from January 31 to February 1, 1902, in an unsuccessful attempt to restore a cut wage. On February 15, 1902, twenty-five employees in the setting-up department at Waterbury Button Co. struck for two days over an "objection to change in system." *

In May 1901 the International Association of Machinists struck the Valley as part of a nationwide machinists' strike. The union claimed that 500 of the 800 machinists in Waterbury struck. Their demands were a nine-hour day for ten hours' pay and a limit of apprentices to "one for the shop and one for every five machinists." The strike also involved Ansonia, Derby, and other manufacturing centers throughout Connecticut.†

The leaders of the strike in Ansonia soon took over the city government.

THE OPEN SHOP

Until the 1930s, the brass companies generally refused to deal with unions. As one of the manufacturers put it during the 1901 machinists' strike, they were "anxious to continue as administrative heads of their own concerns"; they would meet the men but not the unions.

In their opposition to unionism and their refusal to recognize and bargain with unions, they followed the general policy of other Connecticut employers. Scovill maintained extensive files on radical, union, and strike activity among its workers at least during the period from 1918 to 1920. And a delegate to the Connecticut Federation of Labor Convention in 1917 warned, "there is danger . . . for all organized labor in the Valley, in the fact of the operation of the Naugatuck Valley Employment Agency. It was seriously brought home to me when two of our most loyal members have been prevailed upon to go into the American Brass factory [a non-union shop]." ‡

14. The 1919 Strike: "Spreading by Contagion"

The attempt by workers to change their position in the plants and the community was most dramatically expressed in the strikes of 1919 and 1920. These were part of a wave of labor conflicts that swept the nation during this period. In the Brass Valley, tens of thousands of workers took part, and the strikes closed the industry of the area for months at a time. These strikes were based on organizations in which workers grouped themselves by nationality, regardless of their kind of work or which company they worked for. When they struck, therefore, it had the character of a general strike of laborers for the entire region. The strike in 1919 was met with police violence, but was brought to a quick end by concessions on the part of the manufacturers. The 1920 strike lasted several months, involved hundreds of arrests, occupation by the National Guard, and considerable bloodshed. It was defeated by the great wealth of the owners and the lack of competition in the industry; the brass masters could afford simply to wait while the strikers went hungry.

On February 17, 1916, workers at the American Brass Co. in Ansonia walked off their jobs. This was probably the first strike to close down a major brass plant. The workers held daily mass meetings

*Ibid., pp. 512ff.
†Bishop, "History of Scovill Mfg. Co.," pp. 217ff.

‡Connecticut Federation of Labor, *Thirty-Second Annual Report*; the delegate was Frank Peal.

in the town. The company quickly granted a 15 percent wage increase and other concessions. The strike was settled by February 20. It was a harbinger of the massive strikes, led by immigrant workers, that were to come.

The period at the end of World War I combined rapid inflation with an end to war production and insecure employment conditions. The data in Table 16 indicate these trends.

Early in June 1919, a strike movement developed at the American Brass Co. and Farrel Foundry plants in Ansonia. Workers organized a committee of nineteen, with one representative for each nationality, and asked for union recognition, increases of thirty-five to sixty cents per hour, and double time after eight hours.

Charles R. Walker, who arrived in Ansonia about a year after the strike, recorded what he heard about it:

"It was apparently a spontaneous affair, spreading by contagion; had been talked out for weeks, by the men at their jobs but no mass meetings of any kind held. The shop committee had met to consider what became its issues, high cost of living, etc. It originated in this mill, the Coe unit, over among the slitters, some of whom stopped work about ten in the morning, spreading slowly to the rolls. Joe, my blocker, was argued with by bosses and strikers, and finally yielded to the strikers. When he stopped, the other rolls were soon down. The engine was stopped, and Moody gathered the men all over by the door, got up on a box, and gave them a talk; said the mill would start up at once, and ordered the engine started. The engine was started, but when the men saw the rolls turning, they let out a shout and refused to go back to work. After another speech in the yard, Moody told them all to go home; that the mill would open in the morning.

"One man on a draw bench who refused to stop was lifted bodily and thrown out the door. Two Italians cleared the mill with revolvers. Moody tried to hold the door of the casting shop but it broke under a rush of two or three hundred men."

On June 18 the strike spread to Waterbury. Three thousand workers—mostly unskilled Lithuanians, Poles, and Russians in the rolling, wire, and tube mills and casting shops—joined the strike. By June 19 about 5,000 people were on strike, including 500 workers at Scovill. The mayor, William H. Sandland, threatened to call in U.S. troops if local police proved unable to handle the situation.

TABLE 16
Inflation and Production Trends, 1914–1922

Year	Cost of Living (BLS) (1935–39 = 100)	Manufacturing Index of Production (1935–39 = 100)
1914	71.8	55
1915	72.5	64
1916	77.9	76
1917	91.6	76
1918	107.5	74
1919	123.8	65
1920	143.3	71
1921	127.7	62
1922	119.7	73

Source: P. W. Bishop, "History of Scovill Manufacturing Company," manuscript in Scovill collection, Baker Library, p. 221.

State Guardsmen patrolled the streets of the Brooklyn section during the riot of 1919. Courtesy Mattatuck Museum.

The strike was met with massive police and even military repression. John Hollingworth remembers the big strikes after World War I.

John Hollingworth: I was in the state guard at the time. I was on duty when the Lithuanian and Polish were going to have a big do downtown. We formed a military square with loaded rifles. We were told to shoot for the gut. That's how close we got. As soon as we got the order to aim, they pulled away. Broke the strike up. That happened right in the center of Waterbury. They were going to break up the store windows and stuff like that.

We [the State Guard] were on duty at the firehouse, at City Hall, the powerhouse on Freight Street. We were relieved from work, and we were paid by the factory and got government pay at the same time. When needed.

These different ones were trying to start unions and stuff like that. There was always some dissension around. So we were called out when necessary; other times we just worked normal.

I lived on Wilson Street over in Brooklyn. I was called out. They had a certain number of the steam

Firemen ready to hose down strikers on the Bank St. Bridge in the Brooklyn section of Waterbury in 1919. Courtesy Mattatuck Museum.

State Guardsmen in Waterbury during the 1919 strike. Courtesy Mattatuck Museum.

factory whistles. Our number came up, number seven. I ran down from Wilson Street. I got on Bank Street, and the firemen had the fellows pinned up against the side of the wall with a fire hose. So I started running on the right side. The firemen said, "Where are you going?" I said, "Armory." "Go ahead." They knew what the call was.

[The firemen had pinned up] people making a disturbance. In the Brooklyn section on Bank Street. Mostly—you can't mention nationalities, but you know who they were. They pinned them down till we got organized. Then we marched around there and quieted them down.

Peter Kukanskis: Lithuanians took a shellacking, a lot of them did. They beat up a lot of the guys, from what I hear.

I know a guy who had a meat market down on Bank Street. He lost half of his customers after the strike, for the simple reason that the National Guard came in and put a machine gun up on this guy's building, looking down the street. When the Lithuanians saw it there: "You let these guys go up on the roof of your building to shoot at us?" He lost a big trade.

My dad was working on Bank Street. He was going over to work. The guard said, "Hey, where are you going?" "I'm going to work." "You are like hell. Get back in the house." In all this area, you couldn't even peek out of the house.

On June 24, 1919, American Brass announced a general wage increase of ten cents an hour, with time and a half for overtime. The other mills followed suit, and workers returned to work. No union was recognized, but American Brass set up a system of shop committees.

The beginning of the strike, February 1920. New England Workers Association members in their Sunday best paraded along Ansonia's Main St. Courtesy Marie Balco.

15. The 1920 Strike: "We Had All Combination of People"

The 1919 walkout showed the power of the Brass Valley workers to shut down the entire local industry and win concessions from their employers. In the midst of the strike, workers began organizing. The largest organization was the Waterbury Workers Association (later changed to the New England Workers Association). Competing with it was Local 16712 of the AFL, set up to organize unskilled brass workers. Each had many thousands of members.

Both of these "unions" were organized, not by plant or even by industry, but by ethnic group. Each had sections for Italians, Lithuanians, Poles, Russians, Portuguese, French, or other groups. Ethnic community leaders—foreign language newspaper editors, for example—often played significant roles within these sections, even though they did not work in the plants. These were not, in short, unions in today's sense, but organizations of the immigrant social groups.

At the same time, the machinists' union began substantial organizing among the skilled workers in the Valley. Their activities at times supported, at times undermined, those of the unskilled.

The 1920 strike began in Ansonia, where it lasted for several weeks. Just as it began to abate there, it spread up the Valley to Waterbury, where it continued for nearly twelve weeks, hitting nearly every industrial plant in the city. As many as 16,000 workers may have been out in the Valley at one time or another during the course of the strike.

James Tiso remembers the origins of the organization and strike.

James Tiso: We were working in misery. I was working for a dollar a day, ten and twelve hours. All over. If you give me a dollar and this guy gives me a dollar and a quarter, I leave you; I go get a dollar and a quarter.

We started the union over there for a lousy quarter to join. We had a pretty good strong union. But there were rats, agents, that would rat to the boss.

It happened like this: "We'll go to the union. We'll pay dues, we pay a quarter."

Everything was fine. We make a pretty good strong union. They joined at Scovill; they joined at American Brass; they joined at Chase. We want to call a strike.

Then they started making a mess, mixing them up. One union for the carpenters, a union for the bricklayers, a union for the laborers; everybody looking for a buck, like a bird. We're the sucker. You belong to the union for carpentry work; he belongs to the [union for] laborers. I said, make one, one. That's the one they got to be in, one [union for all the workers].

There was a guy from Massachusetts. He came down to organize the people in Waterbury. He started talking. None of the Italian people could understand English; we were all green. When they talked in English, he would explain to us what they meant. He was Italian. We had some people from Town Plot. They were anarchists. Italian people.

That's what happened in the first union. It came in with all the nations: all Italian, French, German people.

This guy [from Massachusetts] talked against the factory, against the people that were traitors to the working people. He spoke against the law, against the police, against the firemen, against the factory.

Some of the police wanted to pinch him. They pinched him. They took him over to the police station. Everybody went. The chief of police told him, "Where are you coming from?" "From Massachusetts." "You go back to Massachusetts, or I'll put you in jail for six months." Just because he was a talker—he didn't do anything, the poor guy.

He opened the eyes of the people in the state of Connecticut. How they're going to do, how they're going to work. And that's how the union was started.

They wanted so much for the people. The company didn't want to give it to you. What you do? You call a strike. You shut off the goddamn motors. You shut off the machines.

The demands of the strike grew directly out of the poor working conditions and the economic needs of the immigrant community.

On April 21 mass meetings were held throughout Waterbury, where votes for a general walkout were taken. On April 24 the New England Workers Association issued the following demands:

"1. Seventy five cents per hour the minimum—Female employees to be given same consideration of rate doing same work.

"2. Eight hours work per day—44 hours per week labor namely Monday-Tuesday-Wednesday-Thursday-Friday from 8 a.m. to 12 and from 1 p.m. to 5—from 8 a.m. to 12 on Saturday.

"3. The re-employment of all members discharged for Union activities without any discrimination belonging to the N.E.W. Ass.

"4. The abolishment of all piece work.

"5. Casters helpers will receive for Brass 20 cents per pot—four rounds limit—for Copper 25 and for Silver 30 cents per pot—three rounds limit. It is asked also an additional helper and should same be absent for any reason his pay to be divided among others doing his work.

"6. The Recognition of a Shop Committee."*

A meeting between the "Unfailing Committee" (strike leaders) of the New England Workers Association and a committee appointed by the mayor brought out some of the basic issues:

"—The majority of members had rejected the idea of dealing with the manufacturers through separate shop committees, and in-

*Copy of demands in Scovill collection, Baker Library.

sisted that they deal with the organization as a whole. Their reason was that different wage scales would result in different factories, and further labor troubles and possibly another strike would follow. They declared that to treat with the manufacturers separately would be to destroy their unity and lessen their chances of winning the strike.

"—The workers walked out of the factories because they realized that they must get more money if prices kept soaring upwards. Agitators might have precipitated the strike, but the increasing cost of living was actually responsible for the labor trouble. The perpendicular climbs in the prices of commodities of sugar, clothes, and other things were cited as examples.

"—Efforts to state their cases to the heads of factories had been in vain. The department foremen paid no attention to them. The 'bosses' in one factory were described as 'kaisers.' Grievances presented to foremen were ignored, and it was impossible to reach men higher up.

"—Favoritism in factories was also alleged. Italians, Lithuanians, Russians, and Poles were given all of the poor jobs on piece work.

"—Many of the married women of the Brooklyn section had been forced to go to work to help their husband support their children.

"—Members of the strike committee criticized the system they

said was maintained by the factories whereby a man's record is passed on from one factory to another. They said if a man is receiving the minimum wage at one factory and becoming dissatisfied decides to go to another, to look for more money, he will find that all of the other factories of the city have been 'tipped off' not to exceed the minimum in that worker's case. The result was that the man was forced to remain in his old position at his old rate of pay." [*]

Because many companies officially kept their plants open, workers developed an unusual tactic to meet their economic needs and still continue the strike. Richard Giacin, a participant in the strike, recalled that workers originally maintained they would rather starve than give in to the manufacturers. Anyone who even mentioned giving in was ostracized, beaten up, or both. However, as money became more and more scarce, people would go to work one or two days a week to earn just enough to get by. This is confirmed by the Scovill strike statistics, which show a decline in absences at the beginning of each week with a return to high levels thereafter.

The role of skilled workers in the strike was ambiguous. Usually of ethnic groups that had immigrated to the Valley earlier than the un-

skilled, they held privileged positions within the plants. Yet their positions were being eroded by new technologies. Thus, they had numerous grievances of their own.

Through the early weeks of the strike, machinists and other skilled workers continued to work. In May, however, the International Association of Machinists—representing the skilled workers—issued demands of its own for a 44-hour week, a 35-percent wage increase, and recognition of shop committees. When, on May 19, American Brass refused to recognize the machinists' committee, skilled workers began to join the strike. On June 13 national IAM organizer Joe Tone arrived to organize machinists, but he announced that union recognition would not be a condition of settlement.

Joe Tone, subsequently Connecticut State Labor Commissioner, recalled that the police would not allow the organizers to address strikers' meetings. However, there was no rule against organizers' talking to each other. Consequently, each meeting was attended by two organizers, seated at opposite ends of the hall, who would discuss whatever pertinent information needed to be relayed—loudly enough for every striker in the hall to hear.[†]

---

[*] Waterbury *American*, April 30, 1920.

[†] M. S. Foucher, "The Labor Movement in Connecticut—An Introductory History," unpublished manuscript, pp. 37–38.

POLICE WITH RIFLES BREAK UP ORDERLY MEETING OF ITALIANS IN CHURCH HALL

Strikers Interpret Unwarranted Action as Provocation to Incite Trouble, But They Keep Cool and No Violence Occurs—Monday's Impromptu Parade Scares Nervous Ones.

Waterbury's police committed the first act of organized violence in the present strike situation last Tuesday morning when a bunch of them armed with rifles broke up a perfectly quiet and peaceful meeting of Italian strikers gathered inside the hall of the Church of Our Lady of Lourdes.

No violent act was committed nor threatened by the strikers which justified this unwarranted interfer-

the strikers were concerned. They were simply having a meeting in the church hall and when the meeting was over they were going on about their business as they do after every meeting. The idea of a parade never existed outside the imaginations of somebody in the police department. As an excuse for sending policemen with rifles into an orderly, legitimate meeting the parade bugaboo may serve. But it doesn't fool anybody in the rank

From the Waterbury Herald, *a "workingman's paper" that combined scandalmongering with local labor news. The* Herald *covered police repression of a strikers' meeting in its May 9, 1920, issue. Courtesy Scovill Collection.*

The strike was met by organized repression from local authorities. More than 100 strikers were arrested; some were held for deportation. Meetings were forbidden; authorities even broke into churches to disrupt meetings. There were numerous charges that employers and police had infiltrated strike leadership. These allegations had at least some basis in fact.

John Driscoll: Joe Tone [of the machinists] told me that his local was infiltrated by company spies. He said he found out later that all but one member of the local lodge executive board were company operatives.

In the 1950s I ran into a barber who told me he had acted as an informant for the Department of Justice. He gave them the names of people who were active in the strike and succeeded in getting them deported. A. Mitchell Palmer had organized the so-called red raids. Apparently a lot of the strike leaders were bundled into railroad cars and shipped out.

The mounted squad of Scovill's private Plant Protection Bureau in 1919. Lieut. John J. Bergin (far left) was in charge of the Plant Protection Bureau. Courtesy Scovill Collection.

Police repression climaxed with the Bridge Street Incident, in which two policemen were wounded and a young striker, Liberto Tiso, was shot dead. Police accused Tiso of firing on the policemen. James Tiso, Liberto's older brother, tells his version of the story.

James Tiso: Over ten thousand on Baldwin Street, ten thousand on East Main. We march—we're walking our own business; we didn't do nothing wrong. Near Scovill we find a set of policemen. "Stay back. Who are you?" "We're not bothering you. We're just walking our own business. We're just showing the shop how many people are out of the goddamn hole."

One sonofabitch of a copper, he goes to the front of the line where all the younger fellows are, eighteen or nineteen years old. He says, "Get the hell out of there, you _____ bastards! What do you think you are?"

There was a rain. My brother had an umbrella. He pushed the horse. Near the bridge. The boy said, "What's the matter?" "Stand back, you goddamn guinea bastard!" Pow! Well, [my brother] didn't want to see him swing the goddamn stick. So he stuck the umbrella in his belly. When he swing the umbrella, that guy [the policeman] took a pistol and boom! boom! He drop on the ground.

Now before he drop on the ground—he had a gun. He pulled the gun. He shoot to left then—

toom! toom! When he got up, blood everywhere. And the cops, they get him. The cop on top of the horse took off, and they took him right in the door at St. Mary's Hospital. Everybody pick up him, help him. Put him in the hospital. Call a doctor.

My brother fell on the street, on the sidewalk. Somebody threw a brick and hit another police, boom! He fall across my brother. My brother still had a pistol in his hand. That guy was afraid they were going to shoot him. He took a pistol, boom! boom! boom!

The police came with a machine gun on top of a truck—it was a big revolution.

The police, after policing the crowd, then they went for the truck to pick up all the fellows that

Scovill factory employees served in the Auxiliary Police of Scovill's Plant Protection Bureau in 1919. Courtesy Scovill Collection.

were hurt. There were eighteen fellows hurt, but not like my brother.

They put my brother on the truck, just like a pig.

Seventeen young fellows were all in one room. But he was bad. They tied him up like a dog. Blood. He couldn't speak. I said, "Tell me what happened to you. Who did that? Do you know?" He said, "Brother, no. You've got the kids."

Before I go, I start to cry.

Finally they say [to my father], "Your son is dead."

My father—I'll tell you the truth—if he knew who killed his boy, he'd get them right on the street, anyplace. We don't say we're anarchists, Fascists, or Communists. We've got tolerance. But that ain't right, what they did.

Liberto Tiso's funeral provided a focal point for strikers' emotions,

and his death became a symbol of their solidarity across ethnic lines.

James Tiso: They took him to a funeral home. We had all combination of people.

All over the state they had to go to send a motor troop from New Haven, Bridgeport, all around. They brought them over to the city: machine guns and everything.

We had one German fellow, big guy, he wouldn't cave in to nobody. He wasn't scared to talk. He picked up on the city, on the police, on the shop, on how they treated the people, how they really are in this America.

The line never stopped, day and night, day and night.

They made a collection, put the money in.

Down there [at the cemetery], all people. The German fellow was with the union. All Polish people, all Italian people, French, German, all mixed. Before putting my brother on the grave. All the police came down on the road.

[The German] made a speech. Against the police, against the factory, against the judge, against the law we've got in the United States of America. Then he rose and said, "The man was on the ground, and they shot him. You've got to have a lot of guts. This is respect in America!" He talk all right.

What was the matter? Was [my brother] an anarchist? Was he a Communist? Was he a Bolshevik? What was this man? He was a Catholic like the rest of the people in America.

And that was the trouble of my brother.

In the wake of the Bridge Street Incident, Governor Holcomb put the state guard at the disposal of the mayor of Waterbury, sent in a machine gun batallion, and stationed sentinels with fixed bayonets around City Hall. The superintendent of police ordered that no permits be granted for strikers' meetings and that policemen carry riot guns with orders to shoot. The newspapers predicted that the strike would immediately collapse. But the strikers, outraged by what they considered a denial of their rights, continued the strike for another six weeks.

After only a little more than a month on strike, the skilled workers returned to work. The Ansonia workers had gone back to work as well. Waterbury strikers held out till mid-July. Ultimately, they were defeated by a combination of repression and the economic power of the companies—the brass masters could afford to wait, while the strikers went hungry.

Despite its outcome, the strike constituted a memorable effort by tens of thousands of people, mostly immigrant workers of all nationalities, to overcome their divisions and use their power over production to make a better life for themselves, their families, and their communities.

PART III

1920 to Mid-Century: The Era of Industrial Unionism

THE PEOPLE

During and after World War I, the flow of immigration to the U.S., which had continued for nearly a century, was largely cut off due to the war itself and to restrictive legislation. The number of immigrants headed for Connecticut fell from 33,000 in 1914 to 5,700 during the twelve months ending with June 1922. This had gradual but profound impacts on industrial communities like the Naugatuck Valley.

First of all, since the war ended the workers' practice of traveling back and forth between Europe and the U.S., those who were in the U.S. had to choose between returning home for good or making a long-term commitment to the new country. A large proportion took out U.S. citizenship and cast their lot with their adopted country.

The balance within the ethnic communities gradually shifted, as the proportion "just off the boat" declined, and the proportion of those who had been born in the U.S. or who had lived here much of their lives increased. By World War II, the Valley was no longer a collection of immigrant settlements, but of American ethnic communities.

The cutoff of immigration led northern manufacturers like the brass companies to look to a new source of labor—American Blacks—to replace the European immigrants. From World War I on, a growing community of Black migrants from the American South developed in the brass industry towns.

A number of factors tended to make the communities of the Valley more homogeneous. The ethnic groups, whatever their rivalries, increasingly spoke the English language, shared American citizenship, and became assimilated to American culture. Marriage between different nationalities, while still frowned on by many parents and church leaders, became increasingly common.

At the same time, changes in the work place were also reducing differences within the working class. In 1909 brass industry historian Lathrop wrote that there was a sharply defined division between skilled and unskilled workers. However, in the 1926 revision of his book, he noted: "At present this line tends to disappear."* An increasing proportion of all workers became "semi-skilled" machine operators, rather than either highly skilled craftsmen or sheer unskilled musclepower—although plenty of buggy lugging remained.

The principal form of collective action that emerged from this

---

*William G. Lathrop, *The Brass Industry in the United States* (Mount Carmel, Conn., 1926), p. 95.

more Americanized working class was the industrial unionism of the CIO era, which began in the late 1930s and reached the acme of its strength in the Valley at about mid-century.

The major efforts of working people to affect the broader social environment during this period were conducted under the auspices of the union movement. They affected both electoral politics and the social policies and agencies of the community. We will deal with them later in connection with the rise of unionism.

1. After Immigration: Mingling and Discrimination

Many of the early immigrants held firmly to their own language and lifestyles, living their lives primarily within the immigrant community and perhaps dreaming of returning some day to the homeland.

Many members of the ethnic groups considered it a point of pride to pass on their language and culture to the next generation.

Hap Lasky: It was compulsory in our house to speak Lithuanian. My father—you couldn't talk English while he was in the house; you had to talk Lithuanian. He didn't want to lose the Lithuanian language. I speak Lithuanian fluently now.

The first generation born in America, however, tended to build bridges to the language and culture of the U.S. The word characteristically used in the Valley to describe the socializing of people from different backgrounds is "mingling." The first-generation Americans mingled far more than their immigrant parents.

Bart Hennessey: [Nationality groups began to mix more with the advent of the] first generation. As the kids went to school, they educated the older people. They got to be twenty or twenty-one, they started to intermarry and everything else.

The issue was particularly sensitive when it came to courtship and marriage.

Caroline Nardello: In those days you didn't marry any nationality but your own. They wouldn't allow you to. The parents wanted you to marry your own nationality. My cousin was going with a French fellow. My mother didn't like the idea. It's best to marry your own nationality.

After they started mingling, the parents got over it. They're more Americanized; they didn't mind.

Hap Lasky: A girl by the name of Clemis married a fellow from out on the West Coast. He was dressed like a duke. She fell for him hook, line and sinker. Then everybody started to complain. That was the first time I've heard of anyone complaining about a mixed marriage. Maybe 1908 or 1909. Most of them married neighborhood girls in those days.

Bergin Center group:

Josephine Tedesco: It was a disgrace to marry out of your nationality in those days.

Mary Cocca: I didn't know anyone [who did]; in those days they always got married with Italians.

Sarah Cappella: All their paisans.

Tedesco: I think that was the way it was with every nationality. Even the Irish.

Cappella: The Irish married the Irish. I'm Italian, I marry the Italian. That's the way it was in those days. Now no more. Now it's a mixed world.

Most of those immigrants who remained in the U.S. gradually accepted it as their adopted home. Peter Kukanskis remembered a trip with his mother to the farm she had come from in Lithuania.

Peter Kukanskis: It was very nice. I saw where my mother was born and my dad was born. Some of the grandparents' gravestones. It was pleasant. It's funny though; I always remember we were leaving her homestead—out in the country this is—and I said, "Hey, Mom, turn around. Take a last look at your old homestead." "Ah, the

An inter-ethnic wedding. Eva Ceriello and Edward Bergin married in 1933, with Mildred Bergin maid of honor and Thomas Colasanto best man. Courtesy Eva M. Bergin.

hell with it," she said. "I'm an American; this is not my home anymore."

BLACKS—THE FIRST MIGRATION

In contrast to other immigrants, Black Africans were captured and brought against their will to America. In the U.S. they were enslaved and deprived of virtually all the rights available to the white population.

Blacks came into the Naugatuck Valley along with other early settlers. In many cases they were slaves or indentured servants. By 1708 there were enough of them in what is now Ansonia that a special balcony was added to the church for the Black community. Over the years they intermarried with other residents of the area. A few local Black families can still trace their roots to these early comers.

The overwhelming majority of Blacks, however, were made slaves on plantations in the American South. Although slavery was abolished during the Civil War, the freed Blacks by no means acquired the same rights as white Americans. A combination of military force and organized discrimination was used to keep them in the South and keep them in agricultural labor. The great majority lived in virtual peonage well into the twentieth century.

During the decades when millions of European immigrants were

Bertha Silva with her parents, Susie and Alfred Carr, and her siblings, in Portsmouth, Virginia, in 1915. Bertha is at far right. Courtesy Bertha Silva.

pouring into American factories, American Blacks were, with few exceptions, excluded from industrial employment. In Waterbury prior to World War I, for example, local Black workers were unable to get jobs in the brass plants, despite the industry's massive need for labor.

With the decline of immigration during and after World War I, however, employers changed their policies. The result was an influx of Blacks from the American South, similar in many respects to the immigration from Europe which had preceded it. Like the Europeans, the Blacks were attempting to escape from social oppression in their homeland— lynchings and Ku Klux Klan activity were at a peak in the early 1920s. Like the Europeans, the

Blacks fled an impoverished, rural, agricultural region in a state of economic disintegration. As with previous immigrants, the men often came first, found work, sent home for family members, and established communities of their own ethnic group in the industrial towns. Again like the Europeans, they relied on family networks and ethnic organizations to provide a degree of security in a hostile economic and social environment.

Until the middle of the twentieth century, Blacks made up a relatively small group within the Brass Valley towns. In many respects, they functioned as one ethnic group among many, and were regarded as such. But in other respects, they were subject to special racial discrimination. They were prevented from living in many

areas, working in many jobs, and receiving many services because of the color of their skin. Despite the obvious advantages of speaking English and being assimilated to American culture, they met serious barriers beyond those experienced by the white migrants and their children.

The number of Blacks in the Valley remained small until World · War I, and the number working in the brass mills was even smaller. As late as the 1920 Census, Blacks formed only about 1 percent of the population of Waterbury. During and after World War I, however, there was a great increase in demand for labor, and the Naugatuck Valley area and the brass industry began opening up to Blacks.

Russell Hunter: When the war was on, they had to send for a lot of guys from the Southland. They even sent for people over in the West Indies. They'd take everything they could find.

Born in 1916 in Darlington, South Carolina, John Gatison came with his family to Ansonia in the mid-1920s. His father, an independent blacksmith and heavy farm equipment repairman in the South, found work at American Brass to support his family of five. He later opened the Southern Grocery Store in an extra room off the family home on lower Main. John Gatison went to work at American Brass in 1940, and was one of the

first Blacks active in the union. "I served on the executive board of our local for a good many years and went through most of the important jobs except president. I was vice-president once, that was enough." He has long been a stalwart of the local NAACP, and is currently its vice president. In 1968 he was elected as a selectman in the city of Ansonia. In July 1969 he was appointed to fill a vacancy on the Board of Aldermen. In November of that year, he was elected to serve a full term as alderman, the first Black alderman elected in Ansonia. He has remained active in politics, as a member of the Black Democrats Club and as the Chairman of the Ansonia Housing Authority. He has long been active in the Macedonia Baptist Church. He and his wife live in Ansonia. He says of himself: "My greatest asset has been that I don't give up."

John Gatison: In the 1900s they migrated primarily from the Carolinas.

Right after World War I was when the big influx began. It progressed right on through until the mid-1950s, when it started to taper off.

My family migrated from Darlington, South Carolina. A lot of people came from Society Hill, South Carolina. That's a rural town made up mostly of farming. Darlington is a city—it's larger than Ansonia at the present time.

The people who came up were mainly farmers.

The members of Luke MacDonald's family were unimpressed when they came to Waterbury in 1914; after Baltimore, where they had lived, it seemed like a hick town. Originally from North Carolina, the family had worked up through Virginia, Maryland, and New Jersey. "My father was a minister. Every couple of years, they'd ship him from one place to another." Luke MacDonald worked at Scovill's in the summertime in 1916 and 1917, when he was in grammar school. After that he worked caning chairs, preparing furniture, bellhopping in a hotel. In 1927 he got a job in American Brass. "I started off in the wire mill. I ended up in the scrap room. I put in forty years and eleven months there."

Luke MacDonald's wife, Lillian, came from one of the older Black families in Waterbury. "I was born on Bishop Street. My family came here many years before I was born. I worked for the Coes for many years. For the whole family: father, mother, grandmother. For thirty years I worked there."

Like other immigrants, the Blacks arrived via family networks.

Luke MacDonald: There weren't so many here in those days. Every time somebody would go on a vacation down South, they'd bring a cousin or son or brother up here. That's how the population grew here.

Some came up on their own; others were recruited and brought in by the companies.

Bertha Silva: My effort was to come here to become a nurse; that was my goal. I intended to go to the school for nursing, because I always liked nursing. At that time you would go to Harlem Hospital and take training there. But Mrs. Coe, who I worked for [as a domestic], was a nurse. She told me, "I don't think it's a good profession." But she wanted me to stay with her—that was her goal, I understood later.

When I first came here there were a lot of young boys who were brought from Virginia to work here. Around 1925. Farrel's and American Brass sent for them. These boys used to take me around in Ansonia. They had a dance hall on Main Street called Foster's

Hall. That's where they would have dances on Saturday night. A lady who was an old-timer used to have house parties; these boys encouraged me to go to parties there. Then she started taking me to Foster's Hall.

These boys came here to work and go back to school. There was no government at that time to help people; you had to help yourself. We used to say: working your way through school.

They had a rooming house for [the boys who came up from Virginia] on Tremont Street. They stayed at Kid Thomas' house. Mary Mendez boarded them. On Tremont Street. One family got a place; they got rooms for different people there. But I think Farrel's had furnished the place for them before they got here. Kid Thomas had a regular boardinghouse. They slept there, but they didn't eat there. Because Mary used to board them.

[The Jamaicans] came in the 1920s. They were here when I came here. They came over on their own; the company didn't bring them over at that time.

The newcomers from the South did not always get along well with the longer-established Black residents.

According to Luke MacDonald, the older Black residents "called [the newcomers] a bunch of roughnecks. Hayseeds."

Black men and women were concentrated in service occupations and the lowest positions in the mills.

Luke MacDonald: [People worked] mostly in the shops. And the ladies—there weren't so many ladies—they did housework for the bosses.

Hard work. They don't bother you, when it comes to hard work. If you were strong and husky, you could get a job anywhere.

Some were working in hotels, restaurants.

The color line was not absolute.

Russell Hunter: We had a colored foreman. That's the only one I know. He was foreman of the slitters.

In 1923, Charles S. Johnson, Director of the National Urban League's Department of Research and Investigations, conducted a sociological study of the Black population of Waterbury. This investigation provides much valuable information, including detailed information on Black employment in Waterbury in 1923:

"Information was secured from 45 . . . plants [which] represent all the plants employing Negroes and approximately 80 per cent. of all employees in industrial establishments throughout the city.

"The total number of Negro employees in these 17 plants is 372, all of whom are men. No provi-

sions have as yet been made for the employment of Negro women in industrial plants. The great bulk of industries manufacture goods requiring male labor; in those plants in which women are employed, employers have been averse to introducing Negro women. The reason is usually assumed, but the implication of such comments as were made was that more serious matters of sentiment were involved in the contact of both races and both sexes. Most of the plants have employed Negroes many years but in small numbers frequently. This limitation has in the past been deliberate. The first considerable increases were made four years ago, the period of the first migration of Negroes northward. Strangely enough, the entrance here was not made quite so much by Negroes just from the South as by Negroes living in the city, who grasped their first opportunity to get into industry after a long confinement to domestic occupations.

"The Chase Metal Works, employing over twice as many Negroes as any other plant in the city, classes all of its Negroes as semiskilled. This refers to Negro workers both in the metal works and the rolling mills. In the Randolph-Clowes Company there are two skilled Negro casters and five helpers. At Scovill's about half of the Negro workers, distributed in sixteen departments, are engaged on semi-skilled work. It is remarked that *skilled* Negroes rarely apply for work. In the American Brass Company, which includes three separate concerns, over 30 per cent. of the Negro workers are semi-skilled. In addition, there are two skilled workers. In the Oakville Company there are two skilled pin-workers, one a man of extraordinary accomplishments, speaking three languages. He is in charge of outside laborers, all of whom are white. Another is a skilled electrician, and still another is a clerk.

"The wages of women are, on the whole, much smaller than those of men. Out of a total of thirty-five interviewed, twenty were receiving $3.00 a day for general housework. This work could rarely be secured for more than four days, however.

"Not one was found to be in an industrial plant. Of the women interviewed, all but seventeen were engaged in some kind of work, principally domestic service.

"The city is distinctly not a labor union stronghold. It developed through interviews with workers that the question of labor unions was rarely, if ever, discussed."*

Paul Garatoni's father, an Italian immigrant, started working for

*Charles S. Johnson, Director, Department of Research and Investigations of the National Urban League, "The Negro Population of Waterbury, Connecticut," *Opportunity* 1 (Oct./Nov. 1923), nos. 10–11: 301ff.

American Brass in Ansonia in 1915, operating some of the more complicated machines. Paul was born in a house on Hawkins Street in Derby in 1917. He graduated from high school in 1937, and went to work soon thereafter at American Brass. He attended engineering school nights. In 1942, he was transferred to the toolroom office and was "on the board" until 1947, when he became the first Italian in the Central Engineering department of American Brass. He worked there until his retirement in 1973. (Paul Garatoni is the father of Quentin Garatoni, introduced on page 218.)

The brass employers were not above pitting race against race as a means of breaking strikes and increasing worker competition.

Paul Garatoni: There was a big

strike at that time [after World War I]. I remember my dad got a job digging the foundations for the Jewish synagogue in Derby. They brought in Negroes from the South to break the strike. Years later I was told that they brought them up in boxcars, like cattle. They were treated as such at the time.

The general manager of a Waterbury brass company that employed sixteen Blacks in its work force of 200, stated in 1923:

"We found our Negro employees were loyal during strike periods that we have been through and always encourage our employment office to engage Negro labor whenever possible."†

The exploitation of racial divisions was made all the easier by the fact that some, if not most, of the unions in the Valley refused to admit Blacks.

Most of the Brass Valley towns had Black communities by World War I. In Waterbury the Blacks settled around Bishop, Pearl, and Vine Streets. The Urban League study described conditions in that area:

"The Negroes in Waterbury live in rather close contact. There are not exclusively Negro sections, but what amounts practically to the same,—there are sections in close proximity in which over 90 per cent of the Negro population live.

†Ibid., p. 302.

Their actual residence area is confined to a few rather thickly populated streets.

"The antagonistic sentiment of whites prevents them from moving outside of the narrow limits of a recognized 'Negro area'. The result has been a much greater degree of congestion and higher rentals. . . . Ten times as many Negroes as whites are forced to pay $25.00 to $35.00 a month rent, although the incomes of both are about equal and frequently less in the case of Negroes who are more often excluded from skilled occupations.

"The garbage and refuse in several streets of the neighborhood was not collected during the entire winter, although collectors were observed attending their jobs on nearby streets occupied by white residents.

"There are . . . seven parks in the city, but none are so located as to be conveniently reached from the Negro neighborhoods. The children play in the streets."*

The Black community, like those of other ethnic groups, developed its own social life and institutions.

Luke MacDonald: You had two churches back in those days, Methodist and Baptist. She's a Baptist, I'm a Methodist. Then another Baptist [church] started up. Then a lot of little storefronts

*Ibid., pp. 300–301.

started springing up about in the 1920s or early 1930s.

They had dances now and then. Not in church. Buckingham Hall, Garden Hall, another place on Central Avenue had a hall. Mostly [colored people]. They didn't mix too much at those affairs.

Hyotha Hofler's family came to Waterbury from Georgia before World War I. His great-uncle lived on Pearl Lake Road and walked to the Scovill plant on Hamilton Ave-

nue to work. His father worked at Bristol Brass, and became a foreman there in 1955. The Hoflers helped found many of the institutions of the Waterbury Black community, including the Pearl Street Neighborhood House and the NAACP. Hyotha Hofler, born in 1955, is a graduate of the University of Connecticut, specializing in demography and cartography. He

is presently a student of communications at Fairfield University. He works as a Marketing Research Analyst at Colonial Bank in Waterbury. He has a deep interest in the history of Waterbury and is currently at work on a history of the town's Black community, much of whose lore has passed down to him through his family.

Hyotha Hofler: The first Black church society, without a building, was founded in the 1890s. Grace Baptist. The building wasn't built till just after World War I. They were building with no capital and not given mortgages. All it was was the support of their parishioners. The amount of effort that was put forth by the people building these things must have been phenomenal.

The churches had a number of organizations that weren't altogether religious. They had an American Red Cross branch that worked within the Black community, stemming from the Pearl Street Neighborhood House, which was a settlement house in its beginnings. It was founded just before World War I, but it didn't get full use as a settlement house till later, in the 1920s. Finally, it gradually worked itself into a society, a clubhouse. It was the focal place for people to meet each other and family members who had come up from the South later than earlier members. It was a place where dances were held, parties, wedding receptions. In the 1920s and 1930s, it was a focal point for entertainers coming to Waterbury. Paul Robeson came. Redd Foxx came.

The Pearl Street House was founded in conjunction with the Grace Baptist Church. It started as a church foundation, a place for people who were seeking shelter until they could find work in Scovill's or one of the other plants.

Bertha Silva: They used to give dances at Gould's Armory. After Memorial Day they would have what you call a midnight dance. Go there at 12 o'clock at night and dance until 6 o'clock the next day. If anyone wanted to go, they would go, but mostly the Black people made those dances.

King David Holmes was born in Fitzgerald, Georgia, in 1922. His father came north to find work during World War I. King Holmes came to Waterbury in 1923, "a babe in my mother's arms." His father worked at Scovill, bought a house with two mortgages, and encouraged his kids to get an education: "You can test the records of Crosby High School; the Holmes name stands there as a landmark of quality." One of King Holmes' brothers went into the ministry, another, unable to support the family, had to go to the CCC camps. "Another brother of mine became very active in the union movement with Mine, Mill in the

Manufacturer's Foundry, which was one of the pioneers of the union movement in the city of Waterbury." King was active in the Youth Council of the NAACP, whose militance did not always meet the approval of the local branch. After completing high school, he won a scholarship to Wilberforce University. After serving in World War II, he worked briefly at Chase and Anaconda. He ended up in Scovill, where he played an active role in the union. "I believe in unionism. It's 'your brother's keeper,' it's cooperation. Working together to provide human betterment." King was involved in setting up the local and statewide UAW Fair Employment Practices Committee. In the 1960s he was an important figure in the local civil rights movement, one of the moving forces in New Opportunities for Waterbury

(NOW), and one of the organizers of community protests. When Scovill began opening management jobs to Blacks, he accepted one. He now works for the Connecticut Department of Human Resources as a Monitoring and Evaluation Representative.

King David Holmes: My knowledge of the Black community was based on coming to Waterbury in 1923, being a baby in my mother's arms. She was coming to join her husband, who had left during the World War I migrations with the Blacks in the South looking for opportunity in the North.

[When my father first came up to Waterbury,] he worked in Scovill's as a laborer. In the old wire mill.

There was a need for laborers. The quality of [Blacks'] workmanship for backbreaking work, menial tasks, was well recognized. It was hard to find people to do that type of work. If you could stand it, you could work.

We had an individual here who was an entrepreneur. He was able to capitalize. He had a hostel, Jones' Hostel and Tearoom. He was able to house those coming in the migration temporarily, until they got on their feet. He was a foreman.

He became a threat to the system, because he could house, hire you. He was readily able to say, "I can get you a job." He operated in that capacity, providing manpower

Pearl Street Neighborhood House in 1931. Courtesy Waterbury Republican-American.

to Scovill's for these menial jobs. He left Scovill's.

If they wanted a place to stay, that's where they came. The population wasn't very large at that time. So he was a very influential man.

Conflicts between Blacks and other ethnic groups closely paralleled those between different nationalities.

Lillian MacDonald: We could walk anywhere we wanted to; it was very safe. Any time of night. Dark. You could walk; nobody would bother you. You could go all over; anyplace you wanted to go.

Luke MacDonald: One place that was kind of bad was Baldwin

Pearl Street Neighborhood House, an important community center in Waterbury, in 1934. Courtesy Waterbury *Republican-American.*

Street. A bunch of Irishmen out there. Sometimes we had to fight to get back from there. Other parts of the city, nobody would bother you.

But in some cases, racial bigotry could aggravate the conflict.

Bertha Silva: My husband told me, when I first came to Ansonia, a bunch of white boys would be [in front of the drug store]; if you came along and you were Black, they would jump you. Finally one day they got a heavy guy. They jumped him. He beat the mess out of all of them. That's what broke it up.

On Main Street, at Vonete's, you'd go along there and they'd call you nigger. Sam's restaurant, you couldn't go past there at a certain time.

2. Homes: Blocks and Triple-Deckers

Most workers walked to work and had to live within walking distance of their jobs. Only a minority of Naugatuck Valley workers had cars before 1945. There were a few streetcar lines, but by and large, the Valley had not developed "streetcar suburbs"; indeed, workers were more likely to take the streetcar from inner-city homes to factories in Watertown or other outlying areas than they were to commute from suburbs into town. Through World War II, Waterbury remained a "walking city"; the smaller communities in the Brass Valley remained "walking towns."

The absence of transportation, combined with the steep hills on either side of the Naugatuck River, made Waterbury a highly congested area. Triple-decker houses and "blocks" were typical; single-family homes exceptional. Overcrowding was a chronic problem. During World War I, rent gouging became so severe that the governor had to appoint a special commission to investigate; he finally ordered a moratorium on all rent increases. During the first half of the twentieth century, however, very little public attention was paid to the continuing shortage of housing.

In 1920 home ownership was more the exception than the rule in Waterbury. There were 19,000 homes of which only 5,700 were occupant-owned. However, the workers with more stable incomes were able to buy homes.

Frank Keane: Unskilled workers went out and bought houses, three-family houses. You'd mortgage the thing for the rest of your life, but the two rents would carry it.

A sign of distinction would be to buy a one-family house. You had kind of arrived if you did that. [It was more common to buy a triple-decker.] You lived on the second floor, others lived on the first and third. The second floor was warmer.

A good many of the mortgages were private affairs, with somebody in the neighborhood, along with the bank. The down payment had to be negligible, because people couldn't accumulate much money then.

Following a common pattern, recent immigrants moved into older neighborhoods near the center of the city, while longer-established groups moved outward to newer and less congested areas. Between 1910 and 1920, for example, native whites and Irish moved out of the First and Second Wards in Waterbury, while Russians and Italians moved in. This process has continued up to the present.

Nonetheless, at least through World War II, most people continued living in areas where their

TABLE 17
Housing Conditions in Waterbury, 1930–1960

Housing type	1930	1940	1950	1960
Dwellings (aggregate)	14,959	25,387	41,410	48,860
1-family	10,283	6,129	1,835*	1,617*
2-family	3,015	4,400	4,395*	2,621*
3-family	1,661†	8,088	8,585*‡	7,489*‡
4-family		1,076		
5–9-family		3,278	4,475*	3,827*
10–19-family			1,465*	1,037*
Total homes	23,078	25,387	41,410	46,860
Owner-occupied	8,164	7,942	20,105	25,355
Renter-occupied	14,914	17,445	21,305	21,505
0 lodgers/family	20,526			
1 lodger/family	1,616			
2 lodgers/family	561			
3 lodgers/family	177			
4 or more lodgers/family	198			

*Applies only to rental units.
†3-family and over.
‡3- and 4-family unit together.
Source: Compiled from U.S. Census data by Peter Rachleff.

own ethnic group predominated. In Waterbury, for example, Italians tended to move from the central city to Town Plot.

3. Families: "Saturday Night Was Known as the Fun Night"

Child labor in the mills declined during the 1920s and 1930s, but children often remained an essential part of the family's economic support system.

Lea Harvey came from the country outside Darlington, South Carolina. Her father was a farmer. "At age five we came to New York City, and my father worked there. My mother didn't like New York, so she went back south. My father moved to Ansonia and got a job at Anaconda. We came to Ansonia. I lived there until I graduated from high school." The only work she could find in the Valley was babysitting and housework, until Chase opened up to Black women in 1942. She worked there fifteen years and nine months, until Chase

closed. She never liked factory work, but stayed "for the money." "I'm a club woman basically; I like working in civic and social organizations. [When I was very young, I was] in a girl's club. I joined a political club when I was twenty-one; I belong to several civic and social groups. I'm very active in the NAACP: I served as president, vice-president, secretary. I worked in the NAACP on a local, state, regional, and national level. I'm deep into that." "If I hadn't had a son to raise, I would probably be in Detroit now, because I would have gone to work for the union." She now has an office job, which she greatly prefers to working in the plant.

Lea Harvey: Most of the poorer kids helped out at home and had little jobs outside the home. You had a lot more responsibility than kids have today. When I was ten years old, I was doing all the family ironing except shirts, and we had six kids. At twelve I got a part-time job, working after school and on Saturdays babysitting.

Anne Zak: I went to do housework when I was sixteen. During the summer. That's what most girls did. Live in. You got four or five dollars a week and your room and board.

There were shirt factories around. Dress shops. Sewing. A lot of people used to take work home. Fill cards with pins and snaps. Laundries.

Waterbury's North Square in 1933. Courtesy Waterbury Republican-American.

Peter Kukanskis: When I was a kid, they used to have sort of cinder block pots. Sometimes in the bottom there used to be a lump of brass. They used to dump it off of Freight Street in back of the laboratory there. We used to pick coke from the furnaces for our fuel for the winter. We'd find those tubes and, boy, that was like finding gold! That was our junk money; that was our cash. We had burlap bags. We'd load them up. Sometimes there was a good harvest, a lot of coke. There were a lot of women, kids, picking. They're scrambling, fighting.

When the curls of brass used to come off the machine shop, they used to flush it down to the river. The Naugie river is shallow. The kids would pick those brass curls, the junkman would come up with a horse and wagon, and there's our cash.

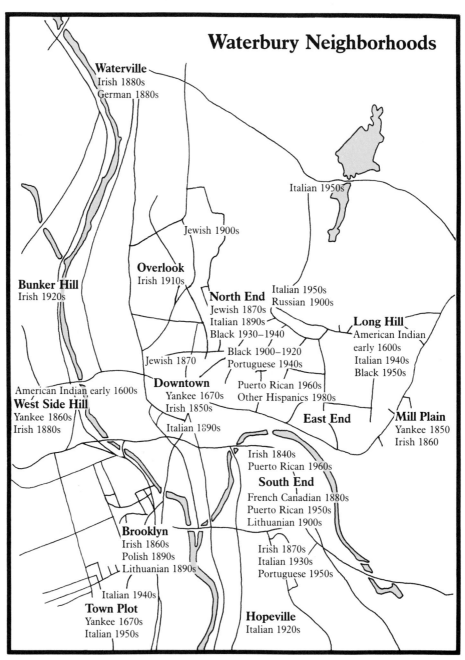

Waterbury Neighborhoods

Waterville
Irish 1880s
German 1880s

Italian 1950s

Jewish 1900s

Overlook
Irish 1910s

Bunker Hill
Irish 1920s

North End
Jewish 1870s
Italian 1890s
Black 1930–1940

Italian 1950s
Russian 1900s

Long Hill
American Indian
early 1600s
Italian 1940s
Black 1950s

Jewish 1870

Black 1900–1920
Portuguese 1940s

American Indian early 1600s

Downtown
Yankee 1670s
Irish 1850s

Puerto Rican 1960s
Other Hispanics 1980s

East End

Mill Plain
Yankee 1850
Irish 1860

West Side Hill
Yankee 1860s
Irish 1880s

Italian 1890s

Irish 1840s
Puerto Rican 1960s

South End
French Canadian 1880s
Puerto Rican 1950s
Lithuanian 1900s

Brooklyn
Irish 1860s
Polish 1890s
Lithuanian 1890s

Irish 1870s
Italian 1930s
Portuguese 1950s

Italian 1940s

Town Plot
Yankee 1670s
Italian 1950s

Hopeville
Italian 1920s

Drawn from an original by Hyotha Hofler.

TABLE 18
Population Growth in Waterbury, 1800–1960

Year	Population
1800	3,256
1810	2,874
1820	2,882
1830	3,071
1840	3,668
1850	5,137
1860	10,004
1870	10,826
1880	17,806
1890	28,646
1900	45,859
1910	73,141
1920	91,715
1930	99,902
1940	99,314
1950	104,477
1960	107,130

Source: Compiled from U.S. Census data by Peter Rachleff.

Despite poverty and work pressure, many old-time residents of the Brass Valley have warm memories of the days of their childhood, when the rural hinterland came right to the edge of town and children could enjoy the pleasures of both the country and the city.

Russell Hunter: When I was a kid [I went] to what they called the golf lots on West Main Street. Some down-and-outers used to build themselves huts. We used to go down and talk to them and listen to their stories. Sometimes we'd bring them cigarettes and tobacco.

When they cut all the trees down, the city began to look like the devil. I remember, when we were kids we used to go in the woods, get apples, pears; any kind of fruit we used to pick. A bunch of us would go picking berries, which is a hard thing to do nowadays, unless you go someplace far out. You were surrounded by woods then. All these plazas, malls—there was nothing but woods. Plenty of woods around. A kid could go and have all the fun he wanted.

In the fall we used to go picking nuts. My favorite was chestnuts.

The games I notice kids playing today are nothing like the games we played in those days. We played release, duck-on-the-rock, roll hoops—we had all kinds of games.

When I was a kid, if somebody wanted ice, they would tell me, "Russell, go down and get me [some]." We used to make our own wagons. A kid enjoyed making his own wagon.

The children would throw parties. I lived down on the second floor, and I could hear them calling me: "We're going to have a party; Mamma wants to know if you'll come over."

We went fishing when we were kids, in the river, up at Fulton Park and Lakewood Park.

The circuses—that was a day for the children. As a matter of fact, that was a day for everybody. They really enjoyed that day.

The circus would come to town. We would get up around four o'clock in the morning and go down to the grounds and watch the circus come in. If you wanted to go in free, you'd have to do some work. You'd have to help put up seats. They could get all the kids they wanted, who wanted to go see the circus. Around 11 o'clock, they'd have a parade. That's where the fun was. They'd parade from down by the plaza all the way to the Green, come up North Main Street, go over Cherry Street and back down to the circus grounds. People would be out there by the thousands. You'd see the lions and tigers and all—they had wagons with cages. It was beautiful. Kids used to enjoy that.

Saturday night was known as the fun night. Everybody would dress and go somewhere to a dance or some function or something like that. [At the functions] they had things to sell or something to eat, mostly to make money for the church. Sometimes they'd give a picnic for the children with it.

I can remember a time when I was playing in my yard and a deer jumped over my head. I looked up, and I saw that deer scooting down the road, and a bunch of dogs were right behind. That was when I lived in the West End.

Eddie Labacz's father came from Vilna, Poland, and went to work at the Seymour Mfg. Co. in 1891 or 1892. Born in 1921, Eddie has lived in Seymour all his life. He followed his father into the plant,

now Bridgeport Brass, in 1941 and works there to this day. He drove a jitney for nine years, and since 1950 has been an annealing furnace operator on the 11 to 7 shift. He has been president of UAW Amalgamated Local 1827 since 1961. He and his wife have seven children. His two sons also work in the plant. "I have one son who turned management, that hurts."

Eddie Labacz: We used to steal from the company and build rafts for the river, build huts in the woods, go up and play house.

Stella Horoshak: We used to go up on the bank and get leaves and roll them up and smoke them. We used to go skating. I played basketball with the St. Stanley girls. We had a lot of activities in those days. We had to be home by the second whistle; when that 9 o'clock whistle blew, we had to be in the house.

I had to work in my father's restaurant from the age of twelve. I washed dishes, made sandwiches.

On Saturdays we used to take a bath, get on a trolley car, go to the Capitol for a nickel. We used to go to Vonete's and have a sundae, all for a quarter.

Athletic clubs and amusement parks served as recreational centers.

Hap Lasky: I'll bet at least 50 percent of the younger people went to

Savin Rock [amusement park in West Haven] on a Sunday. They used to run about ten special cars to take them down to Savin Rock. There was dancing, there was roller skating, there was swimming. When I started courting my wife, I used to take her down with me. In 1917, 1918, through there.

They had good [baseball] leagues. The old City Amateur League had ball players as good as the professionals. They used to get anywhere from 3000 to 5000 people watching them. They used to play down in the old golf lots, where the mall is now.

Brooklyn Athletic Club had a team for Brooklyn. Washington Hill had a team. Then there were the Laurels, from out East Main. Then there was Watertown. [The players were] mostly seventeen or eighteen years old.

Support for higher education and professional careers often came, not just from the family, but from the ethnic community as a whole:

Daniel Zuraitis: The guys in 103 [Lithuanian club] would continually take collections up to help a kid in college. If a kid made grades, then the clubs would kick in periodically. A lot of the early doctors and lawyers that were made were made through contributions of the clubs and the different activities.

But most kids growing up in working-class families during this period had to limit their aspirations.

Frank Pochron: When I was in high school, they gave me a tour of the brass mill and they said, "This is your college."

The family often served as an important bridge to the world of work for the first-generation Americans. In many cases sons were able to take advantage of the economic niches carved out by their immigrant parents, as the following discussion among men who followed their fathers into the Seymour Mfg. Co. indicates:

Sam Kwochka: Your parents worked there, and they were good workers.

Frank Pochron: If you were a loafer, they'd see your old man; he'd rap you behind the ears.

John Chubat: My father used to work in this brass mill, and a lot of our people were here. These people got me in there. Through friendship.

There was no choice at all for the ones who came here. They either had to go to work in the factories or they'd be out of work.

Pochron: We didn't have the opportunity or the transportation to go anywhere else. That's why you tried to pick a factory where your parents were working and could

try to get you in. That helped me, because my father was working there and I could get in there.

Joe Yrchik: Same as my father: he got me into the place, and my brother.

Chubat: Every one of them: they brought their sons there and they followed their fathers' footsteps. A small community, they know everybody. You may know the management.

Kwochka: The company took the attitude that if the father worked here for forty years and did a good job, the kid has to be a little better than some other people. I would say to my kid, "Hey! That's not right; you're not doing it right." They had some pride in the place. So you find a lot of our people had their fathers working. Even some of the boys working now have fathers in management.

DIVISION OF LABOR IN THE HOME

Families found different solutions to the problem of dividing up the work that had to be done in the home.

Mary Toletti's parents came from the province of Avelino near Naples. She was born in Waterbury in 1908. From 1926 to 1944 she worked at Chase's office on Grand Street. She then worked at Robertshaw Control for nineteen years.

She and her husband, an electrician at Scovill's, raised one daughter. Her husband had to work two jobs to send their daughter to teacher's college. Mary has been a member of Lady of Lourdes church all her life, and is presently employed as a bookkeeper at the Waterbury Retired Workers Council.

Nellie Sacco's parents came to Waterbury from Warsaw, Poland, around 1905. Her father worked as a truck driver, delivering vegetables from store to store. Her mother raised eleven children at their home on Rushton Place, off of South Main. Nellie was born in 1914. At fifteen she had her birth certificate fixed up so that she could go to work at the Central Fruit and Vegetable Market. She worked a seventy-hour week for a weekly pay of ten dollars. Later she went to work at Watertown

Manufacturing Company doing "bull work, filing stock off of metal for 28½¢ an hour." She then went to work at U.S. Time as a machine operator on fuses until she got laid off in 1949. In 1950, she married. While she was married, she worked part time at the Fulton Market. She has been a Senior Aide at the Palladino Center since 1975 and enjoys calling bingo there.

Mary Diogostine's parents came to New York from Columbia, Italy. Her father ran a restaurant in the Bronx. She was born in 1920, one of five children. When she was twelve, her parents moved to Waterbury to look for work. During the Depression, her father worked for the city as a "straw boss" for the WPA. At eighteen, Mary went to work for the National Youth Administration. She and other young girls sewed hospital gowns

and bandages at St. John's Church. While she was working at a sewing shop on Mill Street, she married Tony Diogostine. She was making nine dollars a week; he was making fifteen. They had their first child, a daughter. After a year, Mary went to work at Benrus, and then at Scovill's making war products. In 1946, Mary had her second child. In 1948, the family moved back to the Bronx, where Mary worked in a chemical plant and at a five-and-dime store. They weren't making enough money in New York, so they moved back to Waterbury. "We didn't have two nickels to rub together," Mary recalls. "We quit our jobs in New York on Friday, and got jobs in Waterbury on Monday." Both Tony and Mary ended up at Scovill's, now Century Brass, where Mary worked as an inspector until her retirement in 1982. The Di-

ogostines were both active in the union. For the past fifteen years, Mary has served on the Board of Directors of the Waterbury Retired Workers Council.

The following discussion among these women who were married to brass workers was recorded at the Retired Workers Council in Waterbury.

Mary Toletti: [My husband helped around the house] only once, on Fridays. He'd help me with the big dusting.

Nellie Sacco: My husband worked for American Brass as an eyelet toolmaker. My husband would always say to me, "Your job is inside; my job is outside." My husband would never talk about his job at home, never. The only time I heard about my husband's job was when he had fingers chopped off accidentally. That's the only time I saw the people that he worked with. He had to take early retirement. He was a good eyelet maker. They were very hard to get. That's the only thing I know about his work.

Mary said her husband did the dusting on a Friday night: I tried it. My husband would say, "Your work is inside; my work is outside." In other words: Don't ask me. I went to the doctor after an operation. The doctor said [to him], "You could either wash dishes or you could sweep the floor." I knew he wasn't going to do dishes. I said, "Shall I do the floor?" He said, "No, you do the dishes; I'll sweep." He would never, never.

When I went to the hospital, I had casseroles made up. When I came home, there was nothing laying around. "How did you wash these dishes?" He wouldn't answer me. I never got the answer how he cleaned up.

Mary Diogostine: I think years ago a husband and wife, most of them anyway, helped each other out because the money was so little then. You made twelve dollars a week for forty hours.

FAMILY SIZE

One important change in family structure during this period was that families tended to become much smaller.

Frank Keane: [Families started getting smaller] I suppose after the children of the first generation went to school and had children themselves. It's a kind of evolutionary process. If you have eight kids and you saw how hard it was to contend with things, the normal reaction to that is—Not eight for me. I presume this would happen in any situation in this country, where the second generation is not going to act like the first. Plus, things happen; things you want. Cars were coming in, and you want a car; how can you have a car when you have eight kids?

Born in 1946, Frieda Ewen is the daughter of Fredo and Jewel Lucarelli (introduced on page 143). After attending high school in Shelton, she worked in a series of small shops which primarily employed women. She married in 1965. Her husband, like her father, worked at B.F. Goodrich. He later went to work at Anaconda. After getting divorced, she wanted to study to become a history teacher, but discovered there were few jobs available. She went to school to become an LPN instead, and worked for seven years at Bridgeport Hospital until the long hours and the responsibilities of caring for three children became too much for her. In the late 1970s, through the Valley Women's Center, an organization which provides educational programs and mutual support for Valley women, she got involved in a wide range

of community issues and organizations. She became an active member of the LNV Community Mental Health Center, the Battered Women's Project, the Housing Coalition, and the Valley Citizens Action Group. In 1979, she went to work as a paralegal at Valley Legal Assistance. She specialized in housing, and was instrumental in organizing tenants' associations in public and private housing throughout the Valley. She was also active in her union, which is affiliated with District 65-UAW. On weekends, one is likely to find her playing drums in a band managed by her father.

Frieda Ewen: My parents' family was much smaller than the families that they came from. In our family there were four. In my father's there were ten kids. In my mother's there were seven. All of my parents' brothers and sisters had less [than their parents].

Prior to that you existed partly on the labor of your children. That changed; now you had to support them and not gain any benefit from their labors, because more of them were going to school longer and going on to college.

FAMILY AUTHORITY

In many families, parental and particularly paternal authority was strong. Yet it could also be effectively neutralized at times, as the following story indicates.

Catherine Coscia came to Water-bury from Sardinia in 1925, when she was six. Her father worked in the casting shop at Chase. Her mother died when she was nine, and Catherine took care of the three younger children. She "lied her age" and went to work in the Clock Shop when she was four-teen. She subsequently worked at the Box Shop, Plume and Atwood, French's, American Metal Hose, and Eyelet. In 1932, she married her husband, John, an employee of CL&P. They had two sons, Tony Frank and Nicholas John. Tony works as a boss on the tower lines at CL&P, and Nicholas is a vice-president and budget controller and accountant at Clairol in Stam-ford. Catherine still does things the old-fashioned way: "I make homemade macaroni, and cook the old-fashioned way. I don't use canned goods. I made raviolis for my grandson for his graduation. I've got them frozen downstairs, over a hundred of them. Lasagna and manicotti, too."

Catherine Coscia: My father was very jealous of us girls. He loved us. [My future husband] came to see my stepmother. One day my father said to him, "You're not coming to see my wife; you're coming to see my daughter. I don't want you to come here any more."

He came anyway; he found a way. I'd always see him when I went to work in the clock shop. One noon hour the girls said,

"There's somebody outside for you." I said, "Tell them to leave." They said, "He just wants to talk to you." I went downstairs and said, "I told you, I don't want you to come here. Because if you get caught, he's going to get mad at you, and I'm going to get hit." He said, "Don't worry. I love you, and someday we're going to get married." And he did. My father even went as far as to follow me to work. I went to church one Sun-day with my lady friend. [My fa-ther] followed me to church. [My future husband] met me in front of the church, and my father was there. When I went home, [my fa-ther] said, "I thought you weren't going to see him any more."

[We] went out only three or four months. My father said to him, "If you want to marry my daughter, I'm only going to give you six months. If you don't marry her in six months, I want you to leave this house, never see her in the street, and never talk to her.

"You haven't got a job. How are you going to support my daugh-ter?" (He was right, and I didn't realize it in time.) "If she has a baby, who's going to take care of it?" He answered my father, "You don't ever have to worry about your daughter's starving. I'll get a job somewhere." They had told him at the WPA that, if he got married, they would give him a job.

He didn't have a job, but I was working. It was Depression time,

1933. I said to my father, "I never come to you for a dime, for any-thing. I love him and he loves me." (I was only nineteen.) And I said, "We're going to get married. If you want to give me something, fine." (He didn't have anything.) "If you don't, that's all right. I don't want anything, I just want to love you always." So he cooked for my wedding.

4. Social Life: Societies and Saloons

Notwithstanding the assimilation of immigrant communities to American ways, social life in the Naugatuck Valley continued to be conducted largely on an ethnic basis throughout the first half of the twentieth century. Products of mass culture, such as movies and radio, became increasingly avail-able, but they did not replace the institutions of the ethnic commu-nities. The following statements, referring to the post-1920 period, show how much cultural continu-ity there was with the earlier period.

Peter Kukanskis: I know my mother belonged to a club. Once a week or every two weeks, she'd take off for an hour or two or three and get together. They used to work years ago ten hours a day, six days a week. They'd fall asleep on their feet almost. But they had the societies as an out, where they

A Lithuanian community outing in Waterbury in the 1920s. Courtesy Lithuanian Club of Waterbury, Inc.

could go and get away from all this junk they had to hassle every day. That two or three hours with a group of women—at least it was a little pleasure, a little leisure that they had.

Daniel Zuraitis: And they weren't teetotalers. They'd drink boiler-makers, a shot and a beer. This was when they came to their club activities.

Catherine Coscia: If I went out with the girls, we used to go from one house to another. We started a crocheting club for ourselves, a sewing club. Anybody who liked to knit, make embroidery—we'd go to each other's house. Today somebody will come here, tomorrow I go to their house, another day I go someplace else. We weren't allowed to go to movies [or dances].

Anne Zak: When someone died and they had a wake, the men would stay up all night. They had it at the house, they never had it at a funeral parlor. My father was one of them; he was always there.

They played cards and drank and stayed all night. Next day they'd go to work.

In those days, the societies had picnics. That's where people met—I met my husband at one of them. These were Sunday picnics. They had bands. They had food. This was for young and old, the whole family. Nowadays you don't see the whole family going to affairs like that. Dancing. Outside benches. Picnic areas.

Bart Hennessey: If you went to the German hall, you did German

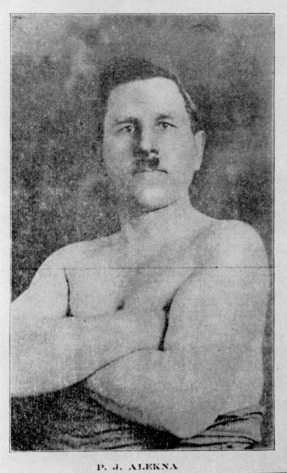

PROGRAMAS
BALIAUS!
Liet. Tautos Fondo 40 Skyriaus
26 dieną Gruodžio-Dec. 1919 m.
48 Green St. Waterbury, Ct.   Pradžia 7:30 v. vak.

Pirk Bonų bus Lietuvoje duonos. Jeigu negali patsai keliaut į Lietuvą apginti priešus katrie apgulė musų Tėvynę, tai pasiųskie savo dolerį su kuriuomi apšarvuosi Lietuvos galingąjį kareivį ir kaip matai lenkus išvarys iš Vilniaus.

P. J. ALEKNA

A page from the program of a wrestling match held at the Lithuanian 48 Club in 1919. Courtesy Daniel Zuraitis.

dances. If you went to the Polish hall, you did the Polka.

Frank Pochron: When I got married, we didn't hire a caterer. The mother-in-law said, "I know these women." They said, "How many are you going to invite?" "So many." "All right, I'll get so many hams, so many turkeys."

Then you rented a club. They had their own kitchen. The women used to go down and cook. They didn't care how many people you had. They all got together and helped each other out.

Joe Yrchik: When my uncle built his house, we dug that cellar by hand. There were about eight of us digging that cellar by pick and shovel. It took us about a month, but we dug it by hand.

John Chubat: My uncle, too. We dug his cellar by hand. There was just some moonshine. Put the bottle there; put a little food there, some herrings, maybe a little smoked shoulder.

For the men, saloons remained an important social gathering place, even during Prohibition.

Peter Kukanskis: There were three or four speakeasies around here. They were "soda shops," "ice cream parlors." Right across the street here was a soda shop. He was bootlegging. There was one on Riverside; he was doing the same thing. Old Smiling John had one on Leonard Street all his life. They made a living out of it.

Every so often they'd close them up for a week or two. Sometimes you'd get warning; they'd say, "John, be careful this week." So they'd try to be careful. They'd be back in business again in a day or two. It was just something where the local gendarmes had to go out and show their feathers a little bit.

Daniel Zuraitis: [The saloon-keepers] were the bankers. If you just had a room, you had a place to eat at the bar that you frequented. So you took your meals there usually. He'd usually loan you the money until your payday came. Write a tab for you. So if you did have some money, you usually put it in his safe. He'd keep a running book. There were even some Lithuanian banks that were started from these kinds of actions.

Many people commented on the feeling of closeness in the communities in which they grew up, something they often miss today.

Bart Hennessey: People were this close: if there was any trouble in the neighborhood, all the neighbors would come over, they'd pick the kids up, they'd bring food. If somebody got sick. If somebody died. Everybody worked as one big family. After World War II or just prior to it, people began to lose that closeness.

While this spirit still persists to some extent, to most people it is just a memory. The following discussion is from the Derby Senior Center.

Mary Poeltl: When I was a girl, all my relatives lived around me, so we were always together. The kids all played together. The mothers got together. Three or four families.

Anne Zak: We're still all together. There were six of us, and we all live on the same street. My children live near me now. We never separated. Have parties together.

Bart Hennessey: As far as my family is concerned, they're scattered to forty-eight states across the nation.

Poeltl: Most families are like that. Once they go to school, they get a job out of town. They never come back to where they were born, the majority of them.

5. Life in the Depression: "What Am I Going to Do, Take a Piece of My House and Eat It?"

Over the long run, the standard of living of brass workers has risen substantially. But their progress has by no means been steady. During economic "hard times," their gains have been lost and their lives thrust back to the severest poverty.

No period of "hard times" was worse than the Great Depression of the 1930s. Tens of thousands of brass workers lost their jobs; the rest worked only short time at reduced wages.

Peter Kukanskis: Eating was a problem. Getting food. Getting money. The only ones that really were well off in those days were any civil servant: politicians, teachers, firemen. They at least got a week's pay. For about three years, my dad didn't do anything. He might go out and work all day. "I got three dollars. The job was worth five. The guy only had three, so he gave me three." So you'd split the three dollars for a loaf of bread, two loaves of bread, some butter, milk, whatever. You survived, but that was the hardest part of living. None of them paid rent because they didn't have the money. Maybe they'd throw a five dollar bill at you every so often.

Then the WPA came in with Roosevelt and made it a little easier; at least there was a little something on the table. I know I'd come home from high school a lot of times: "Hey, Ma, what's for dinner, what have we got to eat?" "Ah, have a piece of bread." Bacon fat or something you'd spread on the bread. That's your meal. And you'd think nothing of it. As long as it was something to put in your belly.

They all raised chickens, they all raised vegetables. I remember our

Unemployment relief in Waterbury, November 1931. Courtesy Waterbury Republican-American.

cellar; we were living in the city, but we had pumpkins and squash and potatoes and whatever you could. And every bit of it went. Because you didn't have money to buy any of that stuff.

Sometimes survival required extreme measures.

Bertha Silva: In the Depression, I would buy moonshine. When things are that bad, you have to make some money. They used to sell me a gallon of moonshine for two dollars and a half. I'd turn around and sell it for five dollars. I carried it in a hot water bag! I had to raffle off all my wedding things to make money. A quarter raffle. It was hard times.

The brass companies adopted a policy of spreading the work among the work force. This provided some income for all—but the incomes were barely adequate to survive on.

Russell Hunter: During Hoover's time, we went on short time. After a while, when things really were bad, in 1932, we were working sometimes five hours a week, one day a week. That was tough. Trying to raise a family.

Nobody lost their jobs completely. They shared it, to give everybody something to do. Still you had to go on welfare. People got by by going on the welfare. At that time people were losing their homes, automobiles.

The cities attempted, at first, to deal with the crisis through charity organizations.

Jim Cusack: At the time of the Great Depression, 1929, 1930, the need for charity was far beyond what the city of Waterbury could carry on. So some of the people prominent in charitable work, through a series of discussions and give and take, set up an organization. It was done very efficiently. The city organized a so-called mutual aid fund, to which those people who were working were asked to contribute. The ordinary worker was asked to contribute 1 percent of his salary. The salaried worker or management employee was asked to contribute 3 percent. Response was almost unanimous in Scovill's.

Unemployment relief in Waterbury, 1931. Courtesy Waterbury Republican-American.

Those funds were used to pay people [to work on municipal needs].

For those with no work and no money, public relief was often the only alternative to starvation:

Russell Hunter: You had to go downtown, and they would give you a bag of food. I didn't get any hard time; they just dished it out to me.

Luke MacDonald: [To get relief food] you had to fill out a form. One time I went down there. My wife was working at the Coe's. Another fellow said, "Let's go down and see if we can get us some help." "Is your wife working?" They asked you how many days she was working; if she was working, you didn't get anything.

Bertha Silva: In the Depression my husband was laid off. He lost everything he had. We had to fall in the breadline, just like everybody else. This is another reason I don't like this town. We had to go down to City Hall and stand in the bread line. It was federal food they were giving to the people. One boy named Tony worked with my husband on the WPA. He would say to my husband, "Vic, did you get any butter?" "No," he said, "they didn't put any in my packet." My husband went back and said, "Could I have some butter?" The man said to him, "It's all gone."

You had to survive the best way you could. My kids will tell you, many days they went without shoes on their feet. How the kids would laugh at them.

Caroline Nardello: My brother went up to City Hall to get something. They would give you beans and rice and prunes. They said, "You have a house." So my brother said, "What am I going to do, take a piece of my house and eat it?"

Rowena Peck: We used to have a soup kitchen. And Mrs. Kellog gave us her skim milk. They came in droves after that skim milk. The soup kitchen used to be over by the bridge in Derby. Some people made the soup in great big vats and brought it down and gave it to the poor people. Just two days a week that soup was given out. We used to have a secondhand clothing place in the District Nurses' Office. There were a lot of needy people in Ansonia, Derby, and Shelton.

Acceptance of relief raised serious questions of pride for many workers.

Art Finelli: When we were kids and times were getting tough in the Depression, 1931, 1932, 1933, right across from the City Hall at the Field Street Dispensary they were giving out food. If you were Italian, you would get oil, flour, macaroni, tomatoes. My mother heard about this. She said, "Come on." I went down there with her. We got two bags to carry home. When my father got home at 5 o'clock that night, my mother was so proud. "See what I've got?" When he saw what she had, he said, "You bring that goddamn stuff back." He wouldn't take it. I can remember my mother crying because he wouldn't take it. He was getting seven bucks a week, raising a family of nine.

Credit within the neighborhood aided survival.

Daniel Zuraitis: Within the old inner cities, all the corners were mom-and-pop grocery stores. During the hard times, they charged. They knew the families that traded with them, and they'd carry them. They'd carry them a year, two years. As long as there was an effort made to pay against the debt. Everybody had a book. Put it on the book. You'd get your salt and sugar and whatever that way.

Under the New Deal, federal programs like the Civilian Conservation Corps (CCC) and the Works Progress Administration (WPA) provided additional local employment.

Frank Keane: I don't think there was ever a CCC in Waterbury. Waterbury kids had about four places around the state they might go. Usually they did some kind of reforestation or cleared the streams. They couldn't be taken care of at home, so the federal government instituted these programs which would take the load off the family. Many friends of mine joined the CCC. They'd be back every weekend in town.

There was WPA like crazy. I think the Post Office building was WPA. A good many of the things that were done in the parks were WPA. Tennis courts and ball diamonds being built. If you were a musician, you belonged to a WPA band. You did your thing and got a little bit of money for it. If you were an artist, you could paint murals on the Post Office walls. They had theater going. They had symphony. This was all WPA. You can laugh at the thing, but it sure helped people through some very trying times. Not just the ones who were paid; I'm talking about the recipients. You could listen to a concert. They'd go around to neighborhoods and do it. Block affairs. And there weren't only forty or fifty people there.

Despite the deprivations, many people remember the Depression years as a time of enriched community life.

Frank Keane: You'd go down every day and wait in line, see if you could get a few hour's work. If you didn't, you did what everybody did: headed for the park. All of a sudden there weren't kids in the park; there were adults in the park. There were adults playing games that the kids didn't play. Volleyball became a big thing. Baseball. They utilized all of these. Local entertainment. Plenty of minstrels and local things.

It was a good time to be a kid. It was a marvelous time to go up and watch these guys cavort around the parks.

Nonetheless, it was also a time of shattered expectations:

Vincent Zak: My father went down to the bank to borrow some money to pay the bills and the mortgage. It was all locked up. Uncle Sam had his big key in there. How is he going to manage with no money? It scared him to death. My mother's hair turned white overnight from worrying. Some finance company finally loaned him the money at 25 percent.

Anne Zak: My family was in the same predicament. No one would lend them money. Nobody trusted the foreigners who came from across. No one would lend them

money for their homes or farms. Finally, Mr. Miller, the president of the Connecticut National Bank, a goodhearted man, gave my parents a mortgage and it was repaid.

Peter Kukanskis: I almost went to college, but I hit at the wrong time. It was Depression time, no money, everything gone to heck. I graduated high school; I had plans of going to college. No money. No money the following year. Two years went by and I started plumbing and that was it.

A Waterbury WPA band in December 1938. Courtesy Waterbury Republican-American.

Unemployed men and women demonstrating on the Waterbury Green, February 24, 1933. Courtesy Waterbury Republican-American.

THE WORK

With the defeat of the 1920 strike, employers were back in a dominant position in the plants and community. The union organizations fell apart and practically vanished. Talk of the possibility of unionizing was met with scorn by many of those who had been through the postwar defeats. Little remained from the early strikes except bitter memories.

John Zampino was born in Montagano Campobasso, Italy, in 1904. He came to America in 1921, and became an American citizen in 1926. He worked in Scovill's West Plant in the Manufacturing Buff Room from 1927 until his retirement in 1970, except during World War II, when he worked in the fuse and case shops. In the early 1930s, he took part in attempts by the AFL to organize in the brass plants. He comes from a wine-making district in Italy and vividly describes trampling grapes in his bare feet as a youth. To this day, he still makes excellent homemade wine.

John Zampino: [In the 1920s] we had about 300 men working in the room. There was a guy who said, "We should have a union in this place. We work Saturday; we've got to work twelve hours a day with no time-and-a-half." But everybody ignored it. Everybody knew what happened before.

Asked if there were any unionism at American Brass in the early 1930s, Russell Sobin replied, "It wasn't even thought of."

Nonetheless, many of the workers' most pressing problems remained: the arbitrary power of foremen, poor working conditions, destruction of craft skills, long hours, low wages, speedup, insecurity. Attempts to address them through collective action would have to await the next great round of organizing activity in the late 1930s.

Before 1920 the major brass companies were owned and run by the local families in the Naugatuck Valley who had been associated with them for so long. After the war Anaconda, the world's largest copper company, swollen with wartime profits and excess capacity, purchased the American Brass

TABLE 19
Waterbury's Industrial Base, 1930

Industry	Number of establish-ments	Number of wage-earners	Value added by manu-facture ($)
All industry (aggregate)	181	24,369	71,181,386
Bread and bakery	32	202	1,106,951
Women's clothing	3	98	148,537
Foundry and machine shop	10	534	2,169,775
Hardware	3	559	1,184,708
Nonferrous metals	15	12,798	39,783,035
Planing mills	4	54	149,805
Printing	16	98	405,321

Source: Compiled from U.S. Census data by Peter Rachleff.

ganization that emerged in the 1930s and 1940s. The union upsurge of the World War I era had involved largely local and craft-based organizations. The next upsurge of unionism, in the late 1930s, took place in the framework of a national organization, which also represented miners and others who worked for the major copper companies in distant parts of the West. Workers in the Naugatuck Valley had become part of a national company and union context.

A typical cartoon from a late 1920s issue of the Scovill Bulletin, *published by the Scovill Foremen's Association and distributed to all employees. Courtesy Scovill Collection.*

6. "Labor Policy": Providing a Docile Labor Force

The brass companies needed workers to run their plants. But workers might organize to pursue interests in conflict with those of the manufacturers. As we have seen, relations with workers were left largely to the discretion of individual foremen into the beginning of the twentieth century. Gradually, however, the brass companies, like other American corporations, developed policies which would provide a steady supply of workers, yet ensure that they stayed unorganized.

IMPORTING LABOR

Maintaining a supply of unskilled labor became a conscious management objective.

Jim Cusack: During the war the

Co., which at that time produced more than half of the country's brass. In 1929 Kennecott Copper Co. followed suit and purchased Chase Brass. Scovill, the only remaining independent of the Big Three, took a different course: It began to diversify by purchasing companies in other fields in different parts of the country.

The effects of this change were limited at first. Most of the corporate organizations of the brass companies were left intact. The same leading families continued to play the same dominant role.

However, the integration of the brass companies into national corporations ultimately had a major impact on the form of worker or-

The American Brass Co.   Ansonia Branch

REPORT ON EMPLOYEE

Date————————191——

To Employment Bureau:

Name————————————————— No.—————————

Dep't.————————————— Operation————————

Working as——————————————————————

(Opposite qualities are shown in the parallel columns below. Place a cross in square before the word which describes employee.)

Regular (In attendance)	Irregular
Punctual	Tardy
Careful	Careless
Industrious	Lazy
Obedient	Disobedient
Patient	Impatient
Sober	Intemperate

Disturber? ☐ Yes   ☐ No

State any other facts of importance——————————————

————————————————————————————

————————————————————————————

Signed———————————————————
                                Foreman

EMP. BUREAU NO. 17--5000-8-21-'18.

American Brass Co. Employment Bureau Form No. 17, circa 1920. Courtesy Adelaide Walker.

mills imported Jamaicans. They were housed in barracks. There was one on what's known as Golden Hill, between Sylvan Avenue and Hamilton Avenue. There was another barracks out in what is now Store Avenue. Porter Lots, they were known as. The government built the houses for accommodation of the people being brought into Waterbury. There were also quite a number of Albanians.

Back in those days, those ethnic groups usually had a self-proclaimed padrone. He's a self-appointed leader. He handles the correspondence. He's a little bit educated, whereas the others couldn't read or write. He handled the financial matters, such as arranging to send money home. He was the intermediary for them with management.

You [the company] were rather forced to deal with the padrone. He would act as interpreter; although he could speak very little English, he could usually be made to understand using a few words of his language and a sort of pidgin English. He would help you to get the people. The hiring was done mostly through a sort of employment agency which came into being for that purpose at that time. That would have been around 1914. Our employment service people would deal with the outside agency, who would ship these people in, according to the number you asked for.

They would come in and usually among them would be a padrone. He would arrive with his gang, or he was already there with the original group. Some of them got homesick and went home.

THE OPEN SHOP

One part of "labor policy" during the 1920s and 1930s was direct resistance to unions.

Discrimination against union members was one simple method of preventing worker organization. Charles R. Walker: "A chief electrician in the Navy. Went to an employer. Said he was an electrician. 'How can you prove it,' said the employer. He showed his union card. 'Sorry.'"

Employers also used their influence with local governments to create a climate hostile to unionism. The virtual reign of terror by the police during the 1919 and 1920 strikes was followed by a continuing informal repression of many forms of labor activity.

Sid Monti: Many of the policemen in town, if they saw four or five guys during unemployment periods were grouped together, they'd disperse them. They were afraid they were trying to talk up unions.

Mike Laban: I happened to be in Lakewood section [of Waterbury around 1932]. Some Italian girls were bellyaching. The girls were

Two Jamaican workers, imported to work for Scovill during World War II, in their barracks in Meriden, Conn. Courtesy Scovill, Inc.

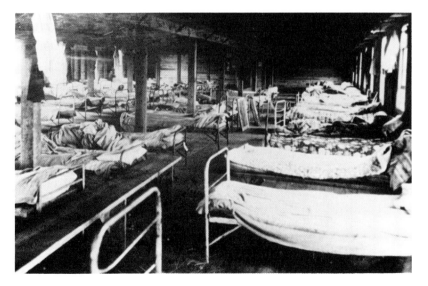

Quarters for unmarried immigrant men in the World War I era. Scovill built these barracks on its property at Golden Hill in Waterbury. Courtesy Scovill Collection.

Jamaican workers, imported to work at Scovill during World War II, preparing to return home in 1945. Courtesy Scovill, Inc.

Former Scovill employees about to board the S.S. Francesca *to go home to Albania after World War I. Courtesy Scovill Collection.*

telling me about the deplorable working conditions, that [the company] didn't pay time-and-a-half. You had to work all kinds of hours.

Some of the girls were around sixteen years old. "Aged 16 and 17 may not work in certain hazardous occupations." They were telling me about some of the machinery, which was belt-driven; they'd get one big motor and run the whole thing on belts. I told them who to contact.

I remember being called a goddamn radical by the police. I think we went to City Hall. I got into a scuffle with a policeman. I was called names, dirty damn Red. I was beaten up and thrown into the cooler. But I was released. No charges were preferred.

WELFARE WORK

Repression was not the only means used by employers, however. The companies developed forms of what was called "welfare work," designed to contribute to the well-being of their employees and keep them contented and "loyal."

Scovill, while not unique, was in the forefront of these activities. In 1913 top Scovill executive John Goss promoted the development of the Scovill Foremen's Association, began a campaign to reduce plant accidents, and opened a plant hospital. The Foremen's Association, in turn, organized recreation for the war workers flooding into Waterbury.

Waterbury garment workers on strike in 1935. Courtesy Waterbury Republican-American.

In 1918 Scovill organized an employment office under its Industrial Service Department to sort job applications. The Industrial Service Department also operated a library and a welfare unit for women workers. During and after World War I, 150 houses were built for skilled workers, and barracks were erected for 500. By the end of the war, such needs were largely addressed by company-sponsored YMCA rooms. In late 1918, a push was made to teach foreign workers English, and a training program for young workers was set up in March 1919.

Jim Cusack describes some of Scovill's welfare activities from the management side:

Jim Cusack: During the later part of World War I and the period immediately thereafter, there was an attempt on the part of management to improve morale. They used to stop work in the middle of a morning or the afternoon for group singing. You would have a leader in a department. I was in the tool room at the time. The toolmakers would all lay down their work for a period of fifteen to twenty minutes. We had one fellow who had a pretty good voice; he

Striking garment workers in Watertown. They are sewing while on the picket line. Courtesy Waterbury Republican-American.

would lead the group in singing. It so happened in the tool department that the assistant foreman was the singing leader. We used to sing all the then-popular songs. In various places throughout the plant they did the same thing.

[The men] laughed at [the singing], but they enjoyed it.

Through private charitable activities, the brass masters' families cultivated their image as benefactors of the workers and of the community at large.

Jim Cusack: The Goss family and the Sperry family were close to their people. Very charitable. The Goss family knew the people in the factory and mills.

Frank Keane: There was a lot of—not collective bargaining, but individual bargaining. You could approach a boss and say, "Hey, my wife's sick, the kid's in the hospital. What can you do for me?" And something would be done.

Over in Scovill, they started the Sunshine Club, where workers could appeal to this club. It was a built-in welfare agency that took care of these people.

Whatever benevolent purposes company welfare programs had, they also served to help ward off such "disloyalty" to the employers as unionism. For example, during the strike of 1919, 53 percent of all foreign-born employees left the plant, whereas only 3.5 percent of those attending the Scovill school were out, according to the company.

Sid Monti: [To keep the union weak,] the Scovill Recreation Association [helped] to meet some of the social needs of the people, so they would get their minds off the oppression that was prevalent in the plant. This was absolutely their strong point.

COMPANY GRIEVANCE HANDLING

The brass companies were interested in developing alternatives to unions, alternatives that might function under employer rather than worker control. In particular, they experimented with ways of handling workers' grievances and giving recourse against arbitrary decisions by foremen.

At Scovill, Goss established what he called the "right to challenge" around 1914 or 1915:

"We publicized very broadly more or less in writing and verbally, when we were talking to

Young Lithuanian women attending an English class sponsored by Scovill shortly after World War I. The book they are using is called Plain Facts for Future Americans. *Courtesy Scovill Collection.*

groups of employees, the fact that they had the privilege to 'challenge' any condition in the plant which they did not like which affected them or affected a fellow employee or which they did not think was to the best interest of the business." *

The "right to challenge" can be seen in operation in John Zampino's story.

John Zampino: I went to Mr. Goss. "Mr. Goss, you're a president of this company and you get so much. Suppose they need another president just like you. Would it be fair if they paid you more than the other one?" "No." "Then why does Mr. Murphy pay one man seventy-five cents average, another

man fifty cents an hour [for the same work]?"

Mr. Goss said, "Mr. Murphy, what do you do that for?" "He had more seniority." Mr. Goss said, "Never mind seniority. You pay that man just as much as the other one." Two weeks later, they told Mr. Murphy, "Either you're fired, or you have to take a watchman's job." From seventy-five dollars a week, he had to go to thirty dollars a week.

During World War I, forms of worker representation developed in the brass plants as they did elsewhere. In the wake of the 1919 strike, a system of shop committees was set up at American Brass. Charles R. Walker describes some aspects of their operation:

"Ballots were passed around today for nomination of the committeeman for the unit.

*P. W. Bishop, "History of Scovill Manufacturing Company," manuscript in Scovill collection, Baker Library, p. 244.

The Chase Brass Co. Girls' Basketball Team versus the Scovill Girls' Basketball Team, 1945. Courtesy Scovill, Inc.

Scovill Case Department workers dancing during their lunch break, September 1944. Around this time, it was not uncommon for workers in various departments to participate in "noon hour dancing to John Madden's canned music." Courtesy Scovill, Inc.

"I found out from the Empl. Mgr. what were some of the matters discussed at the Shop Committee:

"A wall in one of the departments was in dangerous state and threatened to fall over into the room. The mortar had fallen out of some of the bricks.

"This was brought to the attention of the committee and the wall was repaired.

"A pathway in back of the mill, which many men took on their way home, was found to be flooded with water constantly, and it was requested that ashes from the boiler be dumped there. This was done.

"A cooperative store was suggested and approved by the joint committee at the time of the second strike (before the strike) and turned down by the officials of the company."

7. "Rationalization": "We Took That Control Out of the Operators' Hands"

Like other industries, the brass industry has seen a continuous process sometimes referred to as "rationalization." This involves the replacement of traditional production techniques both with new technologies and with systems designed to give management more control over the work process. It could include substituting machines for human labor, science for rule of thumb, planning for tradition, trucks for horses, oil for wood.

The process has had several contradictory effects. It has eliminated much of the backbreaking, unskilled buggy lugging, providing cranes, jitneys, conveyers, and other machines for the movement of materials. But it has often also reduced the skills required of skilled workers, as their manual techniques were built into the machines themselves. The long-term result has been to transform a work force sharply divided between skilled craftsmen and unskilled laborers into a much more homogeneous work force in which semiskilled machine operators predominate.

By reducing the status of skilled craftsmen, rationalization brought them closer to the rest of the work force, easing the way for a unionism which would include all grades of workers in the plant. At the same time, it reduced the privileges which encouraged skilled workers to identify with management. Rationalization thus increased management's power but also helped generate a force which would challenge that power.

New technologies often improved the work itself by making it less heavy and eliminating many sources of accidents. But new technologies also created new hazards,

Guiding a crane at the Chase Metal Works in the 1930s. Courtesy Mattatuck Museum.

such as dangerous new chemicals and higher-speed machines. And the rationalization process was often used to make work more intensive. Workers would have to work much harder in the same amount of time.

Jim Cusack's job was to introduce such "rationalization" at Scovill.

Jim Cusack: I was sent into the mills to study what they were doing and to help to work out what was needed to improve.

It was a very old-fashioned mill from top to bottom, with the exception of the casting.

I went into the least important department first, the tube mill, because it was failing miserably. It had been in operation for twenty-five years, and they had lost money every year. We built a new tube mill over in New Milford, completely throwing out the old.

I next went into the wire mill. The wire mill was noted for the bad odor which permeated the whole neighborhood. It was at the corner of Mill Street and Baldwin. The odor came from the lubricant they were using in drawing wire, which was a mix of bran and several kinds of grains and yeast, which was cultured. The main office was almost directly over the wire mill; that odor permeated the main office, where the president and his people were. "Please do something to get rid of that odor."

We began to experiment with different lubricants, without too much success. We took one of the busy machines out of the wire mill

Drawing rods at the American Brass Torrington plant. Courtesy Western Historical Collections, University of Colorado Libraries.

altogether, set it up in another room, put a very skilled operator on it, and worked out our experiments aside from the mill proper.

Ultimately, we decided that the machinery was too antiquated, there wasn't much you could do with it, there was too much time and expense involved in maintenance and repair. So we went to work with Waterbury Farrel Foundry, and we developed a new type of wire-drawing machine. We told them what we wanted; they designed the machinery. We changed from the hand-tooled wortel steel die to machine-produced carbide dies, which last longer, produce a better job, and would work with petroleum products for lubricants rather than the liquor.

So we decided the best thing to do was to build a new wire mill and almost completely re-equip it and put it in a new building.

One of the principal effects of "rationalization" was de-skilling.

Sam Kwochka: [Now the work takes] no skill at all. You are an operator. The skill goes to the laboratory.

Frank Pochron: You are directed what to do. Years ago it seemed the operators had the technicalities, were proud of their work and able to do their jobs, what the customer demands and the shop wanted. Now it seems they wait for management to tell them what to do and if it doesn't come out right, so what?

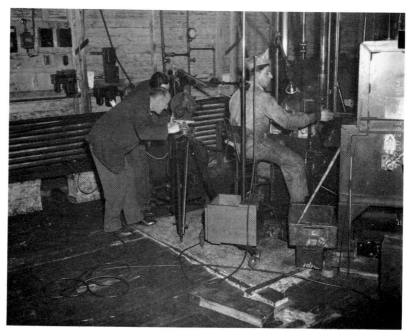

Management personnel taking high-speed movies of a worker and his machine, 1945. Courtesy Scovill, Inc.

Years ago you had to have more skill.

John Chubat: There was a Polish man who worked there a long time. You'd take him mixed-up metal and go to him and say: "What mixture is this?" He knew every mixture. He would just cut it on the shear and look at it, and he'd tell you exactly what mixture it was.

Sometimes he'd take a bite into it to tell you what the mixture was.

In the casting shop now, they cast it, they send a little wafer up to the laboratory, and within ten minutes they know if there is something lacking in the alloy. Next heat you put it in to balance

it off. They tell you what to put in for a mixture now. It's governed by them; it's not the casters any more.

Before the caster used to know what to add or what not to add.

Pochron: Years ago they didn't have all this equipment to check out what you were doing. They relied upon the people to do it.

Another aspect of "modernization" was taking control of production out of the hands of the workers.

Jim Cusack: When I first went into the mill, a roller, for example, established his own passes. A pass means the time a coil or bar of metal is processed through a roll.

Electricians working on an electric motor stator at Scovill shortly after World War I. Courtesy Scovill Collection.

If the rolling mill was very busy, you got out a lot of production. If it wasn't a busy time, everybody was equally busy, but there was less production. That was a result of the individual doing his own planning, in effect, and writing it up to suit himself.

We took that control out of the operators' hands. We put in a group that planned procedures according to the best efficiency. That would have been about 1945, 1950.

We wrote out a mill order ticket which had the procedure printed right there on the ticket. They turned their production, they handed in the ticket, and it was recorded according to the way it was laid out on the ticket.

These techniques were applied to white-collar workers as well.

Jim Cusack: I changed the office clerical procedures. Previously, each mill had its own group in the mill trying to handle production, clerical detail, scheduling, and all of that—each one struggling against the other mills who wanted priority for this or priority for that. I developed a central production control office. We called that the mill production office, wherein we assembled all these outlying offices into one, cut the personnel in half, and did a better job because we had a centralized control.

Rationalization was not always the rule; the brass companies often allowed antiquated production processes to persist. But the consequences could be serious.

Bart Hennessey: When the new wire mill was built, that was tops in the world. But that's when they stopped. Around 1929. They didn't make any changes. They didn't make another change in there for forty years. The competition came along and took all their business away.

8. Time Study and Incentive Systems: "They're Always Trying to Increase Production"

Few questions affect the nature of day-to-day life on the job more pervasively than how fast workers have to produce. For that very reason, it has been a continuing source of on-the-job conflict between workers and managers.

As part of the rationalization process, management has developed such techniques as incentive systems, time study, close supervision, and machine-paced production in order to make employees work harder and faster. Workers, on the other hand, have developed their own techniques for gaining some control over the pace of production, techniques known variously as stints, output restriction, soldiering, quotas, and stereotyping. A study made at Scovill during and after World War I was described by Bishop:

"The investigation showed that in certain departments of Scovill, there were strong tendencies to 'stereotype' the output; that is, a 'standard day's performance is tac-

Pouring molten brass into the continuous casting machine at Scovill, early 1940s. Courtesy Scovill, Inc.

Scovill secretaries being trained to use comptometers, early adding machines, in the 1920s. Courtesy Scovill Collection.

itly set between foreman and workers and is followed day after day. This stint is the amount expected of the worker and no questions are asked if it is achieved.' This phenomenon was particularly noticeable 'in those machine operations where control over the starting and stopping of the machine is vested in the operator . . . and where the work consists simply in the application of a single tool to the material.' Organized labor could not 'be held accountable for this limitation of output, for the [Scovill] plant has few union workers. Nor would it be just to attribute it solely to the management of an individual factory. In a large industrial district such as [Waterbury], the attitude of the workers is formed . . . by the general policy of all the factories in the district . . . [and] . . . it is probable that the stereotyping at the [Scovill] plant is due to a general attitude toward employers which has similar reactions in other plants.'"*

In order to reduce workers' influence over the pace of work, such promoters of "scientific management" as Frederick Winslow Taylor developed "systematic time study," which would allow managers to discover how fast it was possible to do a job, and "incentive systems," which would encourage workers to abandon stereotyping and work as fast as possible.

*Ibid., p. 233.

```
Lesson No. 1.          M.T.A. INSTRUCTION COURSE          Page 34.

  27.  T   F   A SHOULDER Movement generally exerts its heaviest
              pressure on the push rather than on the pull.

  28.  T   F   A minimum SHOULDER Movement requires .00250 Minute for
              its completion.

  29.  T   F   The Time required for a 15" SHOULDER Movement is
              .00180 + .00225, or .00405 (using formula).

  30.  T   F   The Time required for a 15" SHOULDER MOVEMENT is
              .00450 - .00045, or .00405 (using Table).

  31.  T   F   The Time required for the "Start" of a SHOULDER
              Movement is .00090.

  32.  T   F   The Time required for the "Stop" of a SHOULDER Move-
              ment is .00090 Minute.

  33.  T   F   The Time required for the Start and Stop of a 13"
              SHOULDER Movement is .00180 Minute.

  34.  T   F   The "Travel" Time for a 13" SHOULDER MOVEMENT is
              .00195 Minute.

  35.  T   F   The Time required for the "Start" or "Stop" of a
              FINGER Movement is .00075 Minute.
```

A page from a Scovill foreman's Motion-Time Analysis instruction book from 1935. Courtesy Scovill Collection.

Jim Cusack describes the introduction of time study at Scovill.

Jim Cusack: I also worked as a rate setter. That's time study. We set the piecework prices for the various operations.

There always had to be some time study. But it came in on a more scientific basis along about 1925. We brought in a firm of engineers who conducted classes.

You went out to where the operation was being performed, and you studied the motions necessary to do the operation. You tried to improve, in other words, speed up, and make it easier for the operator, through simplifying the handling, or through automatic instead of manual handling. You attempted to improve the process and hopefully to decrease the cost. The hoped-for results of time study were to lighten the work, to make work available to people of more skill and less strength, and to improve quality.

[From the operators we got] mostly stalling. After you become experienced on the job, you know from past jobs. When you set a rate and later restudy them, and when the operator began to run over their time, or if they finished a day's work at 2 in the afternoon and don't do any more because they had their time made, then you knew that you had been fooled to a certain extent. So you got to know what you could expect beyond what you found in the immediate performance that you were studying.

[When time study came, people would] mostly go into slow motion, or make a pretense that the work was heavier than it actually was. Do a lot of unnecessary moving around.

I think it's human nature not to like being studied closely as to what you're doing, put under that kind of observation. So the great majority of people have a great amount of resentment toward it. You could tell if somebody was unhappy: He'd be muttering under his breath, "This so-and-so, I wish to hell he'd get out of here and go someplace else."

When you put a person on piecework, you expect to get greater productivity than if they were on a day-work basis doing the same job. When they were on day-work, a person's incentive was to hold their job, to become known as a good workman. They got a better chance of obtaining the work that was available. If you were a slowpoke or careless or obviously unskilled, you were the first to be laid off. There was no seniority. So it was a matter of ability and willingness to do a good job that kept a person on the job. Whereas the poor worker was let go.

On piecerate—we used to figure that a person should earn 30 percent more after you put him on piecework than before. Up to a certain point. That is the incentive.

Time study was often experienced by workers as just a means of "speedup."

Russell Sobin: They'd have a time-study man come down. He'd check you. He'd know what you could do in so many minutes or an hour. They'd have a watch, and they'd time you. On the rolls, when there were five men on it, he'd stand there and every pass you went through [he would count] how many passes in a minute. On the shears, how many cuts a minute.

Then they even put meters on. Every time it would click. When you stopped, that red needle stopped. They knew how much delay you took.

Time study is how they eliminated a lot of men. There used to be four men. They'd see, this guy isn't doing anything for fifteen minutes, this guy isn't doing anything for ten minutes. So they'd double up the work on another man. That's how they eliminated [men]. They do it to this day.

The purpose of incentive systems was generally clear to workers.

Luke MacDonald: They're always trying to increase production.

They give you a little bonus—do a little more work, you make ten cents an hour more. First thing you know, you make a dollar. You keep on working, you're almost doing double work. That's where you made your money, on your bonus.

It got so they'd find out they could do more, then they'd take a man off the job. If somebody died or quit, they wouldn't replace them. They had you figured out.

I tried to tell my gang: Just make the regular time and never mind the bonus. If you finish your work in four days, stay home on the fifth day. Stretch it out and get more time in. Some of them just wanted that bonus.

Workers often developed ways to produce more quickly or with less effort than time study indicated. Managers and workers, even though they shared many other attitudes in common, often disagreed violently about this.

John Chubat: I want to tell Frank, because he was a time-study man, that you could always break his rates, no matter how tightly they were set. I could break the rates on the slitter. They would time me; I would work normal, just like I've always been doing. But when they're not there, instead of shearing it in one or two pieces, I can shear four or five and put three settings. I can go way over. I put out the work. Just as good as that. But nothing cheating at all. It's my own ingenuity. They never did that before.

Paul Garatoni: If I learn the tricks, that's my business. If the company wants a job done, tell me how to do it and I'll do it that way. But any tricks I know to make it easier for me are mine; you pay me for them. But these time-study men would try to get you to use all of your tricks.

Worker influence over the rate of production required cooperation among workers. Russell Sobin describes how people beat time study.

Russell Sobin: They used to have somebody stand there and "use the finger," so they could have a little time. Each one would take turns. There was a little pedal. Every time the blade on the shears would come down, it would activate the meter.

They even used to have meters in the cranes. Some of them used to rig up a string to that meter. All it was [the meter measured] was the vibration. They'd be shaking their leg just to make it run.

Say you and I were working on the same type of a job and you could put out more. If the guy was decent, you'd say, "What are you trying to do, kill the job? Let's work together. Don't go over me, don't try to make more than me." That's how they tried to do it. Work together.

New workers were often instructed by older workers in just how much work they should perform in a given time.

Frank Keane: You'd make your time, then beyond that you'd make whatever you could make. Up to a point; you didn't want to ruin the job, obviously. You wouldn't kill a job. So if you made your time early, you took a micrometer and walked around the mill and made out you were something else. You'd try to protect your job.

I was tipped off on that when I was in there one day eager-beaver, working too hard. But you had to work. Beyond that, don't ruin the job. "Hey kid, knock it off."

9. Ethnicity and Race at the Work Place: "A Line Drawn as to How Far You Could Advance"

The work force of the brass mills was an ethnic melange, reflecting the various waves of immigration to the area. Until the advent of unionism, struggle among different ethnic groups for the better jobs was often intense.

The Irish, and to a lesser extent the French, having arrived earlier than the southern and eastern Europeans, were well entrenched in the better jobs in most plants.

Jim Cusack: When I went into the wire mill, it was mostly Irishmen.

"Bill Cronin's Rod Mill Champs," a crew of workers at Scovill in 1926. They may have gotten their name from their standing in a Scovill athletic league. Courtesy Scovill Collection.

The workmen, supervisors, practically everybody except the superintendent was Irish. Over the years the other nationalities came in.

[The highest position held by an Irishman at Scovill at that time was] probably superintendent of the casting shop. [Above that was] very largely Yankees.

There were exceptions, however. In Ansonia, the Irish were the objects of discrimination because of their Catholicism well into the 1920s. There were also many charges that members of the Masonic Order were favored. The following discussion is between Bart Hennessey and Russell Sobin, who both worked at American Brass in Ansonia.

Bart Hennessey: When I came in [to American Brass], I was an Irish Catholic, and that didn't rest very well with some people.

Russell Sobin: One time they took a man from outside and brought him in. He was a Mason. Going to make him a roller. He didn't know what the heck a roll looked like. They told me, "He's a roller." I had to be a sticker under him. I was waiting for a job as roller, so I could get more money—I had a family growing. I said, "I'll fix your wagon." I put in the sheets [of a thick size]. He didn't go up on the screw. I stuck it in. Boom, bing! The whole stand broke, and the rolls went up. The sheets went up about across the street. I said, "You forgot something."

Frank Keane: If you were an Irish foreman, you might arrange to hire Irishmen. If anybody was going to be promoted, I'd think you'd do the same. I understand there were complaints about that. But the complaints didn't come way back, since 90 percent of the work force in the mills was probably Irish. When I was working there, there was a big percent of Italian, Portuguese, and Black people. These were Black families who were around Waterbury for a long time.

The newer groups had to fight hard to win access to the more skilled jobs.

Russell Sobin: I worked on the rolls. At that time they used to give three months or better for somebody to break in on the rolls. Like me, because I was of the foreign element, they were prejudiced. One day they told me to go and roll. They put me over with this fellow for four hours. The following night they told me to go and roll. They thought that I would mess up everything and they would have the right to take me off. But I fooled them. I knew what to do with the screw; I knew just how much to pinch. I went along and rolled for two years after that.

BLACK WORKERS

Blacks were concentrated in the hardest, most unpleasant jobs.

Luke MacDonald: There were quite a few [Blacks] in the rolling mill, from way back in the 1920s.

Quite a few. There are some heavy jobs in there, too. You used to have to pick up these great big bars. Two men, one on each side, would pick it up and shove it to the roll. Two on the other side would catch it and pile it on a pan. That was heavy stuff.

Sid Monti: We had more Black employment at Scovill than any of the other plants, in fact, probably more than all the other plants put together. It was only because we had hard manual labor at Scovill's that nobody else wanted; those were the jobs they usually got. In the mills division was where they mostly went, because that's where the hot-and-heavy was.

There were no black foremen at Scovill. At American Brass there was always a Black foreman, since 1937. They didn't hire many Blacks.

By World War II, Black men were admitted freely to the factories but were still largely excluded from the better jobs.

John Gatison: After 1940, we got our fair share up to the point of getting in. But after getting in, we still had to face the same old thing: a line drawn as to how far you could advance. Even though the union contract expressly forbids discrimination, there was discrimination practiced to prevent Blacks from advancing to higher jobs or given their full rights. Both management personnel and labor lead-

ers were aware that there was discrimination practiced. Very little effort was made to correct these practices. I've known of specific cases in which the company and the union worked hand in hand. The better jobs went to the people that had the inside, or were in the know. The Blacks were left out as far as advancement. Since the late 1960s Black workers have overcome some of these practices because there has been more Black participation in the union, new labor leadership and new management.

Bertha Silva: They were very prejudiced [at American Brass]. My husband was a smart man. They made a lot of difference there. They gave them certain jobs, even in the wire mill. Like on the bull block. They were very prejudiced. I think this is why they laid my husband off at American Brass.

[The Black workers] worked on the acid. I've seen many of them with their teeth all green. Underwear when they come home, sweating, all green. They had the hardest jobs. It killed them.

They were against the Black. They'd give them anything [for a job]. They're still doing it that way. I've got a son working right there now. He hates to go into the shop. He [says], "I'd rather do *anything*." He's looking forward to moving out of Ansonia.

Socially, Blacks tended to appear as one ethnic group among many others.

John Gatison: Generally speaking, the Blacks and the whites in the mill got along all right. The ethnic groups separated when it came to sitting around on their own time, like lunch periods. They did that because they got more out of it—it was more relaxing. However, there were many times when they mixed. It was not because they didn't want to associate. I want to talk over something that they're involved with and I'm involved with—it could be some social thing, it could be church—things in which we're associated together which bring the Blacks together. There are a number of Lithuanian people working here. They like to get into their group and speak their own tongue and enjoy themselves that way. The Italians the same way. There are times we sat down with maybe four or five nationalities at the same time, having lunch together.

Frank Keane: Working in the mill, there was no distinction. If you're working on a set of rolls, somebody's sticking it in one end and somebody's picking it up in the other end. He could be a Black guy, that made no difference at all. There was no distinction made there. I presume if you brought him home to dinner, somebody might have looked askance at you.

Black workers had to struggle continuously against discrimination, both as individuals and through union and civil rights organizations. King David Holmes went to work at American Brass in Waterbury after World War II.

King David Holmes: They had somewhat of a weak union. I was in the scrap room of the casting department. I got in an incident where I left. Strictly on unionism. "Unsuitable for this kind of work." The man said, "We're letting you go." I said, "No, I'm suitable for this type of work." They were glad to get rid of me.

I went back to school. I came back, and having a family you have to get a job. I went to Scovill's, went in the employment office, said, "I want a job." I filled out my form. He cried crocodile tears, "College graduate." I said, "Well, how about selling some of this brass?" "Oh, that's reserved for the Gosses and Sperrys." I said, "Look, I need a job."

He said, "I see your uncle works here." He put me in the old North Mill. They make sheet metal.

The union had finally had some degree of recognition. I met a foreman who had some decency about him. Most of the old-timers were in the process of striving to get ahead. There was no absenteeism, and I was more like a spare man. He said, "Learn this job, blocker, then you'll always have a job, because blockers are hard to come by."

I had no problem. A couple of the old-timers knew me and they knew my father. So they taught me the ropes. I'm a spare man, because these old-timers wouldn't stay out. I'd walk in every day, hoping they'd stay out. When they were out, I'd fill in, any job. As a blocker.

There was a lot of resentment. Somebody would call from the testing department. Some metal came back; they wanted somebody to gauge it. "Dave, why don't you gauge some of this metal?" Blacks just didn't get in those jobs. This is late, after the thrust of the union movement; this is in 1948. "Who's this guy Dave Holmes?" The union people resented themselves [that a Black would get such work]. This was very hard to understand as far as I was concerned.

I was a veteran. They had to say, "Well, you've got to give this guy a chance."

[In the 1940s] there were certain departments that were predominantly Blacks. You were relegated to the rough jobs. Casting shop, wire mill, bull block, rod mill. There weren't too many Blacks in the tube mill. It was considered somewhat easy mill work, even though it wasn't easy. There were no rollers, doing miking [using a micrometer], things where you had to show some knowledge.

When I was there, I challenged [the job discrimination] immediately. After we got job posting, seniority. [The union didn't back me up.] We had resentment from them, in the beginning. Even in the mills themselves, if your steward wouldn't fight, you were denied. It was more or less accepted.

I pioneered in the [UAW] Fair Practices Committee in this region. We set up statewide. We had conferences, workshops. There was no money to really implement it, until they came up with a nickel per capita they put aside for it.

[The FEPC made it clear] that we were going to be heard, as dues-paying members. We addressed the school issues that came up, situations in the South.

It led a lot to refining the definition of ability. How can you get experience, unless you have the opportunity? On an educational level, you're denied. You're denied along the line; unless there is some preferential or compensatory consideration, you're never going to catch up. If you've been traveling fifty miles an hour and I've been traveling ten and you say O.K., brother, [from now on] everything is equal, [I'm] never going to catch up. It's a tough situation to resolve.

What do you mean by ability? If you put educational qualifications, that's a bar from the beginning, because of the fact that people were denied equal education. So we said, "O.K., seniority is the determining factor, along with opportunity on the job to prove [that you have the ability]."

[We wanted] the opportunity to go on the job, based on my se-niority, to prove my ability to do the job. In the union I had to argue, which is the deciding factor: which prevailed, experience or seniority? We said seniority prevailed. It was a compromise on our part, as against asking for compensatory education.

10. Working Women: "She Used a Micrometer Just Like a Man"

As we have seen, women worked in the button shops and other parts of the brass companies from the very beginning. They remained an important part of the labor force throughout the history of the industry.

There were many women workers who worked their entire lives in the plants.

Caroline Nardello: In 1918 I was working in American Brass myself. They used to make chimneys for lamps. I used to inspect them. On the bench, benchwork. I worked at Plume and Atwood's. They had the same kind of thing. Some kind of ring you'd have to string them on, from the dip room. The American Ring used to have that. I worked on foot presses there, too. The rest of the years, for thirteen years, I worked in the box shop.

When I went to work sixty-four years ago, I only got seven and a quarter, and I worked ten hours a day, six days a week those days. It was kind of tough to live. Nobody was working when I went to work. I worked quite a few years, helping out [the household].

They had foreladies [at American Brass]. She'd come around, give you the work and tell you what to do. The boss would be in the office; they would hardly bother you.

In those days, they went to work at twelve years old in the shops. One cousin of mine went to work at Scovill when she was twelve, the other I think was thirteen. They worked hard then.

The older women were very nice. They'd try to show you, to help you out. You're green; you don't know what to do, but they'd show you, and then you'd get onto the work. They wouldn't be fresh and say, "You're not doing that right."

[Men and women didn't mix too much on the job.] They would be friendly. But everybody had their jobs, and they would be in different departments. You would stay at your place; you wouldn't roam around in the different rooms.

The American Brass I went into when I was seventeen or eighteen. It was during the war. My cousin got me a job.

I worked in the button shop. We were making army buttons on the stamp press. They used to stamp the eagle on there. A wheel would go around. You'd have to be fast and fill the holes. The power press

Sorting screws at Scovill in the 1920s. Courtesy Scovill Collection.

At Plume and Atwood's, we used to put these things on a string in the dip room. I couldn't take it too long. I was only a kid, and that smell of the acid—oh, it was awful. I didn't work there long.

Louise Lombardo: I worked in Scovill's. I had ten years broken service. I started when I was sixteen years old. I worked on machines: drill presses and knurling machines in the knurling department. I worked fifty-five hours a week.

I was looking for a job. My father worked there. My uncle, later on my sister came. My sister, my brother, my uncle, we were all Scovill people mostly. I went in 1927, and I stayed there about ten years.

It was mostly brass work. We made fuses, electric shells, bushings, which you use for most any plumbing and hardware. At one time we made cigarette lighters, compacts.

We were all friendly. There were a lot of people much older than I was. Sometimes I would sit there and say to myself, "These people are close to sixty years old, and I'm only a teenager." They all had so much seniority, and I'd say, "They'll never leave their jobs. How is the next population going to get a job?" I'd look around and I'd almost get scared. I'd say, "Well, I'm going to stay here forever." (Of course you never know what your life is.) I didn't stay for-

was dangerous; you had to watch for your fingers. I got my finger pierced in the foot press one time. A lot of people cut their fingers off; you had to watch it.

Some men were working the big [dial presses]. I think they paid the men a little better than the women. The women didn't care; as long as they had the job, they worked. That's the way it was in those days.

A press operator in the 1940s. The straps on her wrists pulled her hands away to prevent them from being crushed by the machine. This was a common safety device, and it is still in use. Courtesy Scovill, Inc.

ever, but I worked the rest of my life.

Most women worked out of economic necessity.

Peter Kukanskis: A lot of women worked in those days. I had two aunts that worked all of their lives. They worked down in the button shop, as we used to call it. They were on the presses. They had bull work to do, piecework. They'd come home tired; I don't know how they ever raised a family. But they had to do it. The husband made what the pay was in those days: They'd work sixty hours a week, maybe get fifteen bucks. The woman had to help supply. So they'd go in, and once they got in that habit, the dollar looked nice at the end of the week, and they kept it up. They went out and helped support the family. That was their way of life. They had to go to work to survive.

Catherine Coscia: My father had ten kids. He got hurt. I was very depressed; I said, "I'm not going to school; I'm going to go to work." So I went to work, and the fellow at the clock shop said to me, "Do you really want to work?" I said, "Yes. I need work. I have a father home who cannot work with ten kids." He said, "How old are you?" I lied my age. I was only fourteen; I said, "I'm sixteen." In those days they didn't ask for a birth certificate. So he gave me a job.

I kicked the foot press for twelve dollars a week. I worked ten hours a day. Six days a week.

The first day I went to work, I came home that night, my father was so mad. He said, "Where did you go?" I said, "I went to work." He said, "You went to work at your age?" I said, "Yes. I went to work, because I see we have got no bread in the house; we've got nothing." I got punished that night. Even though I worked ten hours, I had to close myself in the room and go to bed without eating, even though I didn't eat for that ten hours.

[After my first baby] I went to work in the box shop. I figured it was nearer to home and nearer to my mother, so that I could bring my son over there. I used to bring him in the morning and pick him up at night. I worked there about four years.

I had my second son. After a year or a year-and-a-half, I went to work in Plume and Atwood. 1939. That was on Bank Street before. I worked over there for three or four years. I did everything. I worked on conveyers. I worked on soldering. The soldering was different there; they had long points and different soldering. I worked on

The girls' softball team from the Waterville Division of Scovill in 1943. Courtesy Scovill, Inc.

the drill presses. I worked on the foot presses and inspecting.

On the conveyers we did assembly, putting the work together. Like on a lipstick: It has five pieces in there. I did all those five pieces. We used to do eyebrow pencils and brushes.

Sometimes they used to work on lathes. Then, they didn't put the women on the lathes. Now, if there's no work on the eyelet machines, they will put you on the lathes.

In Plume and Atwood there was piecework. If we made 25,000, that was only day rate. If we made 40,000, we would get, say, a dollar bonus on each machine. The men got a little bit more [than the women]. The toolmakers got higher rates. And half of the toolmakers do nothing. When I was working, I used to tell them, "You spend most of your time in the men's room. We take care of our own machines. The bosses don't even know half of it."

I always had a dirty job.

After I had my other son, in wartime, I worked in Metal Hose and I worked in French's. In Metal Hose, I used to test the tubes. There was a table. You put the tubes on. There was water on the bottom. If the water came up on top, the tubes had holes. We put those aside and put another one there to replace it.

I worked 11 to 7 because I didn't want to leave my young son. I sent him to school for a cost accountant.

[During World War II] we made over $100, sometimes if you were fast, $150 a week. We made good money. If you worked nights, you got a bonus.

The union started right after that. I worked in Metal Hose. Then they transferred me to Brass Goods on South Main. I worked there 3 to 11.

We used to make bullets on machines. First, I used to punch them out. Sometimes I was where they punched out the holes in the bottom. Sometimes on the presses where we made the forms.

Over there I had to make the blank. The blank is when you start the work. No matter what kind of work, you start the blank first. The second operation there's the punch that you start for a lipstick or a shell or whatever kind of work. I learned at the American Brass on the eyelets. I worked there two years. Then I left there.

During World War II, as during World War I, far more women were able to enter the plants.

Rachel Doolady: When I went to work during the war at American Brass, I just went in for anything I could do. They put me on a machine where they would solder braided hoses for ships and planes. I was only twenty-one years old then. I said, "Jeeze, I'd love to be

Two women doing benchwork at Scovill shortly after World War II. Courtesy Scovill, Inc.

Scovill's Lipstick Room, 1941. Most cosmetic containers were made of brass at that time. Courtesy Scovill, Inc.

Women cleaning up in a locker room after their shift in Scovill's Lacquer Department, 1941. Courtesy Scovill, Inc.

able to do that soldering. I could do it!" So, after a week or two, they posted me and asked me if I would try it. I did it and I loved it! I would still be there today if they didn't throw me out!

I loved that place during the war. You worked nine or ten hours a day, but you used to enjoy it. The fellows on Sunday morning would bring crates of eggs in, and they would cook them over the solder pot. You would have a big breakfast. It was one big happy family. Everybody really worked and produced. I don't think I ever would have quit there, except that it was told to me when I went in there that it was a temporary job; I would have to leave when the servicemen came back. I worked there for about two-and-a-half years. I got out when the servicemen came back to their old jobs.

A birthday party for Helen Zanavitch in the Manufacturing Eyelet Room at Scovill in 1943. Courtesy Scovill, Inc.

ANSONIA BRASS WORKERS' UNION,
LOCAL NO. 445

(s) Wm. McEwen,

(s) John Porcu,

(s) Fred Rubelmann,

(s) John J. McDonnell,

(s) Raymond Hayes,

(s) John J. Driscoll,
International Representative

(s) Jess Gonzalez,
International Executive
Board Member

Ratified by International Union of Mine,
Mill & Smelter Workers

(s) Alex Cashin,
Coordinator

THE AMERICAN BRASS COMPANY

(s) R. S. Wildman, Vice-President
Ansonia Branch

(s) W. M. Clark, Superintendent
Ansonia Branch

—22—

Exhibit A

HOURLY WAGE RATE

CLASSIFICATION

(Not to include indentured Apprentices)

Class	Minimum
A	80¢
B	82
C	85
D	87
E	89
F	91
G	95
H	99
I	$1.05
FEMALES	
W	70¢

—23—

The 1943 union contract at American Brass in Ansonia. It shows separate, lower wage rates for women. Courtesy Russell Sobin.

She was employed as a coremaker at U.S. Aluminum in Bridgeport, and then as an inspector at Casco. After the war she worked for twelve years as a footpress and machine operator at Autoswage in Shelton. She finally ended up in restaurant work, and has been a waitress at Valles Steak House in West Haven for the past eleven years. Jewel is married to Fredo Lucarelli, a saxophonist and retired B.F. Goodrich employee. She is the mother of four children, one of whom, Frieda Ewen, is introduced on page 109. Jewel is a volunteer counselor/advocate and serves on the board of the Lower Naugatuck Valley Battered Women's Project, an organization that provides shelter and support services to victims of domestic violence. She has lived in Shelton for many years.

That's where I first got a taste of the labor movement. I was doing a job; when they promoted me to the solderer's job, evidently I was getting the same kind of money. So about a month or two later, this fellow came over and handed me a check for $100. I said, "What's this for?" He said, "Well, according to the labor union, you're doing a man's job and you should be getting what the man is getting." He was chairman of the union in the Metal Hose division of American Brass. When he handed me the check, I was flabbergasted. Without me knowing about it, they had gone and grieved and gotten me the money.

Of course, I had to get out when the boys started coming back. I went to work at Lux Time.

Born in 1924, Jewel Lucarelli grew up the child of poor farmers in Madill, Oklahoma. She came to Connecticut during World War II to work in the defense industry.

Women were drawn from rural areas and lower-paying jobs.

Jewel Lucarelli: The day the unemployment man came to town, I went to see him. He told me about a program where the government would train you for shop work and send you wherever they needed you. That's how I came to Connecticut.

The first day of January 1943, we left Oklahoma. They got us into U.S. Aluminum in Seaside Park. They got us a room in Bridgeport. They kept an eye on us for a long time. Some of the girls got caught drinking and partying and got sent back to wherever they came from. But that wasn't my interest. My interest was getting away from Oklahoma, so I wasn't about to louse it up.

I had never had any dealings with colored people, other than just pass them on the streets. I never disliked them; there was never any opportunity because they didn't go to our school or anything. At Wethersfield there was a big house; they had brought girls there from Florida, from Mississippi, from different states. When we walked into the big entryway, there were all kinds of colors and whites. One colored girl walked up to a white girl and put her arms around her, and they were playfully horsing around. I remember the thought went through my mind: "You Black so-and-so, if you ever touch me like that. . . ." I had no reason to feel

that way; it just seemed she was out of place or something. We stayed there for two weeks, and at the end of those two weeks, those colored girls, most of them, I liked much, much better than I did most of the white ones. Once I got to know them. But that first impression, seeing her go up and grab that girl—it just turned me off. It was the way I was raised, really. At the end of two weeks, I was at ease with them, friendly with them. That was my first contact with Black people.

Women didn't work on machines. A stationary job, where they'd put one part in and make a hole in it, yes. But machines that make the parts, screw machines or millers, or those kinds of machines, presses, they didn't work on.

[A friend and I took jobs at Casco's. She was] the first woman roving inspector. I was the second one. Because the inspectors could shut the machines down, the men would end up in fights. So they weren't sure about bringing women in to handle this job. But we found it worked out very well. They wouldn't fight with us like they would fight with other men. They would fight with us verbally; but I understand it was more than words that were used when it was man-to-man.

The more skilled jobs were simply not available to women, even to those who spent their lifetime in the plants. Women were not per-

mitted to be mechanics, toolsetters, toolmakers, electricians, or plumbers.

Catherine Coscia: I like machine work. It's just like cleaning my kitchen to me. Benchwork, no; I did it, but I didn't care for it. To me, it's too boring. But machine work is different.

We took the punches out [of our machines]; we took the fingers out when the toolmakers weren't around. We went on the lathes, we sharpened the fingers, and we put them back on. Of course, if the boss was around, he didn't like us to do that because that was their job. My lady friend and I tried several times to become toolmakers. Our boss said to us, "You took all the men's jobs away; now you want to do that, too." I said, "We could do that, you know." He said, "We know that you could do it." They just said no. But now I see that the girls are doing it.

Before I left, I did it. On one of the machines, we had to change the stamp. We took out the fingers; we took out the punches on top. I said to my lady friend, "Before I retire, you and I are going to do something new." She said, "I've got to stay here; I'm the one that's going to get hell, not you." The boss came by. We were taking the machines apart and washing them down. He said to me, "We have new toolmakers over here!" I said, "Did you say something?" He said, "We have two new tool-

Phyllis Pellizze and Mary Goporozzo, the first female rollers at Scovill, in 1943. Courtesy Scovill, Inc.

Rolling rods at Scovill. Until well into World War II, this job was a male preserve. Courtesy Scovill, Inc.

for drawing shells [during World War II]. She was in the grinding room. She used a micrometer just like a man.

Grace Worthey Cummings was born in 1937 in Chester, South Carolina, near Charlotte. During the Depression, her parents left the South to seek work in the North. Her father worked as a chauffeur and her mother worked as a maid in New York City. When

makers over here." He said, "How much do you get paid an hour?" We said, "We don't know."

He went in his office. We didn't do anything wrong. We went to get him. I said, "Mr. Sullivan, could you come out and see what we did?" He could give us hell; that's all right. He came out, his hands in his pockets. "You did better than that lazy good-for-nothing did." When I retired, they designed a punch right on the frosting of the cake.

During World War II, women were gradually able to move into jobs that had been the exclusive preserves of men.

John Chubat: They worked on the bench, on inspection, drawbench, and jitney drivers, tow motors.

During the war in the wire roll, a woman worked on the rod rolls. She was a catcher. Another worked on a drawbench. Another on a saw.

We had a woman in the brass goods who was making round dies

her father went to Waterbury to seek factory work, Grace's mother came back to South Carolina to have Grace. Grace and her mother joined her father in Waterbury after he got a job in the foundry at Waterbury Tool Co. Her mother got a job at Scovill's. Of her mother's work, Grace says, "I never heard any good stories about it. It was always a thumb lost, two finger ends lost. Those are the kind of stories that used to come home, and that's what we used to talk about. There were never any good things said about the jobs. The companies didn't care about the noise or the safety. When I lived near Plume and Atwood, playing in front of the house, you could always see the ambulance come in there and take somebody who had gotten hurt off to the hospital. It was frequent. Somebody would have a big towel around his hand, he's bleeding, a nurse running around him. My mother used to say, 'Don't ever go to work at Scovill's. It's bad for your health. You get varicose veins from it. Female problems.' So when I got old enough to join the work force, I never worked in a brass plant."

At fifteen, Grace went to work summers at U.S. Rubber, now Uniroyal, in Naugatuck. She stayed on there until 1974. She became active in the union and even organized a wildcat strike. She then worked at Southbury Training School, where she is presently a Mentally Retarded Aide, and a delegate in the New England Health Care Workers Union, District 1199. She is an active member of 1199's Political Action Committee. She is the mother of two grown children.

Black women had been almost entirely excluded from work in the brass plants. Mrs. Lyla Alexander of the Urban League in Waterbury, in cooperation with Mine, Mill and other local forces, put pressure on the brass companies to hire Black women.

Grace Cummings: My mother didn't start working in the shop. She worked in a place called Perry's Laundry; I think it's still there. My mother never did any shop work; most of her friends never worked in a shop, either. They didn't let Black women in the shop then. This is 1942. I would walk to meet my mother downtown. I lived in Wards Flats and she worked in Watertown. She would get the bus for a dime; I would meet her. It was a big treat; I walked back home with my mother for five blocks.

Around 1943, when all the men were gone, they didn't really want to hire Black women to work in the shops. They had ads in the paper. A lot of [Black women] would go down and say, "You just want labor. We're here, we can labor, we'll do anything."

They'd never hire. There was a minister. In the Black community, the leaders are always the ministers. You tell him your problem; not like in Catholic church, where you go and confess. But if you're having a problem, you go talk to your minister. "I can't make ends meet. I want this job I can't get. Can you be my spokesman?" He went down to the Scovill personnel office and talked and argued. So he got the women in there. My mother worked there for many years after.

The whole time she worked in Scovill's, she always worked on a Nash machine. I remember how she would say the work would be real hot; it would come out of the machine and have milky water running over it to cool it down faster. She was always talking about the inspectors. More than once, she lost the tip end of a finger. On her thumb, she had no tip end.

My mother had scars—big, long scars from the machine. She never knew what it was to collect for them. When my husband got hurt in Scovill's, he had a really long scar. They paid him $750. My mother thought that was an awful lot of money to pay for a scar. She had worked there and gotten millions of scars, and nobody had ever given her a dime. At that time, there was no union. There was nobody looking out for your rights. It was fend for yourself, who could be the best informer to the boss, who could be on time, who could bring in the best sandwiches.

Segunda Holland. One of the women who broke the racial discrimination barrier to work in the brass plants during World War II, she stencilled boxes of explosive fuzes for Scovill. Courtesy Scovill, Inc.

When they really couldn't get enough help, couldn't find anybody else, working three shifts, then they hired Blacks.

You were always afraid of getting a real bad job, where you would work real hard and only get day rate. Everybody wouldn't argue with [the boss] too much; they didn't want him to get upset, because he would give you something really, really bad. What you would do was just keep your mouth shut and take it. You would come back home and yell at your kids, but you would never complain in the shop.

I don't remember my mother ever in her life telling me that somebody stood up to the boss and told him he was wrong.

I remember my mother always saying how there wasn't any decent place for them to eat. She worked at a really greasy machine. She used to take a piece of wax paper to work to lay her food on. Now Scovill's has a really nice cafeteria.

My mother used to tell me that the boss used to like this little white girl. Anytime she wanted to make some money, he would find something to get my mother off of a machine. Tell her there was an emergency on another machine, that somebody else couldn't do it like she could. He would butter her up, and then let [the white girl] do it. Even though my mother had more seniority on the machine. It was her job; she was hired to do it.

The workers seemed to get along really good. It's managerial positions that make the discrimination. I worked in a shop twenty years. The workers get along good. They don't have the Black and white friction that you would ordinarily think they would. They help each other out. We're in here, one common cause—unionwise. The only time they try to play each other is a little bit [in the] union sometimes; they try to play that, but it usually doesn't work because workers can usually see a little better than that. It's when they get up

to management stage that they make the discrimination. It was the same [when my parents were working]. You notice that you and your fellow workers get along fine; there's no friction between you all.

Lea Harvey: I graduated from high school in Ansonia and came to Waterbury looking for work. There wasn't much work. I got a job babysitting. I worked as housekeeper for a doctor for about six years.

I went into Chase Brass and Copper in 1942. This was a time when things were opening up. I guess they decided it would be all right to hire Black women. Men were going off to war and the company needed replacements. It made a lot of shell casings and other articles used in the war. Prior to that time, there was always a thing that white women would not work with Black women. But in my fifteen years and nine months, I never had any problem with anybody. So that isn't necessarily true.

I did a number of jobs. I worked in a lot of departments. I started off in the case shop, which is farther up North Main Street. They were making those big shells. I was taking them off the truck and putting them on the counter where the person who operates the machine could get them.

As the service called the fellows to war, those jobs became available, so I got a job working as a

Women Of Today Lead Three Lives

Three Distinct Types Of Clothes Needed

Women of our times are three-way women — they work for the war effort, they guide and mother their children, and they are gay and charming to their husbands and beaux.

For each of these three lives, women need three types of clothes: one, efficient clothes for war work; two, comfortable, easy-going slip-ons for staying at home; and three, glamourous and exciting dresses to wear on nights off.

For War Work . . .

There is little need to discuss your outfit for work, since it is either a simple wash dress or it is one of the company's uniforms.

For Staying At Home . . .

A comfortable slip-on dress for at home is the one illustrated. It has the simplicity and comfort of a housecoat, yet is not long enough to get in your way. It wraps around and is fastened with gold buttons. Its pocket is large

enough to hold everything but the kitchen sink.

What makes it more exciting is the fact that it is made of that new mater-

A typical article from the women's pages of the Scovill Bulletin *during World War II. Courtesy Scovill, Inc.*

Remember Your Lipstick

Lipstick is your badge of femininity when you're in work clothes, and it gives your face a lift. And don't forget the practical angle.

War plant dust chaps lips; your creamy-based lipstick is protective. Take time to put it on right. Fill in your outline with up and down strokes for thorough coverage . . .

Fashion note in the lipstick line — clear, strong colors like rascal red for work; after hours, the new sentimental, heart-throb shade.

Another piece from the Scovill Bulletin *women's pages. Courtesy Scovill, Inc.*

jitney driver. I was the first woman to drive a jitney. I had requested that job. It was a nice job. We were bringing work to the fellows who work in what they call the pickle room. I enjoyed that, because I only worked when they needed work; when they didn't need it, you just sat and read the paper or whatever. So I rather enjoyed that. And it paid very well.

We came down to the main plant. They made all kinds of articles: lipstick tubes, casings for perfume bottles, candlesticks, metal cups—a lot of those small things out of metal.

I had a cousin who worked as a toolmaker—and she was a female—during the war. In Waterbury Mfg., I suppose you could have gone into office work. But I don't know of any Blacks that did work in the office. I don't know of any Blacks that applied for office work. At that time, everybody was looking for the job where you could make the most money, and you could make more money working in the plant than you could in the office.

I was very unhappy. The only reason I stayed in the factory was because it paid more money, and because I knew Saturday and Sunday I would be home—of course, during the war you worked Saturdays and Sundays and every day. For the money, that's why. No other reason. I hated every day of it. I wasn't learning anything. It wasn't uplifting. It wasn't helping me to go forward. It was just: How much are you making, how much is the price of a job, and little petty jealousies between the employees. You'd listen to them, but I didn't like that at all.

As you work, your seniority grows, so you feel that you have security on the job. Therefore you're not going to leave it.

In many instances, men objected to their wives working and insisted that they take care of the home instead.

Catherine Ruggles: I took care of the home and he went out to work. He'd bring home his pay and mother ran the house and put the money where it belonged. He did washing, boiling—all the heavy stuff, he did on weekends. But he'd never let me go to work. He said, "You end up in the hospital or paying doctor's bills." So I never worked. I did want to work, especially during the war. We belonged to a bridge club. They all worked but me. He'd always say, "Can't I work? Ain't I bringing enough home to you? Aren't you satisfied with it?" So I never worked.

In other cases, men and women adjusted their roles in the household to compensate for the women's working outside the home, although the primary responsibility for the home usually remained with the woman.

Mary Diogostine: [I didn't see my husband much;] we used to leave each other notes. My husband was very good. He was very good with the kids. He cooked, cleaned. If I didn't do something, he did it. Lots of times he used to have something already cooked.

Integrating work with childcare was a difficult problem that was solved in different ways. Some women found work hours that allowed them to take care of their children. Others made special family arrangements.

Louise Lombardo: I'm divorced, so I took care of everything. I found myself a job where I could go to work at 8 o'clock in the morning, and I left with the children. I would get home at noon, and we would have lunch together. We'd all leave together; they'd go to school and I'd go to work. At 3:30 they'd get out of school and I'd get out of work. I had a very good boss. He arranged it so I could go to work. I didn't know the man; I just asked if they could accommodate me like that, and they said yes. This was at Benrus. I never took time off; my mother would go up and stay with the children [if they were sick].

Rachel Doolady: When I went to work, my father, who was ill, took care of my son. My son would sleep over during the week. Friday night I would pick him up and take him home. I didn't have such

Rachel Doolady with her son during World War II. Courtesy Rachel Doolady.

a thing as a sympathetic boss. I don't know of any foreman that ever did anything like that to accommodate one of the workers. Where I worked, they'd say you either come in on time, or they'd put you on the night shift or put you on the afternoon shift.

Mary Diogostine: When I came over here and got a job, I was on the morning shift. I had to go to the boss and tell him I couldn't stay on morning shift because I had kids to go to school. So I wanted to be changed on the night shift. My husband was on the night shift, so we had to reverse it. This way, in the morning I was home. The kids used to come home at 12 o'clock to eat. And then they'd go back to school. Their father would come home in the afternoon at 3:15 and the kids used to get out at 3:30.

11. Conditions on the Job: "When I Whistle, I Want You to Come"

After the defeat of the strikes of 1920, brass company management had a free hand. New technological advances and labor policies were introduced; however, basic on-the-job grievances remained.

There were still serious health hazards.

Catherine Coscia: On the jobs, the people got hurt. That happened to me; I got hurt three times. The first time, I was lifting up the metal to put it on the skid. The skid is what you have on the floor. We had to lift it by hand, because the metal wasn't that heavy. Round pieces, sixty, seventy pounds. I was lifting it. In those days, they didn't care whether you had gloves on or not, but I had my gloves on. I put that metal on, and the way it was sharpened, the glove was cut and it cut my hand. It cut the tendon. This finger can never be used. I stayed home for about six months with this.

The second time I got hurt, it was a toolmaker's fault because he was drunk. In the morning, he used to come in drunk. Everybody knew that. They used to call him by a nickname "Fat." So this one morning I said to him, "Fat, I don't like the way you put that punch in that machine." He said, "I'm a toolmaker and I know what I'm doing." "If I get hurt, you're going to pay for it." He said to me, "Don't worry about it."

About 9:45 the machine smashed up. The punch flew out and hit me in the chest, and the piece of steel went into my chest. If it had gone on this side, I would have gotten killed. I went to the nurse, came back and went to work; I didn't feel that pain. When I came home that night, I couldn't lay on my pillow. The piece of steel was in my chest. The punch shattered all over the place. They didn't find the punch. [The toolmaker] hid the punch underneath his toolbox; they found it under there when he passed away. I still have the piece of steel in my purse upstairs.

The third time I got hurt was 400 lb. on my foot. See these toes? I have them, but there's no feeling there. They have the crane you pull from one machine to another. I pulled the cord. The hook snapped. The coil was on my toes. The toolmaker had to get a bar to pick it up from my toes. Over a year, I had a cast on. They're still taking care of me. They still have to give me a needle. It broke my toes and it smashed my instep.

Russell Sobin: On the rolls, they had a magic eye. All you had to do was put your hands by it and it would activate. That's how one of the fellows got crushed to death. He walked in front of it. Just as he walked in front of it, this big thing came over, the coiler, and wrapped him right in it and crushed him. He was only nineteen years old.

There were a lot of dangerous things. I've seen fellows with their fingers off; I've seen fellows get burnt with acid that could take the skin right off you. If you got that in your eye and you didn't get water in there quick, your eye would discolor. It would be just a blank.

On the shears, you could get your fingers cut off. A fellow who worked with me had four off— three off one hand, and one off the other hand. I've seen fellows get caught in the rolls.

One day I was working with a guy, a hell of a nice fellow. I told another guy, "Keep your hands off the button; don't start it." The fellow at the other end pushed the button. It dragged him right up to here. He couldn't go any further. I grabbed ahold of a big crowbar. With all the strength I had, I lifted that roll right out and he fell out. But it took his skin and peeled it right off like a glove. After that gangrene set in, and he lost his hand.

I've seen so many accidents. Oh, my God.

There was a guy who was using a jackhammer one day. Under-

Pulling tubes on a draw bench, Scovill, 1945. Despite technical refinements, many mill jobs still required a lot of manual labor. Courtesy Scovill, Inc.

ground wires. He didn't know where they were. Boom! He was dead. Hit it with the jackhammer. It only happened thirty feet away from where I was working.

[The union, when it first came in,] had a safety committee to go around and check what could be fixed, so it wouldn't be a hazard. I was on a safety committee. For instance, if you went by and saw a pile of coils or a pile of sheets that was leaning a little bit, you'd go tell the boss: "Have that removed. That could slip. If somebody was there, that would be it." That's what happened to a pile of big bars. This guy walked by and it slid. It took his foot right off—he's only got one foot today.

The crane inspector would come down and check that cable all the way through. After a while they eliminated that man. I've seen where the cable snapped and down it would come. If anybody was under it, they'd be nothing but a pancake.

Down in the wire mill, I don't know what happened. That coil, it came out somehow and went right through his stomach. All they heard was sssssssssss, and he was gone. The hot bar went right through him.

One day an oiler was oiling one of the machines. Down came the crane, it crushed this guy right up against a girder. Killed him instantly.

When I first started up there, they used to have buffing wheels. They put a rouge on it. There were five or six men there, and every one of them died of cancer of the throat. Little by little they all went.

To some extent, the health hazards were accepted as an inevitable part of the job.

Frank Keane: When I was a little kid, this man used to visit in our house—my mother's brother. He lost a hand on one occasion, went back to work, and lost three-quarters of the other one. You'll say: That's an absurdity. And I'm inclined to say it is in 1980. But I think you have to go back to the time, put yourself in that position at that time. I presume at that time, this is what people expected.

In my own time in the mill, if I were to get a bad cut in my hand, I didn't stay home. They put me on a bench in the mill and I made bands.

When you worked in situations like that, you kind of expected it. If you're working around machinery in a mill, or you're up in the casting shop or down in the scrap room working in a cloud of metallic dust all the time, you expect that maybe you're going to get a cough out of this thing.

But the "acceptance" was, in part, involuntary.

Grace Cummings: There was always somebody getting the end of their finger cut off in a machine. The tip end. My mother got lots of slices, pieces of finger, really severe lacerations. They would swell up; she'd be out of work on comp, which was at that time about thirty-five dollars a week.

They felt that it was wrong. But when you work in a shop like that, first of all you're glad to get the job. And there's nobody to complain to, because if you complain too much, there's somebody waiting to take your place. So you don't complain.

The foundry at Scovill's Waterville plant, 1945. Modern casting methods had not been introduced here; compare this with the World War I–era casting shown on page 76. Courtesy Scovill, Inc.

There was widespread resentment at the limited responsibility the employers took for those injured on the job.

Art Finelli: In 1940 I lost my index finger. I was out seven weeks. They had to amputate it because it got poison inside.

I was working in the aluminum anodizing. We used to have oil of vitriol in there. When I was nailing some of the aluminum rivets, I just skimmed my finger and broke the skin. I guess I must have got some acid in it.

That afternoon, when I was going home, I washed my hands and I felt a little sting. I went to the hospital. [The staff person] soaked it in a saline solution, put a bandage on, and said, "Come in and see the doctor in the morning." That thing kept me awake all night long. In the morning my finger was as big as my wrist. When the doctor saw it, he blew his stack sky high, because they should have called him.

The next day he asked me, "How old are you?" "Twenty years old." "We have to have your father here." They got my finger off. I went down to St. Mary's and in about fifteen or twenty minutes they took the finger off.

After being out of work seven weeks, I got a settlement of $544. They gave me $11.44 a week for thirty-seven weeks or somewhere around that. That was in 1940.

Before unionization, there were no regular wage rates in the brass plants; two workers doing the same job side by side might get entirely different wages.

Frank Pochron: About raises: When you got married, he gave you a raise. When you had a child, he gave you a raise. If you went to a little bit of schooling nights, you got a raise.

John Chubat: Before the union, everybody got paid different. It was under the table sometimes. Nobody was supposed to know it but you.

Despite the long hours, many workers had to "moonlight" on extra jobs.

Frank Keane: You couldn't exist at that time on just what you did in the mills. My father worked maybe three jobs. He had a team of horses, and when he finished work in the mill, he'd go around and he'd move things. Or he'd deliver things. Ultimately, he had a couple of big wagons. You wanted your furniture moved, he moved it. You wanted a load of hay, he'd move it. This he did on Saturday and Sunday and during the summer. He grazed the horses up on Pine Hill or wherever there was free forage.

Nonetheless, the wages paid by the large brass companies were considered among the best in the area.

Paul Garatoni: Getting into the brass company at that time was a deal, because it was the best-paying job in the entire area. The brass company didn't go sour, until wages were frozen during World War II. I started at forty cents an hour. Forty cents an hour with the cost of living in this area, you lived good. The closest competition to it was Farrel Foundry, and they were thirty-five. The average wage was twenty-five, and food prices were based on twenty-five cents an hour in the area. When I got married, I was making twenty-eight dollars a week, and we were living pretty well.

Wages for women were far lower, as a group of women at the Palladino Center remembered.

Mary Diogostine: I worked in a sewing place. I worked forty hours for nine dollars a week when I started. I was eighteen. I was there about two years and they gave us a raise. I got twelve dollars and I thought that was wonderful. I remember the wage was about thirty-five or forty cents an hour.

Louise Lombardo: I got seven-and-a-half dollars when I first went to work. I was fourteen years old.

Nellie Sacco: I worked up at Watertown Manufacturing at twenty-eight-and-a-half cents an hour, and I had to spend four tokens a day. So what did I come home with? Nothing. And we had to do bull work—with big, big files. And yet, twenty-eight-and-a-half cents an hour. That was about 1937, 1938. You had to be up there at 7 o'clock. Your boss was at the door.

A great source of resentment among brass workers was the poor quality of pension provisions.

Mary Toletti: My father worked in Scovill's forty-two years. When he retired, they gave him a pension of thirty dollars a month. Then he got his social security. When they heard how much he was getting from social security—which couldn't have been too much, because my father's been dead many years—Scovill's took away five dollars. All he got was twenty-five dollars a month.

ARBITRARY AUTHORITY

Since insecurity of employment and the threat of arbitrary firing by foremen were among the most common of workers' grievances, the companies gradually attempted to regularize the process of hiring and firing. One of the first efforts in this direction was John Goss' instruction, during layoffs in 1907, that "not too much attention be paid to ability, but more thought be given to length of service." During World War I, both Scovill and American Brass organized employment offices to deal with job applications. However, until the establishment of unions in the late 1930s, layoffs were still made at the foreman's whim.

Mike Laban: When I started, the union wasn't there. Harry came by and told a guy I was working with that he was all through, that he was on the layoff list. On Wednesday, they told him Friday would be his last day. I figured I'd be told, because I had less seniority and I was single. This guy was married and had a family to take care of. In those days the single guys, regardless of seniority, a lot of times were let go.

Toward the end of the day he asked, "They told you?" But just then Harry came by. I said, "Harry, when am I going to be told that I'm laid off?" He said, "Oh, no, you're not being laid off. Jimmy Buswell likes you. So does Bobby Kilpatrick." I said, "This isn't fair, but I still want the job." So I was kept on the payroll, while this guy was laid off. The reason? Jimmy Buswell would come by, I'd always grab his ear; I'm a gregarious sort of guy. I'd talk to him, knowing that he was an old soccer player.

Workers often were required to do personal favors for foremen in order to retain their jobs.

Mike Laban: The painting and lawnkeeping of some of the supervisors was a common practice in those days. They did it quite frequently, right up to the early 1940s. There were always some people figuring: The boss is going to take care of me.

Emil Antinarella: The boss could walk into anybody's locker, put his hand inside, and get a quart of liquor. Then he got drunk, and he didn't bother anybody. If you were Italian or Polish, some of the old guys made a barrel of wine. If the wine went sour, he was gone for the rest of his life.

Some workers got along well with their foremen.

Frank Keane: The foremen were great guys. You didn't fight these guys. You had to work with them and they with you. There was a good rapport generally between the foremen and the men.

But other workers found the foremen's arbitrary power offensive.

Mike Laban: I had just completed a job and I was standing around, when I heard somebody whistle. The guy was waving for me to come down. He wanted to put me on another job. I resented the fact that he whistled. I didn't pay any attention. He whistled again. Then he finally came running down. "Didn't you hear me whistling?" I said, "Yeah, you've got a good whistle." "When I whistle, I want you to come down. I've got a job for you to do."

I said: "Mr. Wentworth, I have a dog at home. He doesn't understand much English, but when I whistle, he comes running because he knows I'm going to feed him. I'm not a dog; I understand the English language. You want me, you come down and tell me what you want done. Since you're my supervisor, I'll do it. But don't whistle; I'm not a dog. If you whistle, you're going to have a lot of teeth missing and you won't be able to whistle too good." I was young at that time, single—I didn't give a damn.

INSECURITY

A constant preoccupation for Charles R. Walker and those who worked with him was how much work there would be and how long it would last. The following comments are interspersed throughout his diary:

"Too many men for the jobs, and I became a super-helper on Yoxall's rolls."

"Eddie, the foreman, is embarrassed with too many rollers, and helpers, and has no good job to which he can set them."

"Some parts of the Brass mill are only working 4 days a week, on 8 hour shifts."

"An order for 5,000,000 lbs. has come in for the wire mill, which it is said will keep things going there for several months. Men and foreman are keen for news of orders. The West Rod mill is starting two shifts next week of eight hours each.

"A word with Frank Gettlein, Assistant Foreman of the Department. He doesn't hold up much hope for starting the rolls again. Says they had orders to shutdown a month ago. Cherrytree rolls are also down.

"Gilbert moves over from the finishing rolls to mine. Jones, the night boss, steps down and becomes roller on Gilbert's pair. The shop is now filled with the demoted."

Born in 1911, John Mankowski started work at American Brass in Ansonia in early 1929. He was laid off in the Depression in 1929. He came back around 1937. He was involved in getting the CIO union, Mine, Mill, into the plant, and became a staff organizer for Mine, Mill in 1941. He was elected a member of the national Mine, Mill executive board, and was one of the leaders of the secession movement which carried many Connect-

icut brass workers out of Mine,
Mill and eventually into the UAW.
He served as an international representative for the UAW from 1951
until his retirement in 1976.

The problems of unemployment
and job insecurity became much
worse during the Depression.

John Mankowski: I used to stand
out in that main street and look for
a job at American Brass in 1932,
'33, '34, '35, '36. It was an everyday habit to go down there and see
if there was anything doing, along
with 300 other people on the street.
You'd see the guy come over to the
employment office window. He'd
lower the top half of the window
down and point across the street
and holler "You," "not you," as
fifteen guys would start running.
"Not you, you," and he'd try to
pinpoint the guy. It broke down to

TABLE 20
Unemployment in Waterbury, by Industry, 1930

Industry*	Labor force	Unemployed, looking for work	Employed, but laid off without pay
All industry (aggregate)	42,271	2,573	420
Building	1,979	310	28
Iron and steel	2,638	96	38
Metals, except iron and steel	11,005	615	199
Chemicals	279	12	3
Clothing	385	10	6
Food	518	25	1
Paper and printing	415	19	1
Garage work and auto repair	393	30	1
Steam railroads	479	14	1
Telegraph and telephone	431	10	0
Wholesale and retail sales	4,362	131	7
Domestic service (hotels etc.)	898	62	4
Domestic service (private households)	1,884	61	4
Banking and brokerage	353	1	0
Insurance and real estate	492	4	0

*Industries employing at least 300 workers.
Source: Compiled from U.S. Census data by Peter Rachleff.

ten guys, then five guys, and he finally got the guy he wanted in
there. It made you wonder about
what the hell kind of a system this
is. You come down every day for a
job and you don't score.

TABLE 21
Unemployment in Waterbury, by Period of Idleness, 1930

Period of idleness	Unemployed, looking for work	Employed, but laid off without pay
All unemployed (aggregate)	2,573	420
Under 1 week	13	164
1–2 weeks	141	59
3–4 weeks	254	34
5–8 weeks	372	36
9–13 weeks	407	29
14–17 weeks	297	18
18–26 weeks	563	20
27–39 weeks	234	16
40–52 weeks	191	0
1–2 years	60	0
Over 2 years	25	1

Source: Compiled from U.S. Census data by Peter Rachleff.

12. The Coming of Industrial Unionism: "We Had a Signal, Just Like Paul Revere"

Unquestionably, the most successful effort to change the basic power position of workers in the brass industry came with the labor movement that developed in the 1930s and 1940s. Very substantial discontent both with living standards and with conditions on the job developed during the years of the Great Depression. The CIO's International Union of Mine, Mill, and Smelter Workers, representing western miners who worked for some of the major copper companies, began organizing brass workers in the Naugatuck Valley in the late 1930s. By the middle of World War II, elections for union recognition had been won by Mine, Mill at all of the major brass companies in the Valley.

There were several significant differences between the labor movement of this era and that of 1920. The right to organize unions had officially been recognized in law, and the National Labor Relations Act had established procedures through which unions could win the right to bargain collectively by means of an election for union representation. The division between skilled and unskilled workers was weaker, so union organization tended to include all workers in a plant. Nationality groups had declined enough in significance that the plant or company became the natural unit for organization, rather than the ethnic group as in 1920. However, ethnic conflicts still shaped some of the political divisions within the new unions.

The first stirrings of union revival in the brass plants came in 1933, when the AFL organized select groups in the mills.

John Zampino: When Mr. Roosevelt came in, you could organize. So we started talking in the room. Yea, yea, yea, yea. The organizer came from Chicago to organize us. We got a hall. I went outside over there and I saw all my friends. It was the buff room and the plating room that were the first ones to organize in the AFL. We were paying two dollars a month in those days.

I sat with my friend. He said, "What are we doing over here?" "Hey, listen, if we're going to get fired, we're going to get fired. It's the law [that you can organize]. We're not going to do anything bad. Mr. Roosevelt says we can."

They were afraid. They were the ones who remembered 1919, 1920.

We all signed up. We wrote to the company: We're organized.

We went to John Goss, and John

Goss was against the union. But he said, "I believe in a fair day's work for a fair day's pay. We've got bosses in the room; if nobody says anything, we think everything runs smooth. But when people start squeaking, I don't know anything. I'm in the office."

We told him, the [piecerate] price [on compacts we made for Coty] was so cheap! I used to bring home seventeen, eighteen dollars for forty hours in the buff room.

He said to the boys: "I want you boys to go up to the room. We're going to try it for a year. Don't look at your time card. You look at your check next week."

I'll be honest with you. When I saw my check, twenty-eight dollars, I couldn't believe it. Everybody danced in the room. Twenty-eight dollars for forty hours! Hurray!

The buff room, the plating room, and the truckers stood alone quite a while with the AFL. Then all the shop had a vote and went into the CIO.

Born in 1911, Bill Moriarty grew up in a family of Irish extraction in Waterbury. During the Depression, he got a job in the Metal Hose Branch of American Brass. He was briefly promoted upstairs to work in the office, but when a new boss came in, he was kicked downstairs to work in the mill. He was involved in the earliest Mine, Mill efforts to organize brass workers in the Naugatuck Valley. "We

were direct actionists," he recalls. Eventually, he became head of the American Brass local, and then a Mine, Mill staffer. Always a scrapper, he became an activist in the factional conflicts in Mine, Mill, and even ran for national vice-president of the union in the early 1940s. He was one of the leaders of the secession movement and spent most of the 1950s, 1960s, and 1970s as an international representative for the UAW. He has been active in Democratic party politics most of his life. He served as state representative from the town of Wolcott for eight years, as Democratic Town Chairman, and, in the early 1970s, on the State Democratic Central Committee. In the early 1960s, he was the state chairman of Americans for Democratic Action. He is presently serving a second term as labor representative

on the Connecticut State Board of Arbitration and Mediation, and is the president of the Wolcott Lions Club. Bill remains a feisty individual, who tells stories of past struggles with relish.

Bill Moriarty: [By the mid-1930s, conditions were ripe for union organizing in the brass plants, because of] job security and job conditions. You didn't get anywhere, unless you were in the favored group. And they could break you in a moment. The minute you spoke back, they'd just take you and put you back down on the machines or let you go. So when the unions came in, I was ready for a union. And that was typical of many, many other people. People with seniority who had been laid off, while a new guy was kept on. You complained about conditions in the department, and you were the first guy laid off. Those were the conditions that brought about the union.

Sam Kwochka: [The union came in because] there was no representation. There was no vacation with pay.

John Chubat: If the boss favored you, if you brought a little present for him. . . .

Kwochka: . . . or cut his lawn. . . .

Chubat: . . . or brought him moonshine or something, they would [favor you]. That's the truth.

At 12 o'clock he'd clap his hands: "Everybody go to work." All you had to do was answer him back once. If you open your mouth, you're out.

Kwochka: I remember that was a time we used to come into work at 7 o'clock in the morning, the boss would look around: "No work, come back at 9 o'clock. You're going to work two hours, from 9 to 11." You'd come back the next day, he'd tell you, "Nothing today. Come back Wednesday." Sometimes you'd put in ten or twelve hours a week.

Frank Pochron: That's what brought the union in. You'd go in there dressed up to go to work. The boss took his time, looked around, and about an hour later you'd go home. You didn't get paid for it, not a single thing.

Chubat: This was a sweatshop before the union came. The union did a lot for the Seymour workers, especially in brass. The men worked long hours; there was no overtime. We had no vacation.

We got a vacation. We got a pay raise. And they said it was impossible to do it. Even workers didn't believe it.

John Driscoll: Favoritism was one of the all-pervading grievances. Favoritism would be based on whether you cut the foreman's grass or shovel snow from his sidewalk or help him build a garage for free. Women had a lot of griev-

ances about foremen playing favorites. They didn't say why certain women were favored, but that probably is an obvious cause-and-effect situation. Seniority was a big selling point, that the union could get a standard that couldn't be set aside by foremen's likes and dislikes.

At Waterbury Button, one of the issues was the fact that the company rotated the shifts. I believe there were some spontaneous job actions about that. We finally persuaded the company to go for steady shifts. It was the subject of a rather short strike before we got a contract. 1938/39.

Sometimes workers turned to direct action to deal with their grievances.

Of Irish extraction, Helen Johnson was born in 1911 in Burlington, Vermont, where she was raised by her grandparents. Her grandfather, a self-educated man who taught college there, was a great influence on her. After she left home, she worked in a number of Connecticut towns. By the late 1930s she was working at Benrus Watch in Waterbury. Around 1940, she got as job in the eyelet room at Scovill. She got involved with the union, and helped institute a suit for equal pay for equal work for the women in her department. She remained active in the Scovill local until she retired in the late 1970s. She was, and continues to be, ac-

tive in the union's community activities. Today she serves on the UAW's CAP Committee and on the Board of Directors of the Waterbury Retired Workers Council. She devotes a great deal of time to the Connecticut Citizens Action Group, where she serves as the chairperson of their energy program for the state, and as vice-chair of the Waterbury chapter. She says of WCAG, "We're making a quiet revolution in Waterbury."

Helen Johnson: I worked in the Benrus, and we had a beautiful sit-down strike. To this day nobody knows who started it. It had to be in the later 1930s. We were going out one night, and there was a sign on the time clock that Waterbury Clock [now Timex Corp.] was giving their employees a raise. There was nothing said about us. The

Waterbury Battery Co. sit-down strike, March 12, 1937. Courtesy Waterbury Republican-American.

next day, we came in armed with newspapers and magazines. We all rang in and sat down.

We had an awful nice foreman; it really hurt to do anything to him. "What's the matter?" "Hey, you'd better get ahold of somebody. They're going to give them a raise across the road and nothing's been said here." This went on for about a day-and-a-half. Finally, they came across; they gave us the same increase they were getting across the road.

That was really my first time. Nobody ever really knew who started it; it was done real cute. [There was no union at that time.]

Nothing. We did it on our own. It was effective. I don't know how long we could have held out if they'd gotten tough. It was fun.

Meanwhile, the miners in the West were reviving the International Union of Mine, Mill, and Smelter Workers, a union descended from the Western Federation of Miners, one of the most militant in American labor history. The miners had struck in 1934, but the copper companies had gone on producing brass in their mills in the East. The miners decided to reach out to the brass workers.

Sid Monti: An appeal was made by someone to the miners, trying to show them that their self-interest was in getting the fabricators, as well as the smelters and refineries, organized, so they could have one complete, overall union. This was the principal idea behind Mine, Mill coming in.

As I understand it, in the 1930s the miners themselves, at a meeting in Butte, Montana (and other places out there), decided that they would assess themselves three bucks a week in order to send money to guys to help organize the fabricators in the East.

John Driscoll describes the overall organizing effort in the Brass Valley in the 1930s.

John Driscoll: Jess Gonzales, who was the executive board member from this district, was, I think, the

A picket line at the Waterbury Buckle Co. One sign reads "Down with Hitlerism at the Waterbury Buckle Co. National defense demands collective bargaining." Courtesy Ovide Garceau.

first one to scout the area, in June of 1936. He gave a charter to Local 251. The first organizer I remember was Alex Cashin, out of Butte, Montana, previously from the Coeur d'Alene.

Our original way of organizing was, after we got a majority signed up, we'd ask management for recognition. If we couldn't get it, we'd strike. As at Waterbury Buckle or Waterbury Battery.

The first group in the brass mills were people in the Scovill Rolling Mill. A fellow named Art Curtis, really Adolph Curtis, was one of the early activists. He was a roller in Scovill north mill. He had a group around him who were rollers. They were the skilled people in the mills, and they could bring in their helpers. Usually three or so on a set of rolls.

We had an odd group at Scovill

in the powerhouse. They came to us in 1938. We were so unsophisticated that, when they wanted to get a contract on their own, we thought, well, if we could get a foothold this way, we could spread out into the rest of the shop. John Goss, who was in charge at Scovill at that time, was shrewd enough to play it the other way, figuring that if we negotiated a contract, the people would be satisfied and they wouldn't really spread out, because they were isolated from the rest of the mill. That's the way it worked out. We got a signed agreement in 1938, which improved their conditions substantially. But it simply satisfied them; it didn't make them organizers. They weren't disciples after that.

We had people from some of the smaller shops who were actually more active in that early period,

Waterbury Buckle Shop picket line, 1938. The woman in the middle is carrying a cast-iron skillet in her handbag. The strikers had just succeeded in preventing a strikebreaker from entering the plant. John Driscoll is on the left; the other man is Bill Moriarty. Courtesy Bill Moriarty.

people from Waterbury Buckle, Waterbury Battery, and Waterbury Button. We organized those and got contracts, before we did at any of the majors. They were a more integrated group; it was easier to approach them. Scovill, Chase, and American Brass were spread out into so many mills and shops that, to get the whole unit, we had to have a springboard, such as the pay cuts in 1938 and the taking away of the vacation with pay that the companies had first granted in 1937 in an attempt to head off organization.

Conditions were so bad in Waterbury Buckle, women showed me paychecks: five dollars and forty cents for a forty hour week. 1938. We had some very militant people, like the woman who was the chairlady at Waterbury Buckle. She was a French Canadian. She rallied the people around. The men weren't very active at first there, but we won recognition after a strike.

There was a lot of hostility among the various ethnic groups at first. We had a tough time convincing the Italians that they

should trust the Irish, and the Irish that they should trust the French Canadians, and so on. We pointed out to them that the only way to deal with the companies that we had to deal with was to get ourselves together, and that we couldn't afford these ancient hostilities. We couldn't afford to remember 1921.

Some people [still talked about the 1920 strike]. The Italians, for example, said the Irish were the ones who turned pro-company, or never joined them in the first place. That they sold them out,

American Brass workers on strike in Waterbury, 1936. John Driscoll is on the far right. Courtesy Waterbury Republican-American.

American Brass workers on strike in 1937. Courtesy Waterbury Republican-American.

and stuff like that. They were the ones who had the better jobs.

[The companies] all joined in first giving a five-cent-an-hour increase and then, in the summer of 1937, they gave the first vacation with pay for blue-collar workers that the city had ever known. They had been giving their white-collar workers a vacation with pay. And they gave the shop people a 5-percent increase in an effort to stave off the growth of the Mine, Mill union.

Well, we kept coming along, and in the early part of 1937, I think, the local had something like 2,400 members paying dues. Of course, there was no such thing as a check-off; these were all dues paid by hand. But in the early part of 1938, we had another recession. And first of all the 5 percent came off, and then the vacations with pay were discontinued, and, I think, they also got to the first nickel that they had given. . . . With that, there were a lot of layoffs. And I remember we went down to about 400 members.

But in American Brass, there was more militancy than in the other plants, and the American Brass north mill was one section set apart. The north mill workers attempted a strike, so we pulled a couple of hundred people out; the leadership of the local walked out and set up picket lines. And we managed to hold it for a couple of days. We tried to get other parts of the American Brass plant people in those other mills to come out, but we didn't have any success.

However, the strike was a good thing; I mean, it showed the rest of the people what the game was all about, and we filed a petition for an N.L.R.B. election shortly thereafter, even though we had a rather small minority of actual members signed up. And the Blue Card Association was supposed to have a majority in cards, but we beat hell out of 'em in the election.

The first union recognition at a major brass plant was won at American Brass in Waterbury.

Bill Moriarty: The union organizational drive began in the latter part of July 1938. I worked in the American Metal Hose branch of American Brass. We organized in the usual manner: signed cards, held meetings. The union was absolutely new to almost all of us. We didn't have unionization around here, except for the skills and the railroad brotherhoods. We were never involved in that kind of thing. We didn't know very much about it.

We won the election at American Brass. We had fewer than 100 members out of 4,000.

We had fifty-three people on the first negotiating committee. I guess that was all the membership we had. We were trying to impress the company with our strength. The first meeting, Clark Judd insisted that we cut down the size of the negotiation committee. It was O.K.

with us; we just wanted him to think we had so many members we didn't know who to choose. We negotiated a contract, a very meager one, at first; we got mainly job security and a few of the basics. And we were very happy to get it.

Then we began to strengthen the organization, which was difficult even after winning the election. In those days you had no checkoff. Dues were a dollar a month. You had dues buttons. Each month you paid your dollar. You had to go around when the foremen weren't watching because they were still death on the unions. You had to sneak around the machines to get a buck from a guy. If he didn't give it to you, there was nothing you could do about it.

But we survived and expanded. This town was really ripe for unions. The companies were very harsh on the employees at that time. There was no job security. You could work there for thirty years and they could tell you "Fred, you're all through." You'd go home and wait; if they called you, they called you.

At that time you didn't find too many people who were pro-labor. In the city, to the city officials, the cops, you were some kind of people that were causing trouble, you were Communist radicals or whatever.

We were rather loose-knit and new. The word "strike" was some terrible thing that we had been taught they did in Russia.

We were enthusiastic. The people had been kept down for a long time, and now they had new hope. They figured: Now we can stand up and be men; we don't have to go around with our heads bowed and peek around the corner to see if the boss isn't going to put our name on the sheets for a layoff.

Russell Sobin: In 1938 the company gave us a week's vacation with pay. That's the first time it ever happened. The following year we didn't organize. So they didn't give us a vacation. So then we started to think. How about organizing?

We had a vote between the AFL and the CIO, and the CIO won out. Some wanted the AFL. The reason a lot of them didn't want the AFL was that the AFL, at one time, was nothing but a craftsman's union. They would never take in a plain worker in a shop. They wanted carpenters, electricians, plumbers, stuff like that. But the CIO took everybody, and that's why we went for the CIO. We had a vote and we won four to one.

At lunch there would be a bunch of Russians. I speak Russian, so I'd go over and speak to them and tell them about it. A lot of them were threatened by the rollers, that if you join the union, they're going to fire you. [The rollers] didn't want a union. They were like a gang leader.

So the next time they would say,

Stewards' clambake, Local 445 of Mine, Mill, in 1940. Russell Sobin is in the front row, to the left of the man with the bats. Courtesy Russell Sobin.

"O.K. Russ." They'd give me their initiation fee. I'd take them down and sign them in.

Then the next day I'd see a bunch of Polish; I'd go talk to them. The following day, I'd see a bunch of Lithuanians. A lot of them spoke Russian. So I'd talk with them. That's how I got them. I practically signed up over 400 members.

I told them why, the benefits. In case of a layoff—at that time they never laid you off by seniority. You could be there ten years and they could keep a pet that worked there two years and lay you off. When the union got in, they had to lay off by seniority.

I was a steward, until my wife said, "What am I going to be, a union widow?" I was never home. I'd come home from work, I'd be right down at the union headquarters and have to go somewhere.

Me and John Marr were the only two that started the union in our department. Each department had their own steward. You had to have a lot of guts, because at that time a lot of them would say: Oh, if you're going to be a union man, they're going to fire you, they're going to do this and that.

The principal obstruction workers had to overcome to establish unions was the fear of company reprisal,

which had built up over the decades of employer opposition to unionism.

Grace Cummings: My father was always afraid of the union. The boss used to tell him that, if you didn't do what the union said, they would meet you in the parking lot after work and work you over. Even then they were using scare tactics.

He said that the union would tell you how to work. If the boss liked you, he could give you two or three cents on his own, and not give the other guy a two- or three-cents-an-hour raise. He'd say, "It's going to take away your power of doing what we want to do; if we feel you are better than the other guy, we can raise you." He told them that the union goes out on strikes for no reason at all. They would waste your money; you got no benefits from it. It only took care of the guy who was collecting [dues]; he didn't turn it in. If anything bad happened, like on the national news you'd hear about the miners fighting and John L. Lewis making his men walk out and picket in the snow, they would say: "When you're out like that, your family is losing money, you're not able to feed your family. You don't want that to happen to us. We don't have that kind of problem. What kind of problems do we have here? There's no problems here." These people would go along with it.

Subtle hints were dropped. If you were too friendly with the guy who was trying to organize, suddenly you would be given a real bad machine to work on. So you were scared to talk to anybody about anything; you were scared to say anything about your problems.

Frank Pochron: Some of them didn't join the union immediately because they were scared for their jobs. They didn't know what the union could do for them. They didn't think the union would be able to protect them. So they weren't so much anti-union as afraid for their jobs. Especially the old-timers.

The fear was intensified by the sense of being under constant company surveillance.

Russell Sobin: You never could catch [the spies in the union]. We'd have a meeting on a Sunday morning. The next morning the boss would come over to me and tell me everything. I'd say, "You sonofagun, how did you know?" There'd be a stool pigeon somewhere.

Workers active in the union were also subject to direct harassment.

Eddie Labacz: My father used to call it the "bull pen." They would put them in a pit and say, "You, you, you come to work; the rest of you go home." If you were active in the union, they would let you stay home for two or three days at a time. They started to pick out the ringleaders, and they were watching them, harassing them.

There were also serious divisions among workers.

Sid Monti: There was jealousy among the various local unions. They hated one another.

The skilled tradesmen thought they were much better than the regular guys, than the production workers, so there was always a cleavage there.

There's a whole history of real hate between the Irish and the Italians. It got so bad: I used to belong to the Knights of Columbus.

I used to go to the meetings. The Italians would get on one side, and the Irish would get on the other. I said, "To hell with this; this ain't for me." So I never went back anymore. That's how bad it was.

The local guys tried to unify their crew. The Mine, Mill guys tried to unify another crew. There was constant bickering between the two [see section 13, "Union Factionalism," below]. That was one reason it never got off the ground. The left-right fight was doing nobody any good—nobody except the employer. The only ones that suffered were the workers.

John Driscoll: Some places like Chase Metal Works you had a kind of split that we were never really able to overcome for a long time, where you had an Italian faction and an Irish faction. Sometimes you'd have Poles with the Irish and so on.

Blacks were active in unionizing the brass mills, and unions established seniority rights that for the first time gave Black workers some protection against discrimination. But there were also tensions between Blacks and the unions.

John Gatison: The union came in in 1939. The Blacks did support the movement. And that was an awful nasty, tough fight—to get recognition by American Brass.

The unions did not have a Black force. They always had the one or possibly two active to oversee the gains in the fight for rights within the plant. Although the International provided a lot of things on paper that were supposed to protect everybody, what's written on paper, if it's not effectively used, means nothing. A lot that's in the [union] Constitution really didn't mean that much.

Wherever you had active participation by a number of Blacks, there were some gains. I was able to get enough of them interested, so that we were able to make some gains.

There was no Black representation in the early days. And they [the union leadership] dominated and they didn't encourage any Blacks to come out to represent, because they wanted to represent.

The Blacks did not concentrate on getting representation. They were treated pretty fairly, as far as grievances were concerned.

Whatever their limits, the gains were real.

Luke MacDonald: You could never get on the rolls if you were colored. People would go home. After the union, we had two colored rollers.

Outside support for the unions was limited.

John Driscoll: We tried to use the nationality organizations. In some cases the officers were friendly; they let us use their halls, for example. But the Catholic church

was not. When we were trying to organize unemployed workers in 1938/39, I tried to get a local priest to sponsor a meeting. I couldn't get anybody but Dorothy Day [of the radical Catholic Workers] from New York.

I never found any instance of their trying to dissuade anybody from joining, but they never helped. It wasn't until Father Donnelly appeared on the scene that we began to get some help. That was in 1941.

There remained a great many priests who were unfriendly or even hostile. Father Donnelly was regarded as a radical by many of the clergy for quite a while.

Since the union shop was not won at the major brass plants until the mid-1950s, maintaining membership was often a problem.

Bill Moriarty: It wasn't hard to get people to vote for the union, but it was hard to get them to become members, be active, and pay dues on a regular basis.

Helen Johnson: We used to collect dues manually—a dollar. Sometimes, if I knew you well enough, I'd say, "How about about throwing in a couple of extra months, so we can pay the girl [in the office]?" We had them in and out. They wanted something, they needed a grievance, they'd join. Then they'd drop out again.

Checkoff is good, but it's no good for the labor movement. You

don't get too many stewards doing their job. It made them be on their toes.

This problem was probably most severe at Scovill.

Caroline Nardello: The union was there at the time, but there was so very little said about it. Only a few people in our department belonged to it. You didn't have to join it if you didn't want to. A girl that belonged to the union used to tell us about it.

When they got the raise, we got the raise, so why join the union? A lot of them felt that way. We were satisfied the way we were going along.

There were few major strikes in the process of organizing the brass mills. But there were numerous wildcats and walkouts, through which workers asserted their power.

Bill Moriarty: I was fired, after they had the contract. I was told at noon not to come back. Being a small and very cohesive plant, the word spread like wildfire. We went to a restaurant for lunch, and I told them I was fired. So the people lined the streets and didn't go back into work. The boss came out and said, "Come in." They said, "Is Mr. Moriarty coming back?" "I don't know anything about that; that was done upstairs." After about twenty minutes of negotiating from the plant gate to the

Members of Torrington Local 423 of Mine, Mill after World War II. Courtesy Western Historical Collections, University of Colorado Libraries.

street, they decided to take me back. And every bit of victory like that gave us more enthusiasm and more strength and more courage, because we felt that you could see the power of the union if it stuck together.

At American Metal Hose we were particularly strong. We only had 120 people. Each one knew each other. Whether you wanted to or not, you were in the union. As always, you had the weak sisters,

you had the stooges, you had the people going back and forth with tales. But we were strong.

We had wildcat strikes. We had a list of grievances as long as your arm, and they weren't being settled. During the World War II preparedness period, the unions were supposed to be nice, to be 100 percent patriotic Americans and all that. So we weren't getting anywhere, and we had two main switches in the plant. I was co-

chairman and, with the other one, we decided we were going to put on a demonstration. So we pulled the two main switches that shut down all the machines.

The superintendent got on the phone and told [the union officials] what was going on. So [they] called us and said, "You guys get those machines rolling. You stop this stuff and stop this nonsense. We've got a war to win." My response was, "You sit up in that office and man the telephones, and we'll run the Metal Hose."

Helen Johnson: We got to find out a few things about the eyelet room. We found we were really being taken for a ride. The discrepancy in the pay between male and female was really sad.

We knew that they were trying to organize, so we called and had a meeting. We instituted a suit. We didn't know anything at that time. But we went to Boston and we fought it. After the first meeting, the company gave us an increase.

It was a win in a lot of ways, because that time they kept telling us that in wartime you can't give any increases.

That intrigued me, so I began trying to organize our department. I got one of these lads, and we organized the department pretty well. Those that didn't [join], I felt sorry for, because nobody talked to them. We were trying to hold down production, not do too much. We were only supposed to be there for the duration, since we took a man's job. One gal said, "I'm going to do what I can, to

hell with them." One day she came over; she had a card and she was crying, "Sign me up, please; nobody's talking to me."

From my experience in Benrus, we pulled a little work stoppage. There were two other eyelet rooms in another building. We got them together and we pulled it.

We just stopped, turned off everything. We wanted so many things. We wanted better working conditions. We had no place to change our clothes. We had nothing. Second and third shifts, if somebody got hurt, God help

From the Scovill Union News. *The newspaper considered women's participation in union organizing noteworthy in 1941. Courtesy Scovill Collection.*

them; you had to wait till somebody came around to take you over
to the hospital. Everything was
wrong.

We had nobody tell us; we just
decided all of a sudden: We've got
to get to these people. They've got
to do this, they've got to do that.
We gained their respect; that made
a big difference. They found out
we'd fight for them.

At that time they were going
south and bringing carloads of
Blacks up here. They knew nothing. It scared the life out of you,
watching them work, because you
thought they were going to get
their hands cut off. We didn't want
any of the working conditions. We
didn't have proper dressing rooms,
we had nothing. So we used them
as a target.

At that time there was a lot of
discrimination—I had to come to
Waterbury to find out about discrimination. The superintendent
started about how we have to accept these people. It started off
nice. We tried to tell him: These
people are going to cut their fingers; they're going to cut their
hands and worse; they're going to
be riding around up at the pulley.
Finally he got really snotty. So I
said, "How many Blacks have you
got in your office?" His face got red.

There was a lot of resentment
against the Blacks, don't let anybody kid you. And I was just as
bad as anyone else. I've learned
since. We just thought they were
dumping all this trash in there.

Russell Hunter: Once we walked
out. It was something they
wouldn't agree to. We didn't go
home; we just let them settle it in
the factory. We walked out in the
yard, stood around talking, played
ball, until we were told: "O.K.,
boys, come back; it's settled."
That was just to show them that
we would do it. That was just the
slitters.

Russell Sobin: We had a signal,
just like Paul Revere. Some guy
would walk down and say, "We're
going out." Nobody would ask any
questions. Next thing, you'd see
this group putting their stuff away,
taking their overalls off, taking
their safety shoes off.

We had a steward in the casting
shop, and he was a thorn in the
boss' side. So they finally put him
on the carpet, and they gave him a
week off for what he'd done. We'd
get notified and, the next thing,
we'd all walk out or call sick. That
would last a week or two, until
they hired him back. In the 1940s.
A couple of times it happened that
way.

We had little walkouts. Maybe
something wrong with working
conditions, you'd all walk out.
One department after another.
We'd stay out, until it was settled.
That's how we used to do it. You
had to get some action. We'd get
together and settle it. If they
didn't settle it, then that department would start it and the others
would follow suit. They would be

sympathizers. So we'd tie it all up.
They couldn't fire everybody.

[When people walked out in one
department,] the other departments would follow. Maybe they
wouldn't walk out that day, but
the next day, they wouldn't come
in because we'd have a few guys
out there picketing.

Management considered unionization a threat to its power.

Jim Cusack: Those were very difficult times for supervisors and management. As they organized, they
appointed stewards in the various
departments. Pretty frequently
they appointed rather tough individuals for stewards, persons who
would be willing to stand up and
challenge the supervisor. About
details of the job, wages, whatever
you could think of.

For workers, however, organization was a means of gaining some
influence over the conditions of
their life.

Luke MacDonald: When we got
the union in there, you got a week
off with pay. That's a whole lot different. Some years you got two
weeks off. I worked up to three.
Now some of them get five weeks.

If you saw a job vacant, you
could ask for it. Anybody could
ask for it. They'd try you out; if
you could do it, you had it. The
men with seniority had preference,
if they could do the job.

After the union, if the foreman

Mine, Mill Local 445's baseball team, the CIO League champs for 1940. Courtesy Western Historical Collections, University of Colorado Libraries.

said something you didn't like, you'd take it to the union and they'd fight, find out who was wrong and who was right.

Russell Sobin: You couldn't be a roller at that time. After we got the union in, that's when we broke the barrier. I became a roller. We had a Russian roller, a Polish roller. I think I was about the first one. That was in the 1940s.

[After the union,] we had Italian rollers, we had Russian, Polish; we had everything, we had a League of Nations. And after, we even had a colored guy who was a roller. That was in the late 1960s.

Peter Kukanskis: In the factories where people worked where unions were, the fellows used to say, "Hey, you should have a union in your place. Look, we work less hours, we get more money, we get a little benefits, we get a day off." They'd brag about it. Gradually another shop would

get in and another one. That's what turned the page over, and all of them did unionize eventually. Because they did do a lot of good. They made working conditions better for the people. You weren't afraid of the boss so much; you wouldn't get fired so quick. So when the unions came in, they were glad. A lot of them went for it, because, they said, "At least we've got a little more say-so about our job."

Reid Robinson, international president of Mine, Mill at the 1947 Mine, Mill convention. Courtesy Western Historical Collections, University of Colorado Libraries.

13. Union Factionalism and Secession: "If We Hadn't Had This Type of a Fight, We'd Have Been a Hellofa Power"

Nationally, the CIO was built by a coalition of forces ranging from relatively conservative bread-and-butter unionists to devout Catholics to members of the Socialist and Communist Parties. Through the CIO's early years, these groups worked together with little overt conflict. In the early 1940s, however, many CIO unions, including Mine, Mill, began to become polarized into what were called at the time left-wing and right-wing factions.

The conflict first surfaced in Connecticut in the form of a power struggle between the first generation of Mine, Mill organizers, including Alex Cashin and John Driscoll, and a new group, headed by Donald Harris, sent in by Mine, Mill president Reid Robinson in 1941.

At the 1941 convention of Mine, Mill in Joplin, Missouri, the factional struggle broke out into the open. On the one side were the national officials of the union, led by president Reid Robinson. On the other side were a number of top local officials from Connecticut, led by John Driscoll.

John Driscoll charged that Mine, Mill had been infiltrated by the Communist Party and that union policy was being shaped to the Communist Party line. Mine, Mill president Reid Robinson portrayed Driscoll's attack as a personal power grab.

The brass unions in Connecticut rapidly divided between those who supported Reid Robinson and those who supported John Driscoll and the Connecticut leadership. Some supported one side or the other because of political agreement or because they believed their charges. But rivalries between different local unions, leaders, and ethnic groups often played a role in the choosing up of sides. Bill Moriarty was a major figure in the Driscoll group.

Bill Moriarty: When we came back [from Joplin], the lines were divided. We had been on the telephone, telling [local supporters] what was happening, and they went right to work spreading the word out. That's when the lines started to form. They formed rather quickly. Guys like John [Mankowski] and Ovide Garceau had set the thing up. They [the other side] had already formed their groups they thought they could trust, and there was a sort of a nucleus on both sides of the warfare that was to come.

Important support for the Driscoll group came from a Waterbury priest, Father Joseph Donnelly.

Father Donnelly: One night I was called upon by the president of the Scovill local and the secretary of the Scovill local. They outlined to me a story of their attempts to prevent the Scovill local union from being taken over by the Communist element in the Mine, Mill, and Smelter Workers. They were fighting what apparently seemed to be a losing battle. They wanted some help, and I heard them out. I thought they deserved some help, so I discussed it the next day and the day after with my superiors. I suggested we should start an educational program in Waterbury for the union members. It was the fall of 1942 when we started our first labor school in Waterbury. With this, the whole controversy sort of erupted in Waterbury.*

The fierce competition between the factions was very disruptive to the labor movement in the Valley. Sometimes local meetings broke up in fist fights, as the factions battled for control. Russell Sobin remained a Mine, Mill supporter.

Russell Sobin: There were factions for a long while when the Mine, Mill [secession was happening.] We had problems. At the meetings we had arguments. Different sides: half of the hall would be this, the other half would be that.

Helen Johnson supported the Driscoll group.

*Interview with Father Joseph Donnelly in the Historical Collections of the Pennsylvania State University Libraries.

Helen Johnson: [The left wing] would get organizers who spoke Italian, Lithuanian, and send them in. It was hard for us because we were all English-speaking people, most of us. Even the ones that were Polish or Italian—they sort of forgot it. It's one of the sad things of this country: We forget where we came from.

They would pull meetings, mass meetings, say on a Holy Thursday. This was practically a Catholic town.

You'd walk in [to a union meeting], here were your friends that you worked with all day, all lined up on this side, you over on [the other] side—that used to bother me.

They tried to buy me, when they found out other things wouldn't go. They knew I wanted to finish school. They offered to send me to Columbia, pay all my expenses, set me up in an apartment.

[The company] never came right out, but I always figured they were with us. They knew; they were smarter than we were. I think they would have used them, or whoever it was, but they didn't want them in control.

Once the battle lines were drawn, each side attacked the other on every possible basis, from the details of local contract settlements to positions on international politics. An evaluation of the truth of these charges is beyond the scope of this book; the issues are complex and clouded by years of charges and countercharges. Some of the issues included:

Isolationism and interventionism. Prior to 1940, virtually all parts of the labor movement opposed U.S. involvement in a European war. During 1940 and 1941, the national CIO leadership began moving toward an interventionist position. The local CIO leadership in the Naugatuck Valley remained predominantly isolationist, in part because its Irish component did not want to go to war in support of the British empire. The American Communist Party also supported isolationism until Germany invaded Russia in June 1941, after which it became resolutely interventionist. The Mine, Mill national leadership made a similar change. The "right wing" immediately charged that the "left wing" was serving the foreign policy interests of the U.S.S.R., and that the Mine, Mill national leadership, by switching from isolationism to interventionism when Russia was attacked, revealed that it followed the "Communist Party line." The left wing, conversely, charged that the right wing was really still isolationist, while the left was made up of patriotic Americans who proved their loyalty through the sacrifices they made for the war effort.

Proper role of Communists in the labor movement. The right wing generally held the position that members of the Communist Party should not be allowed to hold office in unions, on the grounds that they were bound by loyalties which would lead them to serve interests others than those of the unions. The left wing replied that Communists had played an important role in building the unions and had acted as loyal followers of CIO policy.

Actual role of Communists. The Driscoll supporters charged that Mine, Mill was dominated, at the top, by the policies of the Communist Party. The Robinson supporters replied that the union leadership had been democratically elected by the membership, had served them loyally, and that the charges of "Communist domination" were merely means of Red-baiting by ambitious union politicians.

Militance and national defense. Both "left" and "right" claimed to represent militant unionism and simultaneously to support the national war effort and its needs for production. The left regularly attacked the right as "phonies" who were not really militant unionists. They urged all-out production for the war effort, eschewing anything that might impede production. At the same time, parts of the right attacked them for being entirely unwilling to use slowdowns, walkouts, and similar tactics to defend workers' rights, and for thus submitting to the will of the employers.

Democratic control. Each side portrayed itself as the representative of the rank and file, the other side as a leadership clique.

Local control and national solidarity. The Driscoll group, composed largely of leaders from Connecticut, maintained that they were the legitimate leaders of the brass workers' union movement and resisted efforts at domination by the national Mine, Mill leadership. Robinson and the left wingers argued that the basic strength of the workers lay in the unity of brass workers, miners, and all others who worked for the large copper corporations. They advocated industry-wide bargaining and argued that the Connecticut insurgents were destroying the unity on which industrial unionism was based and rendering the workers powerless.

Leadership. Each side presented itself as a body of skilled and dedicated trade union leaders, able to make gains for the membership and, therefore, worthy of their loyalty. Each portrayed the other as incompetent and self-serving. A great deal of the literature on each side was devoted to claims of their own collective-bargaining success and denunciation of the other side's failures.

Personalities. Individuals were charged with secret sell-outs to employers, seeking loans from employers, using union positions to evade military service, and seeking personal power and union job plums. Much of the support on each side flowed from personal loyalty to or dislike of individual leaders.

Political chicanery. Each side accused the other of using vote stealing, violence, bribery, and political wheeling and dealing.

General political orientation. Both sides claimed to operate within the general framework of good trade union practice and, more specifically, within the limits of official CIO policy. Each side accused the other of violating that framework.

Values. Each side saw the other as a threat to certain important values. The right portrayed Communism as a threat to religion, to personal liberty, to the nation, and to free enterprise. They presented its aspirations as based on unrealizable fantasies in conflict with human nature. The left claimed that the right opposed the very things that brought social progress. Its leaders identified a set of "progressive forces" in the nation and the world representing the interests of the oppressed, downtrodden, and exploited, which were struggling against privilege and reaction to make a better world; they included the Communist Party and Communist countries among these forces and viewed anti-Communism as an attempt to destroy them.

By early in 1943, the union in Connecticut had become so disrupted by the battle that the national CIO appointed an administrator to run the district. Driscoll ran for president of Mine, Mill but was defeated by Robinson. The factional fight continued until early 1947, when the Driscoll group, charging that Robinson had been reelected

COMPARE!

13 YEARS YOUNG—CIO Shipbuilders is aggressive, militant, battling for the workers every day. It fights for and wins the best working conditions.

COMMIE CONTROLLED Mine Mill is run-down, broke, conniving for the comrades. It hasn't won a decent new wage contract in our industry this year.

"We pick the FORWARD LOOKING Union—
CIO SHIPBUILDERS!"

VOTE AMERICAN • VOTE FIRST COLUMN!

SHIPBUILDERS -C.I.O.

SAIL YOUR UNION INTO CALM WATERS WITH

Progressive Metalworkers Council of the

Industrial Union of Marine & Shipbuilding Workers of America

CIO

CIO Shipbuilders election handout, circa 1947. Courtesy Western Historical Collections, University of Colorado Libraries.

by vote fraud, seceded from Mine, Mill and set up their own organization—the Provisional Metalworkers Council (later changed to Progressive Metalworkers Council, PMC). In 1947 it affiliated with the CIO Shipbuilders' union. Meanwhile, Mine, Mill and PMC battled in union meetings, referendums, and National Labor Relations Board elections for the support of Naugatuck Valley brass workers. By 1950 the PMC controlled all the brass locals in Waterbury, while Mine, Mill held those in Torrington, Thomaston, and Ansonia.

These divisions had long-term effects on Connecticut's brass workers. The PMC merged with the UAW in 1950. The locals that stayed with Mine, Mill joined the Steelworkers' union in the 1960s. Raiding continued through the 1950s and 1960s. Bitter feelings persist to this day.

Whatever the merits of the struggle, those who participated on both sides agree on its disruptive effect on the local labor movement.

John Mankowski: You were dividing your attention in trying to create the union on the one hand to fight the company, and on the other hand you have these fights in the local union, on the floor and everyplace else. Instead of spending the time to organize and strengthen your forces toward the main target, here we are dispersing

(Above and opposite) *Anti-union cartoons from the* Scovill Bulletin, *1946.*

our strength into all these other skirmishes.

Because of all of this going on, you had on the one hand to fight this political battle, on the other side you were still fighting to gain something out of these companies for our members. I'm sure that everybody would agree; if we hadn't had this type of a fight, we'd have been a hellofa power.

Russell Sobin: When we first started the union, there was Torrington, Waterbury, and us, and

we all would strike at the same time. [After secession] they had squabbles. If all American Brass plants would go out: Kenosha was AFL; we're steel in Ansonia, I don't know what Detroit is; I think there are four different unions. Different factories have different unions. Everybody wanted to get their finger into the pie and get those union dues. I always thought that one big union would have been perfect.

Employers were not unwilling to take advantage of intra-union conflict. Courtesy Scovill, Inc.

14. The Industrial Unions at the Acme of Their Power: "The Process of Brotherhood Was Exemplified, Because There Was a Basic Need"

Born in Waterbury in 1928, Tony Gerace's first introduction to the labor movement came not at work, but at church. "I was under the influence of Father Joseph Donnelly [see page 173], who I was an altar boy under at St. Thomas Parish in Waterbury. During my grammar school days, he approached me one time and said I ought to go into labor law. Father Donnelly was a very dynamic person. He was a very stern disciplinarian. He emphasized the basic human values of respect and dignity. It had a tremendous impact on my life. He was constantly fighting for a cause. I was a member of an organization known as the St. Thomas Boys Brigade that he instituted in the parish. It was a marching unit, a drum unit. He had us engaged constantly in competitions throughout the state." Tony started working at Chase in 1944 when he was sixteen years old. After a stint in the Marines, he returned to Chase.

His reputation was such that, in a
sharply divided union local, he was
repeatedly called on as someone all
parties could trust to serve as election chairman. After Chase closed,
he went to work at the Vickers'
machine shop, and then at the Miller Co., a small brass plant. He became head of the union there, and
later was elected president of UAW
Amalgamated Local 1251. He is
currently a UAW international representative. Whenever there is a
strike in Waterbury, whether of
brass workers or nurses, Tony
Gerace is likely to be found putting in his time on the picket line.

When Tony Gerace came back
from World War II and went to
work at the Waterbury Mfg. Co. of
Chase Brass, he found a lively
union presence.

Tony Gerace: In those days, one
person's cause was everyone's
cause. If one person was wronged
in one department, he was not isolated; the entire union knew about
it. We rallied around to assist each
other. I can recall going to union
meetings where the hall was always
overflowing. We used to make it a
point to get there early, so we'd get
a seat.

   I drove a tow motor, and I got
around the plant with ease. We
worked very diligently with other
groups who had needs. We banded
together, for example, in refusing
to work overtime, because someone had a cause or they were de-

*Pickets in front of the Waterbury Mfg. Co., 1946, part of a wave of postwar strikes.
Courtesy Waterbury* Republican-American.

nied something. The process of brotherhood, really, was exemplified, because there was a basic need in those days. There wasn't the sophistication there is today; it was almost starting out brand new.

Everyone was more informed of what was going on, because everyone really cared about what was going on. There were so many new areas to conquer that, if we didn't have the solidarity, we could never have achieved.

A primary union goal was to address the needs of workers and their families outside the work place.

Helen Johnson: We took a big role [in politics]. Of course, we were mostly Democratic Party. If some of our members wanted to run on independent tickets, we would support them. We used to get our people out; we used to provide cars and drivers and work in the polls.

[The independents] never got a whole slate, but once in a while we could slide in somebody.

When the legislature was in session, we used to go up one day a week. We were briefed on the bills that were coming up. We knew what we were talking about; we could tackle any of the legislators we wanted. We went in and actively lobbied. Got onto the floor, when we were able.

Now they've changed that. You're not getting the people. We had better participation. With

more participation, you broaden your scope. We used to [organize politically] by locals. Your local had more to say.

I liked the opportunity to help people. Even outside of work. If they had trouble at home, illness, separations, a child that's retarded—you were able to steer them and get some help and use the agencies which we were all supporting through the payroll plan. I really liked that; you really felt as though you were doing something. Make them realize the union wasn't just for collecting your dues and to heck with you. That was good, although I liked a good fight myself, too.

I remember a big parade on meat. The meat was going out of sight. I don't remember how it started. Right in the middle of the war.

Most of your people in the shops came from another country; they went to work, they worked long hours, they went to school long enough to get their citizenship papers. If they were lucky, they had a little plot of ground. So they had no hobbies. All they knew was work, eat and, sleep. You'd say: As of such and such a date, you're retired—that used to kill them. You'd go down to the Green and see these men sitting there—you'd want to cry. They were helpless. At home they were in their wives' way; it started trouble at home. I kept saying: You've got to teach them, so they'll know what to ex-

pect so they can plan. And we have to have centers, we have to have somewhere for those people to go.

At that time, every month the entire executive board of the [union] council met, so we knew what was going on in other shops. We were more of a cohesive group. A few of us decided: Let's see what we can do about getting some place for these people. We started going around to the agencies. Everybody thought it was a good idea, but no help at all.

I used to go down to Duggan School on Wednesdays, run movies, we'd play bingo and things like that. They looked forward to it. Now we have quite a few [centers]. We were all busy and tired all the time, but we always found time to do things for other people. It's a good feeling.

I've made a lot of friends through the labor movement. A lot of hard work, but I learned a lot, too.

Tony Gerace: Getting the company to buy sickness and accident benefits [was important]. I, for one, was never able to purchase sickness and accident benefits. For me and my family, it became very important to have that protection.

First and foremost was the establishment of the company-paid pension plan. In the late 1940s and early 1950s, that was the rallying cry. That certainly added some sense of dignity and security to employees who otherwise were

UAW regional summer school at the University of Connecticut, 1956. Bobby Lombardo, now president of UAW Local 1078, is in the dark shirt in the foreground. Art Finelli is standing third from left in the back row. Courtesy Art Finelli.

forced to work when they were unable to work, because they had absolutely nothing to fall back on.

At the same time, workers struggled to get some degree of control over conditions of daily life at work.

Tony Gerace: After the war, overtime was not as accessible as during the war years. That was always a constant fight. In my department we finally were able to achieve equalization, where the union and the company both worked on scheduling together. There was a board set up in our locker room charging hours to the employees who had worked. The system allowed everyone to get an equal, fair share of the available overtime.

Workers tried to gain a degree of power, not only through collective bargaining, but also through direct action on the job.

Eddie Labacz: We had a wildcat, second shift in the wire mill. They had a boss who came out of the guard force. Every time a guy would do something, he would write in a little black book. So the whole second shift sat down. The company said: We can't get rid of the whole second shift. So they transferred the boss out and brought in another foreman who wasn't keeping a little black book of what everybody was doing. It was just a sitdown. Everybody said: "We're just going to sit here; either fire us all or get rid of him." So they got rid of him. 1956, 1957. You do that now and you'd be hung off the rafter by the government. I think it lasted about five hours.

Tony Gerace: One department had a problem. Since we were the transportation department, they would say: Gee, fellows, we'd appreciate it [if you would join our refusal of overtime]. We'd go along with them. The next time around, we may have had a need and they would help us.

The brass plants were known for their own style of unionism. Gerace, who worked in the manufacturing and mill departments at Chase, as well as the Vickers' machine shop and the small Miller Co., describes their differences.

Tony Gerace: [What gave the brass mills a special quality was] the solidarity. The determination of the people; they're a more determined group. Their vocal exhortations of the leadership. I can immediately tell if they're in a brass plant, by virtue of their tradition. Everybody speaks out, everybody jumps up. They're determined. If you say to them, "Fellows, we need this," if you convince them, you've got it. They'll stick right with you.

There's not that namby-pamby situation. You'll find this in any mill. American Brass. Century. They'll tell you the same thing. It's accepted: If you come from the mills, you're a fighter, you're a different kind of person.

In the early period, management resistance to the unions was often intense. As time went on, however, accommmodations were generally reached.

Tony Gerace: The first week I went to work, there was a floorlady who used to display an anti-union button on her posterior. There were conflicts between line supervisors and the workers almost daily. Charges, innuendoes about belonging to a union. That improved drastically as time went on and supervision began to get a little more sophisticated. By the mid-1950s, they were more in line to accept that we were here to stay.

Some workers, especially those who had been with the companies for many years, objected to being required to join a union.

John Hollingworth: In the Brass Goods, around 1952, they decided to have a closed shop. So the union man came to me and said, "You'll have to join the union." The superintendent found out about it and came down and put me in the engineering department. I was always grateful to the superintendent for doing that.

The unions made at least a token effort to address the problem of racism.

Lea Harvey: In about 1950 the national union (UAW-CIO) made an FEPC committee. They formed this committee in our local union, too. I was honored when I was asked to be the secretary of that group.

I worked with that committee for several years. Of course we never did anything, never really accomplished anything to my knowledge.

In 1952 the union sent me as a delegate to a convention in Chicago. They sent nine men and myself. This was a mobilization of unions and the NAACP. I got to meet Walter Reuther and had a picture taken with him. I met many people who held high positions in the union, some of whom I remained friendly with over the years. My union also sent me, its first woman, to union school at the University of Connecticut for one week, which was very beneficial to me.

Black workers used unions as a vehicle for their struggle for racial justice, but they also had to fight for justice within the unions.

John Gatison: I went on as the chief steward in my department in 1946. To get recognition by the supervisors, I had to fight. We had a few of the people in management that swore they were not going to

recognize me. For two reasons: my color number one and, secondly, they didn't like doing business with a union leader anyways.

The foreman had provoked me by telling me that no union steward is going to tell him that he has to change a decision that he made. Whether it is a violation of the contract or not, his law is law. I told him, "Please don't tell me that again, because if you do, and if you keep that attitude, then we're going to settle it one way or another once and for all." A few days later he did, and I said, "That's it; let's go."

I got the personnel director down who handled labor relations. I demanded that he tell me personally, in front of everybody, that he will not tell me again that he's not going to cooperate with the union.

I said: "I'm going to tell you what I'm going to do. I'm getting pushed around, being misused, and I'm just sick of it. I'm not leaving here. If we leave here tonight without me getting what I want, tomorrow morning, you can bet your bottom dollar, we will have plenty here waiting for you. And it won't be the labor leaders, either." That's when they called a recess. They knew who I meant. I said, "If you think that I'm just threatening you, just try me."

In about ten minutes they were back and they told me.

I believe that decision paved the way for respectability. From then on I let them know that this is the way I operate. I'm not going to give up. I don't use violence. I don't use vulgarity. I don't think it's necessary. I can use force in my way when necessary. I believe in insisting that you respect me. And I will always give you my respect. I believe in endurance.

Outside of the mill, within the labor movement: I've been in many state and national conventions. The International always had civil rights committees, and we always had the right to meet on a state level and on a national level. We got many things beneficial to us on civil rights in our contracts. But if you didn't have people to uphold those good things in the contract, then it was meaningless. This is where I felt the worst. This is one of the things I did not achieve: the participation of Blacks in the labor movement as deep and as large as I had hoped.

The reason is that there was never encouragement from the labor leaders to actively participate. They thought that if you had too large a number of Blacks participating there would be less for them to handle. Somebody like me would be the one to try to encourage them. We succeeded on a small scale, but far below the number of Blacks participating we had hoped to get.

Within the unions, a gap could easily develop between the leadership and the rank and file. A union leadership that sought an accommodation with management still had to deal with its own rank and file.

Frank Pochron: The union/management thing is a pretty tricky proposition. I remember one time they were negotiating. They were going past their strike deadline. They were going around the clock. Later I found out the union was ready to agree something like a couple of weeks before the deadline. The company negotiator at that time stated: "Don't do that now, because your membership is going to say you didn't fight hard enough. Stick to the last minute. You have to put on this big act to have the membership stick behind you." So the union stayed there down to the wire.

Nonetheless, the brass unions were marked by widespread, active participation well into the 1950s.

Tony Gerace: So many people were involved. It isn't like today, where there are just a few really dedicated people that are doing the job and the rest just go about their daily work. There, everybody was involved. We had veterans' committees, a union label committee. One of the biggest thrills back in the early days at Chase was if you got selected to be put on a committee. You felt that you were recognized. There was never anybody lacking in any office; it was a fight to get onto an office. "Hey, I got chosen to be on union label com-

mittee!" You had a sense of satisfaction. Everybody wanted to participate, while today they're reluctant.

The key thing in those days, I believe, was the time that people gave outside of the work place. It was not unusual that every day of the week there was something down at the union hall after the shift.

It was very common to stop in at the union hall. It was a meeting place where people used to gather, which you don't see today.

I believe it's apathy. Also, society in general. The close-knit neighborhood or the close-knit family or the church organization or the fraternal organization—that was the place to go. Today, people in this hectic society have so many other things to do that they find it an obligation to go to some of these things. We have to exhort people to go to union meetings. If we need a quorum, we have to get on the phone and say: We have a very important thing, we must have a quorum; you must be here. In those days, if you didn't get there early, you stood up at the meeting. Everybody was interested in the movement.

THE SCOVILL STRIKE
OF 1952

The final solidification of union power in the brass plants and the community came with the Scovill strike of 1952. Although union

Mine, Mill Local 445 in the late 1940s. Among those pictured are Mike Laban (at table, on right) and John Gatison (three rows behind Laban). Courtesy Mike Laban.

recognition had been won at the Scovill Mfg. Co., the area's largest employer, during World War II, the union had remained weak throughout the 1940s. This weakness resulted both from the factional struggles that divided the union and from the deliberate policy of management to accept unionism but to keep it ineffectual. Vice-President Alan Curtiss, chief of Scovill labor relations, spelled out his approach in a speech to managers in 1944:

"Many negotiators enter negotiations with the attitude, 'What will I have to give the union this time?' Rather the attitude should be, 'How can I negotiate a better contract from the company's standpoint?' By this I do not mean a contract unfair to the employees and their representatives. After living with a written contract, I believe it better to have one than to be without one.

"Management should enter negotiation for a contract with the definite policy that it will not give away or dilute management's rights. Of course, many companies have already given veto power on certain matters. In such cases management should try to regain full control of its rights. Management should have no hesitation in proposing at the end of the contract year amendments which will strengthen its position.

"As an example of the effort of unions to get a veto power on a management function, I cite the following.

"An existing contract had a clause concerning work shifts:

Signing the contract that settled the 1946 Scovill strike. Bill Moriarty, Ovide Garceau, and John Mankowski are sitting at the extreme left. Alan Curtiss, vice-president for employee relations, is sitting sixth from the left.

'The setting of the time of work shifts is a function of management. The Union will be consulted before shift schedules are changed.'

"In the amendments proposed by the Union was the following clause: 'Any change in a regularly scheduled work shift shall be mutually agreed to by the company and the Union before going into effect.' This obviously would tie the Company's hands in a very vital matter.

"I hold that a strong management clause is a very important part of a contract. A contract should be educational, as well as an agreement on various points involving wages, hours, and working conditions. I believe the following management clause a definite asset:

"'The management of the operations, the manning of the plant, the direction of the working forces, and the maintenance and develop-ment of plant and worker efficiency are vested solely in the Company. Unless specifically set forth in this Agreement, there shall be no abridgement or diminution of any authority, right or responsibility of the Company necessary to further these functions."*

*Alan C. Curtiss, "How to Negotiate a Labor Contract and Make It Work," unpublished paper in Scovill collection, Baker Library.

The weakness of the union at Scovill was apparent to all.

Frank Keane: [When I went to work at Scovill,] there was a steward, but nothing to bother anyone about. He probably was dominated by the company at that time. It wasn't very strong.

Scovill had long been considered a good place to work, but that reputation gradually deteriorated. Sid Monti eventually became head of the Scovill local.

Sid Monti: When I went back in wartime, anything goes. The bigger you goofed off, the better they liked it. Because they were working on cost-plus in most cases. So they didn't give a damn.

After the war was over, they started putting the pressure on, like they did in the old days. Grievances going unresponded to. Unfairly handling the problems of the people. Generally just being anti-union and anti-people.

Monti explains some of the problems that led to a major strike in 1952.

Sid Monti: At some time or another, everybody in Waterbury had at least one member of their family working in Scovill's. They were the largest employer in town. Such a resentment had been built up against that company.

In negotiations, I used to turn to our guys and say, "What's the cheapest commodity this company has?" They'd say, "What do you mean, commodity?" I'd say: "What's the cheapest thing they have? A piece of machinery? A roof over their head? A piece of equipment to work with? A ton of steel? Copper and brass? The cheapest commodity is you. If you get killed, all they have to do is pick up a phone, call up the employment agency, and say 'Send me a guy.' It doesn't cost them a nickel. But if a piece of equipment goes on the bum, they have to spend money to fix it. So they think more of that piece of equipment than they do of you."

Then I'd turn to Curtiss and I'd say, "I think more of the little fingernail of our guys than I do of your whole goddamn company and all its money."

The issues were manifold. We were probably the lowest-paid brass plant in the country, on any job. Grievances were manifold. They were a very big issue. We also wanted life insurance improvements. Night shift differential was a big thing.

The sickness and accident benefit was the lowest in the industry. I think we were getting twenty-five or thirty bucks a week.

[Before 1952] the contract gave the company the right to re-study the job if they made a change which was 5 percent or more of the entire cycle. They'd always find a way to get 5 percent. So they'd make the woman make two steps, for example, and that would take five seconds off the total cycle time, if the total cycle time was twenty-two seconds. They restudied every job. In fact, we were doing more work for even less money, in spite of a wage increase.

One of the major issues at Scovill [in 1952] was a funded pension plan. You want a pension plan which will not be based on payments by the company each year out of the cash drawer, so to speak, but will be set up on an actuarially sound, funded basis. That was the strong UAW policy.

On June 21, 1952, thousands of Scovill workers—only a small minority of them members of the union—walked off their jobs in the most serious strike in the brass industry since 1920. The strike took on many of the aspects of a community struggle.

Sid Monti: The Scovill strike I'm very, very proud of. We didn't have a union shop. We had maybe 600 or 700 dues-paying members, and there were about 7,000 or 8,000 people in the plant. I was holding my breath: I didn't know how many people would cross that line.

The thing that I liked about the strike was the cohesiveness of the people. They felt that they had to be together, not from a trade union philosophy, but from the standpoint: Look, they beat our brains

Sid Monti arrested on July 11, during the 1952 Scovill strike. Courtesy Waterbury Republican-American.

in; now it's our turn to get even.

Everybody was with us. We had no problem getting pickets. If we ever ran short, we'd call up one of the locals and they'd send 100 people down as quickly as you could say "shift."

It was a real testing ground. All the people really worked their butts off.

There was a lot of help from the UAW. The strike may have collapsed if it wasn't for the UAW strike benefits. When we called it, we didn't think we were going to get benefits; we didn't think we were entitled to them because we'd only been with them less than a year. But there was never any question.

At one meeting we had to rope off four square blocks downtown; no traffic could even move.

We had complete cooperation from the railroad workers. Nobody'd come through. We'd put up one picket, or just a stick with a sign on it, at the crossing where they came into the company property. They'd bring it up to that stick and that was the end of it. They'd all climb off the engine.

Grace Cummings: That was when I learned to like spaghetti with butter. That's without the sauce.

They stocked up the warehouses, they had people working overtime—they prepared for the strike. When the strike happened, my husband was working there. The work started running short,

and the customers started yelling about orders; that was the only reason they settled. Their intention, as I understood it from my husband and guys I talked to, was that they just wanted to break the union. They figured a good, long strike would do that. The union had just gotten strong, but they could break it. If they broke it, people wouldn't be interested. If they lost the strike, got no benefits after being out all this time, all this money lost, mortgage payment, people lost cars for nonpayment of bills, they would have no faith in it. But in this case it worked in reverse. The union got stronger.

My husband was afraid to be out because he was going to get fired. He just knew. The company was saying: If you stay out, you're going to get fired. They had a whole bunch of scare tactics. He was petrified, I'm not going to have a job. One of the things [in the settlement] was no reprisals against the strikers.

Helen Johnson: That was where you learned things in a hurry, about your agencies and about your antiquated state laws, too. We set up strike committees. The UAW patterned some of the things we set up here in Waterbury into their national program.

I'd come about 5:30 in the morning on the picket line. I was a roving picket captain; wherever you're needed, you go. After that I'd go home, change my clothes,

come back down, and we'd have the people come in that needed help. In the afternoons, I'd go calling on people that were ill. At nighttime we did our dirty tricks. We had to do some of that; we had to get back at them some way.

I did more walking. We'd get word someone was going in or we'd see them. We'd take off and follow them all around. They'd try to lose you, so they could sneak in some gate. You got threatened. The guards at Scovill's were really with us, but they couldn't do anything.

Mike Vernovai was born in 1913 in Millinocket, Maine, home of the Great Northern Paper Co., the largest paper mill of its kind under one roof. His parents had come from Italy. "I didn't appreciate being a captive of a one-company town," and so he came to Water-

Pickets at Scovill's Hayden St. gate, Scovill Co., July 11, 1952. Courtesy Waterbury Republican-American.

bury in 1937. A tool- and die-maker, he was made union chairman of the Oakville Pin shop of the Scovill Mfg. Co. on the first day of the big strike in 1952. In the early 1950s he was active in the UAW International Skilled Trades Council; from 1954 to 1968 he was chairman of the Region 9-A Skilled Trades Council; he was a charter member of the UAW International Skilled Trades Advisory Council, and was its chairman from 1963 to 1968. He went on the staff of the UAW international in 1968 and was assigned to the Conservation and Recreation Department. In 1970 he was transferred to the servicing staff of Region 9-A. He was assistant director of Region 9-A from 1975 to 1978, when he retired. He currently heads the retirees' chapter of UAW 1251 in Waterbury.

Mike Vernovai got involved in politics in Watertown, just north of Waterbury, in the early 1950s. He helped build the Democratic party from a minority of perhaps 10 percent to a plurality of 500. He was elected to the Watertown School Board in 1957 for a six-year term. In 1958 he became the first Democratic representative from Watertown to the state legislature in fifty years. He served two terms in the Connecticut House of Representatives, where he was chairman of the subcommittee on workmen's compensation. He has been chairman of the Watertown Democratic party since 1964.

After more than four months, the strike was finally settled.

Mike Vernovai: Fourteen of us got fired [at Oakville Pin, then a subsidiary of Scovill]. We were rocking a car back and forth. The boss wouldn't let his brother out of the car. We said we'd let the boss in; we wouldn't let his brother in.

[At the end of the strike,] Scovill had settled. It was on a Sunday night. Then the company met with us at the Elton Hotel, and we finally came to a settlement. In the meantime, Sid Monti had sent his boiler room guys in to get the boilers ready for Monday morning. All of a sudden, I thought about the fourteen guys. It wasn't all guys; there were some girls, too. I said, "Wait a minute. The fourteen guys are called back?" "Oh, no," Mr. Leavenworth said, "No way." I said, "O.K., that's it; there's no agreement."

I called Sid Monti and told him about it. Sid got on the phone, called the boiler room, and called the boiler room guys out. Two hours later, we were back in the hotel. We sat down and settled the whole thing. The fourteen people were taken back; all suits were withdrawn. I was being sued for a million dollars at that time. So was the international union. I told them it was a good thing they didn't sue me for any more because I wouldn't be able to afford it.

The gains were substantial. We asked what was different after the strike.

King David Holmes: Recognition. Foremen would understand people had a right to question. They beefed up their time-study department to give answers and process grievances. We had a good stewardship.

Sid Monti: [In the 1952 strike,] we built a union, and for the next years they really functioned like a good trade union in all aspects: trade unionism, community activities, political action. On almost every level, we had good guys and good committees going out and doing the work that was necessary.

Immediately following the strike, we had some twenty-one arbitration cases. We had grievances coming out of our ears—we had 500 or 600 piled up. I think we won twenty-one or twenty-two straight arbitration cases. The result was that we commanded a lot of respect.

We were the first ones to get five-dollars-a-month pensions in the brass industry, although they had already gotten them in auto and steel. That was a result of the 1952 strike.

Grace Cummings: After that, there were always scraps. I think people got brave. They started making demands. They started asking for safety things. When my husband worked there, I think it was 1956, they made a demand for safety goggles and safety glasses. He wore glasses; they were always getting broken, and they never even paid for them. Then they started paying for the glasses; that was a big thrill. They started paying for safety equipment in Scovill's; it was a union-won thing.

Another thing the union won was a fifteen-minute break, instead of ten. This happened when my mother was in there. She said, "I'm going to take my big thermos; I can have two cups of coffee."

Perhaps most important, the union itself was transformed.

Sid Monti: Every steward had to be elected, they couldn't be appointed; that was my doctrine. So we used to have membership meetings of the departments—there were 200-odd departments. We had people coming there, giving vent to their emotions, and telling what the hell was wrong in the department. If there was a problem in the department and everyone was saying they had a grievance, we'd immediately call a meeting of that department. We want everybody to let us know what's going on. We had organizational-type meetings. We began to properly elect people to lead the department on shifts.

It is interesting to compare the Scovill strike of 1952 with the Brass Valley strike of 1920.

Both strikes were mass struggles, in which thousands of workers actively participated day after day, week after week. Both tried to use the workers' power to halt the production process as a means of forcing concessions from the employers. Both strove to win concrete demands that grew directly from the needs of workers and their families. Both tried to shift the balance of power in work place and community, so that workers, as an organized force, would have a voice in decisions that affected them. And despite the fact that the 1952 strike affected only one company, it—like the 1920 strike— was a community-wide struggle, drawing support from workers at many other work places, and was seen by both sides as a test of the future role of unionism in the Valley.

The legal context of the two strikes was markedly different. In 1920 police and National Guard functioned as direct agents for breaking the strike, beating pickets, disrupting meetings, and conducting a virtual reign of terror against the strikers. In 1952 there was a substantial police presence, but workers were allowed to meet and picket. The company went to court, however, and secured an injunction which forbade mass picketing at the plant. In contrast to 1920, the workers generally accepted, however unhappily, the limits set by the "forces of law and order"; there were no riots in 1952. Class conflict had been directed, to some extent, from quasi-military to legal channels.

In 1920 the manufacturers had simply refused to meet with union representatives. By 1952, the employer was legally required to meet with the elected representatives of his workers. The union already had a contract and an ongoing relationship with the company, albeit one in which the company was by far the dominant partner.

The type of worker organization involved was very different. In 1920 the most important group was a local organization with different sections for each of the principal nationalities; there was also a union of laborers affiliated with the AFL and a union of skilled workers, the IAM. In 1952 there was one industrial union, the UAW, representing all industrial workers in the plant, to which hundreds of thousands of workers in other metalworking industries throughout the country belonged.

In 1920 the workers were defeated. They returned to the shops, unorganized and demoralized. In 1952 workers returned to work with many significant concessions from the employer. Most significant, workers were able to establish themselves, within the plants and the community, as an organized counterpower to management.

PART IV

Mid-Century to 1980: The Era of Brass Industry Decline

The U.S. economy since World War II has been marked by two contradictory trends. On the one hand, there was a sustained period of economic growth and prosperity, based in part on American domination of a devastated world economy. Yet there were also the problems of economic stagnation, growing international competition, and declining industries, which grew increasingly severe through the 1970s. Naugatuck Valley brass workers experienced the effects of both these trends.

The years following World War II were generally ones of economic advancement for American workers. Owning automobiles, many were able to move beyond the confines of the "walking city" to live in new suburban areas. Ethnic traditions remained, but became less important, especially as more and more young people married outside their ethnic group.

Starting in the 1950s, many factors, including the mechanization of southern agriculture, generated a new migration of Blacks from the South to northern industrial areas, including the Brass Valley. They were followed, in the 1960s, by a new immigration from such traditional sources as Italy and Portugal and, increasingly, from Puerto Rico and other parts of Latin America.

The brass industry, however, was unable to provide employment for the new migrants as it had for the old. First, the introduction of automation had steadily reduced the number of jobs, especially at entry level. Then, reflecting a process now widely seen throughout the northeastern United States, the brass industry itself began to decline. Competing materials, such as plastics and aluminum, reduced the market for brass. The large corporate owners, with little commitment to the local economy, allowed their plants to run down and become antiquated. The brass companies reinvested their profits in other regions and other industries. Unemployment in Waterbury reached 15 percent in the later 1970s. By 1980 only a handful of brass plants remained in operation, each employing a few dozen or hundred workers where once there had been thousands.

Their numbers and economic power decreasing, workers in the brass industry have also seen the power of their community organizations and unions decline. They have been forced to take wage cuts and to give up the improved working conditions that they had won in earlier struggles. The problems of their industry have been compounded by the more general problems of the American economy in the 1970s and early 1980s.

TABLE 22

Family Income in Waterbury, 1949

Income level*	Number of families
Families (aggregate)	27,315
Under $500	1,420
$500–999	770
$1,000–1,499	1,060
$1,500–1,999	1,220
$2,000–2,499	2,130
$2,500–2,999	2,980
$3,000–3,499	3,645
$3,500–3,999	2,450
$4,000–4,449	2,280
$4,500–4,999	1,655
$5,000–5,999	2,640
$6,000–6,999	1,410
$7,000–9,999	1,600
$10,000 and over	770

* Median income, $3,700.
Source: Compiled from U.S. Census data by Peter Rachleff.

TABLE 23

The Waterbury SMSA Metal Workforce, 1930–1960

Occupation	1930	1950	1960
Blacksmiths, forgemen	111	91	187
Filers, grinders, buffers, and polishers	411	517	367
Furnacemen	32	302	138
Machinists, millwrights, and toolmakers	2,667	2,687	2,526
Molders, founders, and casters	318	172	130
Rollers and roll hands	276	337	195
Male operatives:			
Iron and steel	513	187	53
Other metals	2,264	3,247	2,804
Female operatives:			
Iron and steel	215	54	12
Other metals	1,514	1,377	987
Male laborers:			
Iron and steel	303	63	20
Other metals	2,146	697	449
Female laborers:			
Iron and steel	17	2	0
Other metals	109	29	43

Source: Compiled from U.S. Census data by Peter Rachleff.

THE PEOPLE

1. The Newest Immigrants: Minority Workers

Starting in the 1950s, large numbers of Blacks again began to migrate from the South into northern industrial areas, including the Naugatuck Valley. There was also a new migration from Puerto Rico.

The newcomers faced many of the same problems as previous immigrants; they were forced to enter the work place at the lowest rung, to live in ghettoes, and to develop the skills necessary for work and life in an urban, industrial area.

The new migrants faced two additional obstacles, however. First, they arrived at a time when industrial employment was stagnating and entry-level jobs in industry

TABLE 24

The Occupational Structure of the Black Community in Waterbury, 1960

Occupation	No. of wage-earners		
	Men	Women	Total
All employed (total)	1,375	856	2,231
Professional and technical workers	39	42	81
Managers and officials	16	0	16
Clerical workers	35	39	74
Sales workers	14	16	30
Craftsmen and foremen	306	7	313
Operatives	611	422	1,033
Domestic servants (private households)	12	190	202
Service workers	131	109	240
Laborers	211	31	242
Unemployed	n.a.	n.a.	388

Source: Compiled from U.S. Census data by Peter Rachleff.

TABLE 25

Black Family Income in Waterbury, 1950

Income level*	Number of families
Families (total)	339
Under $1,000	50
$1,000–1,999	43
$2,000–2,999	59
$3,000–3,999	39
$4,000–4,999	35
$5,000–5,999	42
$6,000–6,999	33
$7,000–7,999	12
$8,000–8,999	4
$9,000–9,999	8
$10,000 and over	14

* Median income, $3,449.
Source: Compiled from U.S. Census data by Peter Rachleff.

were actually decreasing. As a result, they did not benefit from the tremendous demand for their labor that earlier immigrants had experienced. Instead, many of them were condemned to extended unemployment and lower-paid, nonindustrial jobs.

Second, they faced the traditional barriers of racial discrimination. Unlike the European immigrants, most of them differed from the dominant population, not only by language and lifestyle, which they could change, but also by skin color, which they could not. Black people met racial discrimination in employment, education, housing, and other spheres of life.

Hyotha Hofler: [The migration of the 1950s and 1960s] was more from places like Alabama and Mississippi. The jobs the migrants would have done had been automated. There was a fast track for people already living here working in those particular jobs. Because of [the decline of brass industry employment, the newcomers were] not succeeding in finding new opportunities or other means. Not to say that all the people who came didn't find jobs. I know a few people who came up during that time who did manage to work at Scovill or Chase.

[The people who came up were] sharecroppers mostly. A lot of Blacks coming up from Louisiana at that time were Catholics. You get the inroads of Blacks into the Catholic church at that time. That

The Goodwill Lodge of Elks, Waterbury, 1956. Courtesy Grace Cummings.

A mural on a wall of the Goodwill Lodge of Elks building, Waterbury, 1981. Photo: Jerry Lombardi.

migration began tapering off around the Kennedy era.

You hear stories of immigrants coming from Italy; they look down at the newer ones: "They're just off the boat." It's the same thing: Just off the farm, country girl or country boy. There were new people coming from Alabama and Mississippi. People would tease them. They had a much different accent than people from the rest of the South, much harder to understand from a northern point of view.

I would say that 60 percent [of the current Black population of Waterbury] came in the 1950s, if not more. More Blacks living in Waterbury now were born here than migrated here, but [a large proportion were kids of the 1950s' and 1960s' migration.] People coming in the 1950s are now grandparents.

The biggest stumbling block to the later migration was the lack of work. The brass factories really just collapsed here, and related industries just collapsed. The clock industry collapsed. So there is no source of income.

[Organizations created by the 1950s' migration include] the Elks Club on Cherry Street, the Dukes Club, and Alpha Omega Psi, a Black fraternity of the elder sons and daughters of the generation who came up during the 1950s and who got into U. Conn. or Yale.

There seems to have been a large number of people of that migration whose children made it to college. In earlier migrations, there hadn't been a large number to make it through college. There had been a large number of professional people, but usually they had gone to school in the South. [Funds for education came through] church scholarships established in the 1950s, and from the NAACP nationally.

The area [where Blacks lived] spread out. It reached up to Cooke Street, all of Pearl Street, Bishop Street except the northern part, to North Main, North Square, Abbot Avenue. Cherry Street to North Elm, and up to Vine Street, except the places on East Main directly. Vine Street seems to have been a center more than Bishop Street, although Bishop Street had a number of Black businesses.

Capell Bacote represents the generation of Black workers whose families came to the Naugatuck Valley in the 1950s. Born in Darlington, South Carolina, in 1954, Capell came with his family to Connecticut in the late 1950s. His grandfather and uncle worked at American Brass. The Bacote family was and continues to be very active in the church. In the early 1970s Capell's father built the Star of Bethlehem Church on Lester Street in Ansonia. Capell went to work at Anaconda in 1973 as a centerless grinder operator. In 1981, he left Anaconda to work as a foreman at his father's construction company

in New Haven. He lives in Ansonia with his wife, Maxine Young.

Capell Bacote: I was born in South Carolina. At about the age of three, my folks moved up here. I've been living here all my life since then.

[They came up] because of work. From around Darlington.

My father worked farming sometimes, hauling wood, whatever.

My father's father was already in the brass. My father's brother is there now. So I've got a family of three down there. My grandfather. His half brother, my uncle, and me. Mostly in the brass rod department. Block area.

[My family was active] in the Star of Bethlehem church. My wife and I are members of it now, my mother and my sisters. My father built most of the church himself. He worked till 5 at night on

his job, then he'd go straight down there and work for four or five hours at night. Every Saturday he'd work down there. It took him a few years to complete it. There were about three who worked on it steadily. I'd give them a hand every once in a while.

We used to go around collecting money. We had a building fund. We had donations. We'd go around ringing on doorbells. We would sell dinner sometimes. We'd have a building fund service.

There used to be a Vacation Bible School in the summertime. After school they used to have Bible study for high school kids. We help the needy whenever we can. We have services during the week. The whole body in Connecticut [gave scholarships.] My sister got a scholarship, about $500; she went to South Central.

Frieda Ewen: There weren't many Blacks in Shelton. I was really not aware of racism in high school and growing up. I can recall three Black families in Shelton. In my class I went to school with two Blacks. Both of them were very close friends of mine. I never saw that there was a problem with racism. Billy and I were real close friends; we used to talk on the phone for hours. There was never any problem that I saw with doing that. I never expected a problem.

It wasn't until I was out of high school and working in the hospital with a Black woman from Shelton.

She would talk about the racism in Shelton, and I would deny that it existed and say: "No, that's not true in Shelton; in Shelton there wasn't any racism. There were Black people there and everyone liked them; they were everyone's friends. The class in back of mine had only one Black person, and he was president of the class."

She said to me, "Of course, everyone knew them and liked them; they were a novelty." It was true. She made me start thinking about it. Plus some of the other Black workers at the hospital sat me down and taught me the facts about it, in a good way, realizing my naiveness about it.

Then I started to talk more openly about it with people in the community, people I'd gone to high school with, and found that there was a very strong feeling of racism there and that there was a very strong Klan movement there, that it was the center for a lot of Klan activity on the East Coast. It was in the early 1970s that I found out about it, but I'm sure it had been there before because these were kids that I had gone to high school with and I'm sure they didn't start it.

I became aware of it and it was everywhere. It was the police department, the politicians—it was just there, very blatantly, but still covered up.

It was in people's attitudes, the things they said. I had a friend in high school and many years be-

yond. There was one grandparent on each side of her family who was Black. I never thought anything about it. After high school I got a few comments about that. There was one incident where I was dating a guy and fixed up his friend with her. They had a good time, he liked her and called her back again and talked to her. Then someone told him that she was part Black. He came to me very angry and upset and asked me if that's what I had done to him. I just couldn't believe it. I said, "So what, who are you? Are you something great that somebody should worry what their background is to please you?"

Many Blacks have told me that they are literally afraid to go into Shelton.

Racism was deeply ingrained in the white community.

John Yrchik: I remember as a kid the incredible racism that was displayed by all the whites, no matter what ethnic origin, toward Blacks. When there was a Supreme Court ruling that you couldn't discriminate against someone on the basis of color, everyone was talking about how they would never sell their house to a Black person. Or they would never rent a house to a Black person.

I think that's related to the tremendous amount of de-skilling that was going on at that time. Blacks, along with women, were being incorporated in the labor

force in ever-increasing numbers and occupying the same status as whites in the labor force.

What it did was reinforce racism outside the work place that had no basis in the work place. Side by side whites and Blacks would work together. But when they got out of work, they all went to their separate communities. They were each taught that the other was somehow very different.

Seymour is a very white town. Ansonia is not so white. You have to this day in those towns predominantly white and Black sections. We have one Black family that lives up the street here. But when I went to school, there was not one Black kid in the entire grammar school or junior high school I went to.

At lunchtime [in the plant] all the Blacks would eat together and all the whites would eat together. It was like there were two different clubs, the white club and the Black club. You wouldn't see that on the job until lunchtime. Everything that had to do with leisure, free time, was segregated. Production itself wasn't.

William Freeman is a poet and fiction writer who was born and grew up in Waterbury. His first published poem appeared in the Crosby High School newspaper. His work has since appeared in *Greenfield Review, Westbere Review, Obsidian*, and other small press magazines, as well as in the

1981 *Anthology of Magazine Verse and Yearbook of American Poetry*. His father came to Waterbury from Pittsboro, North Carolina in the 1940s; his mother's family has been in Waterbury for several generations. After high school, he worked in the brass mill at Scovill's while studying data processing in New Haven. Later he worked in the data processing department at Scovill's. He has lived, among other places, in Alaska and London, and has held a variety of jobs while completing two unpublished novels. He currently lives with his family in Waterbury. He recently completed a poetry collection about Connecticut under a grant from the Connecticut Commission on the Arts, and is currently working on a novel based on Waterbury history. William Freeman is the nephew of Russell Hunter, who is introduced on page 63.

William Freeman: I had a lot of white friends while I was going to grammar school. But as we became older and were moving more into a larger world, they tended to fit into the cliques that were more or less white cliques; Black kids fitted into Black cliques. They were based more on color and on what you were studying.

I grew up on Orange Street; we lived until I was seven on Vine Street, right around the block. The neighborhood was Polish, Black, Italian. Everyone there were children of factory workers; it was a factory worker community.

Orange Street stayed pretty racially balanced until the 1960s, when we had civil disturbances. Then most of the whites left Orange Street. Various parts of Orange Street became predominantly Black.

I don't think I was aware of racism until I moved into the work world. I was at home in the Black community. It never was anything other than the Black community, until high school and looking for a job.

Racial conflict also occurs occasionally in the schools.

Capell Bacote: At the high school. I was there one time. A Black guy and a white guy got in a fight. Then all the Blacks got on this side and all the whites got on that side. They had to call the cops. Ever since then, it's been getting worse and worse. Especially at the high school. [The papers] blow it out of proportion. It's two or three kids, maybe a dozen. Stereotyping. It is getting worse at the high school; that's why my sister didn't go up there. Racial things, there's more fighting, more intimidation. It's not only the high school, it's getting worse everywhere. People just trying to dominate everybody else, trying to be Mr. Bigstuff.

Blacks have conducted a continuing struggle against racial discrimination and prejudice.

John Gatison: The first major incident in the Valley happened in Derby, which ultimately was the reason for the formation of the NAACP in the Valley. A young man was accused of raping a white girl. He swore to everybody that he did not do it. Since they figured they had enough evidence to prove his innocence, they banded themselves together and said: This is not going to happen to one of ours when we know he's innocent. It was in 1943 or 1944. The formation of the branch in the Valley took shape in 1944. That was the beginning of the major racial issue in the Valley. He was eventually set free—the NAACP won the case.

In the 1950s we got involved in getting the younger girls and boys an opportunity to be store clerks. After that we went into the hiring practices in the Valley, in indus-

NAACP youth center, Cherry St., Waterbury, 1982. Photo: Jerry Lombardi.

try, on the blue-collar level. We achieved many things along those lines. Then we got into discrimination in places such as the YMCA. You were allowed to participate in certain activities, but you were not allowed to become a member. We took issue with that one. They played a little tough on that one for a while, and then they threw in the sponge.

We followed the same line as the NAACP has always followed. We are taught to always try to resolve whatever problem we can without a lot of fanfare. We're not looking for a lot of publicity; we're not looking to make a big fuss out of something. If we can resolve it without going into all of that, then we do it. However, if we cannot resolve it through peaceful means, then we keep on moving. If it has to get nasty to get what what we know are our rights, then this is what we do. We do whatever is necessary.

There was no such thing as a Black worker in industry doing office work. We had to use quite a bit of the government literature and laws.

We went after Farrel's first. This is where the ice was broken as far as hiring practices in blue-collar jobs.

We had a number of Blacks that were interested in school teaching. It has only been within the last eighteen years that we have a Black teacher in the school system. Local Black teachers still don't apply in the city.

Blacks also organized in the political arena.

John Gatison: Back in the late 1930s, they had the Black Democratic Club. It operated until about 1970. It was organized through interested, community-minded Blacks.

In the beginning the fight was to get Blacks interested in participation in the mainstream of political life and political struggles and get out interested people to become registered voters, to try to get Black representation on some boards. We were not successful for quite some time as far as serving on meaningful boards.

When it really got into high gear was in 1948. We had a number of interested people participating. Finally, we got a Black as chairman of the planning commission—that was one of the biggest political gains we made.

The 1960s saw a new wave of "Black consciousness."

William Freeman: How did "Black consciousness" come into Waterbury? My awakening may have been with Mohammed Ali, or Cassius Clay as it was then. Martin Luther King, of course. That's basically it. The big thing was the march on Washington; it was very big around here.

Hyotha Hofler: In 1963 or 1964 we had workers from Dixwell Legal Rights coming up from New Haven to work in Waterbury. "Everything you wanted to know about your legal rights but were afraid to ask" type of meetings. It got people hot and bothered. I was only seven years old. I remember going to them with my parents. I was very scared. I didn't know what was going on; I thought the end of the world was going to happen at any day.

There were numerous incidents in 1967 and 1968. I was thirteen years old. The disturbances were a few windows being broken, fires, shooting between police and people who broke into stores and stole merchandise.

If you had a problem, stealing is the worst thing you could do to solve the problem. Causing disturbances won't solve it. The positive side of the disturbances in the 1960s is that it did create, in 1968 and up until fairly recently, a consciousness. People were saying: "I'm mad as hell; I'm not going to take this anymore. Maybe there's redress." Sit-ins. Protest marches. Stand-ins on the Green. Churches that opened their doors for different meetings. They had an all-night sit-in at City Hall because of the lack of police protection in the Black neighborhoods, the lack of fire response, lack of services in general in Black neighborhoods.

It caused an immediate effect on recognition. Large numbers of people—Hispanic, Black, white, poor, professional, rich, blue-collar, white-collar—many people sympathized with it.

The Brass Valley also experienced a large migration of Spanish-speaking people, primarily from Puerto Rico.

Hyotha Hofler: The Spanish migration was still at its peak period until the 1970s. They were experiencing problems that were more dramatic than we had experienced. There was practically no work for them. There were no immediate foundations for them to come to. A language barrier. Although there were many Spanish-speaking Waterburians who arrived here from New York and had lived a generation in New York.

There was nothing in Waterbury. Public assistance and anti-poverty programs that had been started, hoping to fill the void for lack of jobs temporarily, became a long-term thing in many instances, in the Spanish community and the Black community.

By the 1970s, the majority of Black people living here were born here or had been here for at least twenty years. Many of them had had some time of gainful employment, working in the brass indus-

Waterbury, July 2, 1969: "Black militants mill around Hubie Williamson in front of a North End pool hall Tuesday evening before moving through the square asking people who had no business there to move on. Armed with bull horns, as is the youth at left, the men agreed to aid police in keeping order after Mayor George P. Harlamon cancelled a city-wide curfew imposed earlier in the day." Courtesy Waterbury Republican-American.

City Hall sit-in, Waterbury, February 7–8, 1968. Demonstrators camped in City Hall to protest poor housing conditions. The city quickly agreed to their demands for leased housing. Courtesy Waterbury Republican-American.

try or some other type of job related to it, like the clock industry. But for the later populations, the problem was that the economy was very depressed in that period. It made it very difficult for people. That is why the Black community and the Spanish community turned to each other: the fact that we were fighting the same problems.

Alejandro (Alex) Lopez was born in Jajuja, Puerto Rico, in 1929. When he was four years old his father died; after that he was raised by his father's uncle on a coffee plantation. At the age of seventeen, he left the plantation to look for work. Jobs were not easy to come by in Puerto Rico at this

time. For a while he cut sugar cane by hand on a coastal sugar plantation, then returned to his uncle's farm. After a short stay in New

York City, Lopez settled in the Naugatuck Valley, attracted by the possibility of a factory job. He did manual labor in an iron foundry, and in 1953 was hired by the Scovill Mfg. Co. Since then, his only periods of unemployment have been "whenever there's a Republican president." Lopez joined the union there in the early 1950s, even though union membership was optional at that time. For the past twenty-nine years he has given critical support to his local, UAW Local 1604, and is a steward in his department, the Blanking Room at Century Brass, the successor to Scovill. At home, Lopez likes to play Spanish folk music on the guitar—he is self-taught—alone, or with other amateur musicians. He is a permanent deacon of St. Cecilia's Church, which serves the Puerto Rican community. He is also active in a Puerto Rican social organization and helps conduct voter registration drives in his community. His wife, Anna, works in a bilingual education program in the Waterbury public school system.

The experience of Puerto Rican immigrants, and the development of the Puerto Rican community in Waterbury, is strikingly similar to the memories of previous immigrant groups.

Alex Lopez: I came to this country on August 6, 1950. I came to New York. My godfather's stepbrother was there. He sent me up to Connecticut, because there used to be some Puerto Ricans working here who would go back and forth every weekend. He figured I'm better off, because in New York I might have gotten lost. In those days in New York, anybody working in the hotels or something like that made maybe thirty-five dollars a week. It was good money then, but you had to wake up at 3 o'clock in the morning to get to the job at 6 o'clock.

I came down with these guys who worked at the foundry. They lived in Naugatuck, in a boardinghouse. On South Main. [It's not there anymore] because they built the highway. It used to be a nice place.

When I came, everything was strange for me. I didn't speak [any English] at all. There were about fifteen Puerto Ricans living in that boardinghouse. These friends of mine took me to the foundry. They gave me a job.

The job was nothing like I expected. It was with a shovel. The sand comes in on the wagons, and you've got to shovel out by hand. I had a tough time in there. They had a guy, he was like a little supervisor; if the boss went away, he'd take over.

One day it was raining, very heavy. Sand fell. The guy wanted me to go down and get that sand. "You go; you go." I didn't want to go because I didn't see any sense. Why? It was a little bit of sand.

Just enough to make me wet. So I hit him with a shovel. Not too bad. The way I saw it, he just tried to force me to do something, and I knew he was taking advantage of me. I felt I had to defend myself. I hit him in the back.

He got mad. He went away. Then the boss came down. The boss didn't say anything. I kept on doing my job.

The boardinghouse was cheap in those days. You only paid ten dollars for a room. I got my lunch. The lady was nice. Treated us good. [She was not Puerto Rican;] in those days there was nobody with any position like that. In those days I remember only one Puerto Rican who had a wife and kid living in an apartment. [The lady who kept the boardinghouse was] Italian. A nice lady; she gave a good meal for that kind of money.

Sometimes we had to share the room, maybe three beds. That part wasn't bad because we understood each other; there was nobody else in there besides Puerto Ricans.

Some worked days; some worked nights. The ones who worked days couldn't sleep because the ones who worked nights came down in the middle of the night.

Later on some of the guys went to New York and bought some rum. On the weekend they'd go crazy. The place took a name: They call it La Casa del Diablo because of the noise. After I got out

of the house, a Puerto Rican took over.

The main problem for us Puerto Ricans was that there was nobody to communicate with. Usually we like to joke around, we like to talk; one talk another listen. That's why, when you go around, you see a bunch hanging around. They want to talk, laugh, joke, as if they had nothing to do. We like that. I think it's from the Indians we get that kind of manners.

We'd do that in the beginning, but the policemen used to come around and say, "Break it up, break it up, break it up." Without reason. We noticed they'd only break up the Puerto Ricans' group. But we couldn't say much.

Some new guys came [into the boardinghouse] and started working in the foundry. These guys became my close friends. We'd go out together to the bar, hang around. So we made a very close friendship. They told me, "Why don't we get a little apartment someplace?"

We went to Union City and found a nice apartment with four rooms on the third floor. We lived better out there, because there was nobody else.

This guy told me: "My mother is going to come from Puerto Rico. I want you to go meet her. She's going to come to New York." I said O.K. But he didn't tell me that he had a sister. I went to see his mother and I saw that girl over there. "Who's she?" "Oh, she's my sister." That's my wife today.

I started to go to New York, because I met the girl who is now my wife. Every weekend I'd go back and forth.

I came in 1950 and by 1953 I got married. After that I lived around different places.

I was in the foundry because I didn't want to jump around. If anybody is going to look for a job in some other place, they had to know good English. I wanted to get out of there because I didn't see any improvement. I kept working with the shovel. Another fellow and I decided to quit, because somebody came up and said, "What are you doing there? why don't you come to work in Megin, construction work?" That used to be a company in Naugatuck; it doesn't exist anymore. "We're making out there $1.65 an hour." We only made $1.35 in the foundry. So we quit.

We went to work for Megin and we made a few more pennies. But it started to get cold. For him, winter was a new experience. Some guys told us, "You've got to be careful; it might be too cold." They started to scare us. So we sent a notice to Mr. Jensen, who used to be the personnel in the foundry. He wanted us to work there because we did a lot of work. If he would put us inside, we would come back. We were afraid to be outside. He said, "Yes, come down; we've got something for you." The other guy got a job

grinding, so he made more money. But me, he needed a man to cut the sand. About the same job, only inside. The worst part was you had to start at 9 o'clock to get off at 8 o'clock.

There was a Pole doing that job with me. When all my friends would go around 3 o'clock, I couldn't talk to the guy. The guy didn't know English. So I hated that part from 3 o'clock until we finished. To stay there with a man and not talk to each other, like we were mad. I put in a year like that.

I told them, "I want to make more." The boss didn't want to take me out of there because that job was the kind of job nobody wants to do. It was very hard to get somebody in there. So he played games with me. Like one time he said, "Yes, I'm going to make you a molder, but you have to wait."

They never put me in there. So I decided to quit. But I worked one-and-a-half years before I quit.

You can see what happens to somebody who doesn't speak the language. I wanted to be independent. In the beginning I had no choice. But I didn't want somebody always to have to help. So I started to pick up here and there a little English, so I could defend myself. One day I wanted to go home because I didn't feel good. There was a guy who used to be an interpreter for everybody. He said, "You want me to tell the boss?" I said, "I'll tell him." I went to

the boss and said, "Me sick; you go home." He understood; he laughed. He made a joke out of it after that.

After I met this girl, my friend decided to bring his mother down here. He got an apartment in Waterbury. His sister, who is my wife today, came too. So I decided to move up here to Waterbury. I found a room on Meadow Street. I considered these people family already. Her mother reminded me of my mother. We got closer and closer; before I knew it, I had a family.

In the beginning we had a lot of problems. It is very hard to come into another culture. Some people work their way into the American people more easily. For Puerto Ricans it's hard. Puerto Ricans have been here thirty years now, since 1950. If we're here another hundred years, we're still going to speak Spanish, and we're going to keep on doing the same things we do in Puerto Rico. That's the way we are. A very small amount of the ones born over here go to American ways of living. [Our kids] speak Spanish; they eat what we eat; they do things like we do.

You go to South Main, you see all the kids, any way, jumping— it's just like two cultures in one. When we came from Puerto Rico, we didn't used to do that. You might think: When I go to Puerto Rico, am I going to see that over there? You aren't going to see that over there. Most of these habits of the street, noise and that, are from New York. Puerto Ricans from New York are different from Puerto Ricans from Puerto Rico.

[Puerto Ricans are "summer people."] "Summer is too short." We are "sons of the sun." It's in our blood to be going out. How can you keep a Puerto Rican inside the house? Maybe an American will stay inside, not come out because the neighbors don't like that. We don't care. We go out on the porch; we might have a little noise; we might sing; we might talk. Because the summer is too short. Don't forget, we are mixed with Indians. Indian people are like that. To me, I pay respect to what they're doing. I don't have time for hanging around, and I have different ways of living. But I'm not going to say I am better.

Opening the hydrants is an idea from New York. Puerto Ricans who came here from the beginning don't do that. It's only a handful—out of a hundred, you only need two or three to open a hydrant. Just like when you live in a three- or four-family house, you only need one who throws garbage in the stairs; then it looks like everybody is the same.

In the beginning people didn't understand the Puerto Ricans. But now they get in there. Got no choice. If you see something every day, all of a sudden, even if you don't like it, you start to get to feel comfortable. I see American people now are getting to be much

better with Puerto Ricans. After all, we Puerto Ricans like to spend a dollar.

The main organization that we are associated with is the church. Almost everybody, directly or indirectly. It's a place for everybody. Besides that, we've got a club; we've been working since 1958. We've got a place up on Baldwin Street. It's an old place we bought there. It's very hard to get good members. We've got a book full, but there's only about thirty-five who are working to keep the place. It's a social club. We get together sometimes. We celebrate family parties. We have little dances. We make some money to keep up with expenses, with the mortgage. It's almost paid now. The whole idea of this club is for everybody. For the future: Maybe somebody, my children, will have something. We say that, but most of the people don't understand that, don't believe that. It's a tendency of Puerto Ricans here to say, "I'm going back to Puerto Rico next year."

Another thing you didn't ask me, but I'm going to tell you: People don't want to go out and vote. We should have a big political power here, "Political muscle" they call it. We don't have it. We should have at least 10,000 [voters]. We might have 500. It's hard to get into people's minds the idea of the system in this country. Which is no different from our country, because we have the same system. Out there everybody

votes. Here, I don't know what's the matter. We tried to put it across.

2. Housing and Urban Reorganization: From Walking City to Suburban America

In the decades since World War II, the basic spatial organization of urban areas in the Brass Valley changed drastically, as it did in cities throughout America.

Until World War II, Waterbury and the other towns of the area were basically "walking cities," with most workers clustered within walking distance of the major plants. As most workers became able to afford cars, suburban areas began springing up both in the fringes of the factory towns and in surrounding, more rural towns. New plants were built primarily outside the inner city, since most workers could now reach them by car. Stores moved to shopping malls based on auto access.

John Yrchik: When I grew up, this area here began to become part of suburban America. It changed its character a great deal. There was a lot more occupational mix in this town than it had ever seen before. When people have to do shopping now, they rarely go downtown. They go to all the malls in this

Urban renewal in the 1960s. "This strip of land on Bank Street in the Brooklyn Section, left barren by highway demolition, used to be the center of a thriving business community." Courtesy Waterbury Republican-American.

Bank St. Bridge during the great flood of August 1955. The flood devastated Waterbury, particularly the Brooklyn section, and Torrington, as well as other Naugatuck Valley towns. Courtesy Waterbury Republican-American.

area. You can see the whole thing just splinter apart.

Daniel Zuraitis: The biggest thing that changed [Waterbury] was the flood in 1955 and then the advent of the highway system that cut the heart out. Plus the brass mills slowly closing and the industrial parks beginning, which pulled it away from the communities, which left the inner-city community hanging.

Peter Kukanskis: Between the flood and the highway, I think there were about 200 Lithuanian families that got out of this area. Plus the fact that a lot of the younger generation just moved out of it.

The tie between work place and residence has largely been broken.

Eddie Labacz: We had more Seymour people [at Seymour Mfg. Co. in the old days] than we have now. Now we've got them from Waterbury, Bridgeport, Ansonia, Derby, New Haven. [The change came] when cars became more plentiful.

The new Black and Puerto Rican migrants moved into the declining inner-city areas.

Hyotha Hofler: After the war people were not going back to their old neighborhoods, but were out settling new areas in Waterbury itself. Waterbury, up until World War II, had been a very congested town. Most of the outreaches had

been very rural. The newer neighborhoods were being established out east, further up North Main Street. Town Plot was more settled, lower South Main, Hopeville was more settled than it had been. So you found the housing not being abandoned [in the face of] an onslaught of Blacks coming in, but just because after the war there was more money to spend on single-family homes. Triple-deckers and that kind of living were out of fashion for the soldier coming back and his wife and the baby-boom children.

Because of that, there was housing available for expansion [of the Black community], probably not being owned by Blacks living there, but maybe owned by people who had bought new housing in other areas, and charging exorbitant rents at that time for living there.

Often the ghettoization process was deliberate.

John Gatison: The neighborhoods that are run down were created by greedy people who wanted to make a buck and not pay anything for making a dirty dollar. They would let the building run down, collect all the money they could get out of it. The only place you could get a rent was there. But this is disappearing and I'm glad it is.

You were forced to live under certain conditions to start with. Then when you wanted to move

out of that neighborhood and buy a house, they'd say, "You're from that neighborhood; you couldn't even get a mortgage." Neither did you have any way of forcing the landlord to keep it up to standard. This is what created ghettos. It's not the attitude of the tenants. This sort of practice was kept up and kept up. The landlord, of course, gained by it. Usually you would find that he wouldn't own one house. You could take a street with twenty houses on the block, maybe two or three people owned those houses. Very little money was put back in to keep the property up.

There were many Blacks that wanted to move into neighborhoods, and there were many efforts made by neighbors to deny them one way or another. This is a matter of record. But they were unsuccessful. After the Blacks succeeded, they were accepted; the fight was over, and they have been welcomed and they have been enjoyed since they've been in the neighborhood. And people have admitted, "I was wrong." This, again, is a matter of record.

Daniel Zuraitis: The city was left high and dry, with basically the old, hanging on, and the influx of the new, because now these became cheap rent areas. Many of the properties were picked up by absentee landlords which further deteriorated the neighborhoods. The neighborhood while it was

Community action, March 24, 1967. "Bucket brigade was held by tenants and area residents at 189 Orange St., in protest against lack of water in three of the apartments in the building. The lack of water is due to a broken water pipe, which tenants say has not been fixed since Saturday. Tenants are also staging a rent strike against the owner of the building." Courtesy Waterbury Republican-American.

owned by the individual who lived in it, he took care of it, made sure that the tenants took care of it, and the next thing that happened was the landlord who was an absentee just seemed to be interested in whether the rent check was in the mail at the right time, and didn't give too much concern to the neighborhood or the unit itself.

Policy decisions also changed the space of the city. Major highways were built, crossing in the very center of the city; large residential areas were razed to make way for them. Large areas were cleared through urban renewal.

Hyotha Hofler: They took down most of North Square in the late 1970s and put a park in its place, a housing project on the south side. It will never be the same. It was kind of a classic area. It had buildings that were kind of old, but formed a kind of unit. People could identify with where they were standing. The bus stopped there on both sides. There were cleaners, businesses; people lived there. It wasn't the best of housing, but what makes good places to live probably is not all the time sparkling surroundings; it's a place where you can commune with people, share common experiences, and somehow grow up, grow older, and grow wiser. I think they destroyed that. Even looking back with the least of rosy glasses, it is something that was probably much better there. Not only the build-

ings, but the community was much better than has survived.

It was deliberate. Most Black people believe it was done to lessen any sort of power or cohesion that we could have. Pearl Street Neighborhood House—it would have been like burning St. Peter's, if they had torn that down. They didn't do any remodeling on Pearl Street, which was held in private hands by nonabsentee landlords. North Square, up until the time it was torn down, was primarily owned by absentee landlords. Mostly white, a few Black.

[North Square buildings] were used in the riots of the 1960s as stations for creating disturbances, melees. The same things that go on in Ireland now: throw rocks at the police, call the policeman pig, or whatever. Places to meet and gather; people stood in the corners there and talked. This seemed like it would breed tension. People were upset, lack of work. It was a center point, and people who were aware of it knew, and that's the reason it was destroyed, in my estimation, and in most Black people's minds.

It was our most focal point of meeting at that period. A lot of storefronts at the time in the area were meetinghouses for different organizations. [The Panthers'] headquarters was two doors down from North Square, in a building that was similar to the architecture on North Square. Late Victorian, high, overhanging the sidewalks a

little, pretty nice storefronts. If they fixed it up nowadays and it was in a different town, they would get $600 for the apartments. They were brick buildings, pretty sturdy.

[The destruction of North Square] was fought [by the Black community]. We had hoped better would be built. We had hoped, by building better, we would get an upgrading effect on, at least, the image of North Square. With two different factions fighting against each other, it was hard to come up with any one plan on how to save it. So it was leveled and nothing was done.

More has been taken down than built up [by urban renewal in general]. I don't call parking lots building up. It's sad. Waterbury is characterized by this emptiness, the ghost town image of itself. I don't share it. I think it could be a wonderful place to live. There are great places still remaining. Hopefully they will remain, until people begin to wake up and get to see that something can be done here.

Class divisions took a geographical form clear even to children.

Frieda Ewen: [When I was growing up,] the owners did not live here. They lived in Woodbridge and places like that. In Shelton, where I grew up, the division was: Shelton people, Huntington people, and Pine Rock people.

Huntington was the rich area.

More than four years after being cleared, this urban renewal site in the largely Puerto Rican South End of Waterbury had still not been developed. Photo: Jerry Lombardi.

People had money, they had big houses, they had the nice clothes, they had the cars later on, and went on to college. Most of [their parents] didn't work in the Valley; they worked in Bridgeport, Westport, places like that. They weren't real Valley people. They lived in Huntington because Huntington was a ritzy area with spacious land and trees. It was [suburbia], but we all had to go to the same high school. They were better dressed. You could tell Huntington people.

Then there were the Pine Rock people. Pine Rock is actually a part of Huntington, which Huntington denies. Pine Rock is a real low-income place. People lived in shacks. They had old Indian trails for roads. They had their own community, too. That was where the tough people came from; they were tough. You'd be afraid of them. You could also tell Pine Rock people.

Then there were Shelton people, who were midline between the two. Most of the Shelton people came from homes where the parents worked in the factories.

There were clear lines. I remember being younger [than high school] and being aware that they were Pine Rock kids. That is more when kids are into punching each other or whatever. Real young they used to fight, and it would be the Pine Rock kids that would win.

The urban areas of the Naugatuck Valley have moved increasingly from thriving industrial centers to depressed areas. In Waterbury in 1976, unemployment reached 15 percent. It was 21 percent for Blacks, 34 percent for Hispanics, and 28 percent for Vietnam veterans. The head of the Central Naugatuck Valley Consortium for Alcoholism Services, reporting that alcoholism was "significantly higher than average," explained that "unemployment is a determining factor. Of those in the detox unit at present, I would say at least 60 percent are unemployed."* Per capita income was 125th out of 169 Connecticut towns, many of them impoverished rural communities. As white workers moved to the suburbs or migrated elsewhere, the concentration of Black, Hispanic, and elderly people greatly increased.

Claude Perry was born in Mount Dora, Florida, in 1942, one of nine children. His father was self-employed in timber, truck farming, and citrus. Perry attended Florida A&M, and in 1963 was awarded a degree in agricultural education and technology. While he was in school, he traveled around the country with his friends, picking up various kinds of farm work as he went. "I was following the season to see how things were done. Tobacco, cotton, citrus, everything. And just travel-

*Quoted in Geoffrey Douglas, "Waterbury: A Long Time Dying," *Connecticut Magazine*, Nov. 1976.

ing and enjoying myself." He ended up in Ansonia in 1962, and returned a year later after completing his degree. He worked for thirteen years at B.F. Goodrich, until it blew up in 1975 and he found himself unemployed like hundreds of other B.F. workers. He recalls those days: "Being unemployed was tough, plus I was laid up for a year because of an auto accident." In 1977, he got a job under the CETA program as a business developer for the Ansonia Economic Development office and as a social worker for the Board of Education. In 1979, he was employed by the Economic Development Commission as a business developer, and by 1980 he was the administrator of that office, a job he still holds today. He is very involved in community affairs and is an active member of many organizations, including the NAACP, the A. Philip

Randolph Institute's local chapter, the Black Democrats, Ansonia Community Action, the Valley Housing Council, Congressman Ratchford's Advisory Committee, the Valley Citizens Action Group, the Connecticut Fair Housing Association, the Incorporators of Griffin Hospital, and Valley Citizens for Racial Equality. An informal advocate for the rights of Black citizens in the Valley for many years, he was recently appointed the Fair Housing Officer in the City of Ansonia. He and his wife, Virginia Martin, a psychiatric aide at Fairfield Hills State Hospital, have raised nine children.

During the 1960s and 1970s, a whole series of movements developed around the issues of urban life. North End Community Action started in Ansonia in the mid-1960s.

Bertha Silva: Sis kept on talking to me about how we should do something about [the housing situation]. She said, "I'm going to do something about it." They started asking different ones if they would participate in it. They said yes. They started it in Frances' kitchen.

Then they said, "We aren't just going to ask certain people, we're going to ask anybody." That's how they did it. They asked me and I was ready for it.

[A candidate] came up there and was trying to become mayor. In the backyard there. He said, "How

Women playing bingo at the Rocco Palladino Senior Center of the Waterbury Retired Workers Council, 1982. Photo: Jerry Lombardi.

Housing demonstration, Waterbury City Hall, January 16, 1967. A committee presented a petition to the mayor, signed by nearly 3,000, demanding slum clearance, low-income housing, code enforcement, and integration of city housing boards. Courtesy Waterbury Republican-American.

are you going to vote?" We said, "What are you going to do for us?" He said, "After I get in, I'll do something for you." When he got what he wanted, he didn't care any more.

The big march [on City Hall] was to get better houses. None of them got any, not one. If the people had stuck together, they would have gotten the kind of houses they wanted. But they turned around and left it in somebody else's hands.

Claude Perry: We were trying to explain to the welfare moms that they had rights under the law. We were trying to get people who were receiving welfare to educate themselves, so they could get off of welfare. Out of that group, there were only one or two that didn't do that. Everybody else moved on and became something, accomplished something with their lives.

This was Black and white. Once they realized, "This is a real problem; we can do something about it ourselves," then they started to do it. But there was too much success too fast. The establishment, Black and white, was opposed to that. You had a place. They didn't want women, especially Black women, to become anything. Black men were not even interested in helping Black women improve their stock in the community. 1969, 1970.

Silva: This is something the people wanted. They didn't want to stay on welfare; they wanted to help themselves. They didn't want to help. So we went to Hartford to see the governor. We had a march down Main Street.

During the 1970s, community organizations and community-based public interest groups became a major phenomenon throughout the country. In the Naugatuck Valley, the most visible group is the Connecticut Citizens Action Group. Originally started with the support of Ralph Nader, it defines itself today as an organization working for the interests of low- and middle-income people. In Waterbury it has several neighborhood organizations, took the lead in fighting a city tax revaluation, and has organized community support for strikes and job actions by nurses, firemen, and brass workers. In the lower Valley, it has worked primarily on housing issues.

Frieda Ewen: One of the problems at Beaverbrook was rent increases. The management was asking for a rent increase every six months. Most of the time they got almost all the increases they wanted.

The rent increases bothered people the most. The tenants began to get together and talk with each other and developed a tenant union, a tenant association, and decided to fight the rent increases. They put up a big struggle against the first one that came and got it substantially reduced, down to

about one-third of what was requested. About twenty-eight days later a new request for a rent increase went in, for sixty dollars. The tenants had just gone through this big battle, so they knew some of the ropes. They investigated some of the practices of management. Management had set up a dummy corporation. The dummy corporation would buy cheap carpeting and sell it to Beaverbrook at a high price. Then they would put in for a rent increase because it cost them so much to do this carpeting.

The tenants presented it to HUD and to court, and the rent increase got stopped cold. HUD, in their decision, said they were going to look into some of the practices at Beaverbrook. It was the first time in the state of Connecticut that one of the 221-D3 housing rent increases had been denied completely.

The tenants picketed the Beaverbrook offices. When people applied for apartments, they would tell them what was going on.

They had the help of VCAG. VCAG is the Valley Citizens Action Group, which is a chapter of the Connecticut Citizens Action Group. VCAG's primary work in the Valley is working with housing groups on housing issues. They are also working on hazardous wastes and statewide issues that CCAG chooses to work on.

VCAG has taken what was already here and developed it a lot

further, organized new tenants' and neighborhood groups. Now representatives of these groups meet together, interact, and tell their own stories. The groups are not actively supporting each other yet—like if one is having a problem the other showing up to help with it. That, I think, is the ultimate goal, to build an association where everyone feels a part of it all, and if there's problems in one of the associations in another town, it's your problem also and you should help them with it, with your expertise or with just your body, if that's what's needed.

3. Social Life: "They're All over God's Creation Today"

After World War II, conditions changed greatly for workers in the Naugatuck Valley. Unionization and economic expansion increased wages and job security. Younger white workers began moving out of older, ethnic neighborhoods in the inner city to newer suburban areas. Many of their children went to college or pursued opportunities outside the brass plants. Television in the home created an ever-present alternative to other social activities. Peter Kukanskis and Daniel Zuraitis describe the situation in the Brooklyn section of Waterbury.

Peter Kukanskis: A lot of it happened after World War II. The war had the whole thing to do with it. The boys came back from the service. They had seen something that they had never seen before. They tried to better themselves. A lot of them went to school on the G.I. [Bill.] They got the education. The housing was another problem, too. They liked to live wherever the job was closer. So little by little they just petered out, and they're all over God's creation today.

Before [World War II], they were still all in the area here, their parents were here. But once the parents passed on, there were no strings really attached to them.

There's television, automobiles, moving away; the attraction wasn't here anymore. Before, you used to come down [to the club] and see this one, that one every week or two. How are you doing? The young generation, like our children, will have nothing to do with it. They like rock 'n' roll; their way of thinking is entirely different, and there's no way of stopping them. So these clubs are hard to make a go of.

The church has the same problems, too. The young generation doesn't care to go. Donations are tough. They're just about making ends meet. It's hard.

Years back in our parents' [time], there was no transportation, no place to go, no other entertainment really to speak of. Baseball, football, or any of those sports were not in their line. So

you'd hang around the corner: "Hey, there's a big dance tomorrow night" and they'd all go to it. So they'd have a good turnout.

With transportation, with different activities, little by little this is something they don't care about any more.

Daniel Zuraitis: There came a time in the early 1950s when it became almost stigmatized to push your ethnic background. You were only supposed to be proud to be an American. Everybody's proud to be an American and fortunate to partake of all the benefits. But the name-calling got louder and many of the ethnic clubs closed. Now everybody wanted to be American and forget their ethnic origins.

Older neighborhoods and their traditions remain only as enclaves.

Catherine Coscia: This neighborhood of ours is just like years ago. If somebody dies, something happens, we make a collection; we make a cake; we bring flowers. They stabbed my lady friend's husband about two months ago. We made a collection, we got about $200 or $300 for her. We bought fruit; we bought mass cards; we even bought her groceries. But we don't go into each other's houses. We call each other on the phone.

Many people also see a fundamental change in attitude:

Frank Pochron: When people started getting cars and all that, they became individualists. Instead of going to the clubs, they wanted to have their own times by themselves. After World War II, instead of associating, you didn't have any more communities, community gatherings. They started going off to their own distant things by themselves.

John Chubat: After World War II, they started having the Cold War with Russia. Our people were sort of afraid that they would be taken for Communists.

Today we are not so free. The old-timers knew how to enjoy themselves. They had clubs; they had picnics; they had dances. They had beautiful choirs, beautiful music. Today it is dying out. Because everyone is afraid or ashamed.

But much of the change is seen as a result of changing conditions of life.

Lea Harvey: I don't know my neighbors. I have not known my neighbors for at least twenty-two years. I've been in this house fifteen years. I don't have any reason to know them. I come out of my house, I go in my garage, I get in my car, and I go. I come back, I drive in the garage, I close the door, I make ten steps across the yard to the porch, and I go upstairs. How would I know them? When am I going to see them?

One of the many food booths at the Holy Rosary Church Italian Festival, Ansonia, 1979. Photo: Jerry Lombardi.

Band playing at the Holy Rosary Church Italian Festival, 1979. Photo: Jerry Lombardi.

One of the most striking changes in working-class life since World War II is the steady decline in the importance of ethnicity.

John Yrchik: Already when I went to school, there was a great deal of ethnic diversity. You didn't have just Polish and Russian kids.

We grew up saying things like, "No, I'm not Polish; I'm an American." When I was a kid, it wasn't important to be identified with any one group or another.

When my folks were kids, they played with other people who were Polish or children of immigrants. They all lived in pretty similar cir-cumstances. Their families always worked in the town mill.

There is a consciousness of op-pression that they had. Like racial oppression, you could call it. They would say, "We were just like Blacks." My uncle won't tolerate anyone saying Polack to this day; he gets very mad. He was turned down for a job at National Cash Register when they asked him his name and he told it to them. They were going to give him a job, and then they said, "We don't need anyone with your qualifications, or with your background," or some-thing like that.

That changed after the war.

Maybe part of ethnicity not being important is that the whole econ-omy opened wide up. There were opportunities for everybody that didn't have them before.

Perhaps the most important aspect of the change was the frequency of intermarriage between members of different ethnic groups.

Eddie Labacz: When the war came, it changed. People started to marry one another; it wasn't that the Polish had to marry a Polish. They started building houses in Seymour; a lot of out-of-towners came in.

TABLE 26
First- and Second-generation Immigrants in Waterbury, 1930 and 1960

Country of origin	1930	1960
Immigrants (aggregate)	72,125	51,681
Ireland	14,179	5,949
Italy	23,942	20,724
Canada	6,803	6,818
Lithuania	6,390	4,228
Germany	3,320	1,703
Russia	3,040	1,919
England	2,824	2,401

Source: Compiled from U.S. Census data by Peter Rachleff.

TABLE 27
Waterbury's Population, by Citizenship, 1950

Citizenship status	Number of residents
Native citizens	84,675
Naturalized citizens	14,085
Aliens	4,360

Source: Compiled from U.S. Census data by Peter Rachleff.

Residential integration among white ethnic groups also played an important role.

John Yrchik: [The ethnic groups] were forced to live in the same area of town pretty much.

[Now] the people next door are Lithuanian; there's Russian down the street; Russian and Polish next door; up the street, there are names like O'Day, Welles, Cretella, Hogan.

Victor Vaitkus represents a different generation of immigrants than most of those met in this book: He came to the U.S. in 1949. Born in Lithuania, he hoped to become an actor, but spent the war years running from the German and Russian armies. After coming to Waterbury, he spent twenty-seven years as a crane man at Scovill. He has been very active in Lithuanian cultural activities, including an amateur theatrical group. He is now retired from Scovill, and runs the Spauda Bookshop in the Brooklyn section of Waterbury, where there is an array of books, magazines, and records representing Lithuanian life, both in the U.S. and in the old country.

Ethnicity remains a real, if less significant, aspect of many people's lives. Ethnic organizations carry on.

Victor Vaitkus: A women's club still exists. An international organization, American Women's Federation, Lithuanian section. They support the church; they support students, scholarships; they send packages to Siberia and to Poland, to the Lithuanian population. Their cooking is beautiful. Good buffet.

Frieda Ewen: When I was really young, people were more into the ethnic groups than they are now. There was a lot of closeness there. They would go to the halls, to the clubs, and bring their problems there.

When my grandfather came over from Italy, a lot of Marchegians came. They weren't very well accepted. So they felt the need to create their own little community. They did it for economic reasons. They would support each other. They started the insurance—they had life insurance they paid for collectively.

Every family function that we had on that side of the family was

The Lithuanian Club of Waterbury. The club was still an active organization in 1982. Photo: Jerry Lombardi.

held there. Everybody had their weddings, parties, dances, and things. It wasn't a community club as far as doing things for the rest of the community. There are those clubs all over.

I can recall, when I was younger, working there and it was really strong. The leadership was really strong. I think what happened: There was one girl there who was daughter of the president. She was going out with a man who was Irish. Then she married him. She continued to come to the club because all her brothers and sisters and her father was there. Her husband came with her, but everybody was angry about him; they didn't like him. As time went on, he gradually became accepted and he started to work with the club and everything. He eventually became president of the club! I have mixed feelings about this. I saw that as a good thing, that he was doing this. But I think that intermarriage and the watering down of the ethnic group was the beginning of the decline. The tie that held them there to begin with was them against the world, and this was breaking down. This was, at least, one of the reasons for the decline. People didn't need it anymore. They didn't need to hole up together because the rest of the world was so cruel to them.

Traditions continue to be passed on within families.

A traditional wooden crucifix. Carved by a Waterburian of Lithuanian descent, it was exhibited at the Lithuanian Club of Waterbury in 1980. Photo: Jerry Lombardi.

Mary Sabot: Tonight is our Christmas Eve. We have a big supper. So yesterday we made the pierogies. We made 200 of them. So tonight we're going to eat like pigs.

The holidays—cooking, baking, and preparing. Every year I say I'm not going to make any cookies. My daughter-in-law says, "Oh, Ma, if you don't make cookies, it's not Christmas." I make a big tray for her and a big tray for my daughter. And then I make a pizza snack.

Education played an important role in establishing a sense of social mobility.

John Yrchik: After Sputnik the big thing was science: Study science. I went to college as an engineering student. Go to college and be good in science and math. Everything else is not really worth studying.

Part of it was government encouragement. Part of it was that state university systems were being established. U. Conn. grew phe-

nomenally. It offered programs in a wide variety of subjects. It was affordable for most working-class families. So, for the first time, it was possible.

Frieda Ewen: It wasn't, in general, that people should go on [to college]. There were chosen people who they would pick out: These would be the ones who would go on to school. The ones that could afford it; that had a lot to do with it. The decisions were almost made prior to high school, in what direction you were going. Kids would take college courses in high school, so those would be the ones the guidance people would focus on. You chose [college or vocational tracks] before you went to high school. They presented you with a paper which had these things on it and you said [which you would take]. There was the college course, which meant you were zipping on your way. There was the academic course, which was a medium thing. Then there was the business for girls, so you could all go into little offices and type your little brains away. The boys had shop, where they learned mechanics and tool making. The boys were allowed to take some business courses if they were in the academic or college courses, but the girls could never take any shop courses.

Strangely enough, when the girls took the business, they had home ec. for four years. The girls in the academic and college courses only had it for one or two. The boys didn't. I wanted shop, and they wouldn't give it to me.

Born in 1951, Quentin Garatoni is the son of Paul Garatoni, introduced on page 97, and Eileen Denihan. He grew up in Derby, one of seven children. After attending Derby and Notre Dame High Schools, and South Central Community College for a short time, Quentin went to work at

Anaconda. When he was laid off, he went to work at B.F. Goodrich. He quit when they decided to sell the plant, and in 1974 got a job at Anaconda. He worked on the extruder for three years, and is presently a coil packer in the Rod Mill. He got active in the union during the 1977/78 strike, and soon became a steward. He is a member of the Valley Citizens Action Group, Norwood's Athletic Club, and the National Rifle Association. He was married for nine years, and has one daughter.

Young people in the Naugatuck Valley, as in the rest of the nation, experienced a deep alienation that originated largely in the Vietnam War.

Quentin Garatoni: Back in the 1960s, I grew up in a crazy time. I saw friends of mine going off to a war that we didn't know what it

was all about. I was a patriotic American: they should go. But then I saw my friends coming back from Vietnam, and they're telling me what's going on over there. And I see in the papers, about these people are Communists, or this or that. They're just guys right next to me. They come back and say it's wrong being over there and this government keeps pushing this war on us. And that made me question the whole idea of where we're coming from. Then it seemed like every aspect of society I looked into the government was dictating the way we should live. It made me very cynical about our society and the way it's run.

4. Families: "Now It Takes Two, and You Can't Make It"

The family probably remains the most important institution for most people in the Brass Valley. But families themselves have changed greatly. In the post–World War II era, extended kin networks became less important as nuclear families scattered and public services replaced many of the functions once performed by the extended family. In the 1960s and 1970s, an increasing proportion of married women were in the paid work force, making the two-breadwinner family more the rule than the exception. Male and female roles in the family were challenged, both by these structural changes and by the new values articulated by the women's movement, but no clear new pattern in working-class families had emerged. One-parent families, however, became increasingly common.

Frieda Ewen: For men, for the boys, [the expectation] was to grow up and get a good, steady job in a factory, in one of the better-paying factories in the Valley, which would have been Sikorsky's, American Brass, or B.F. Goodrich. I don't think they paid that great; I think some of them are still large sweatshops, like B.F. was. That's what was expected, and you made it, once you got into one of those steady jobs. People got into there and stayed there for the next twenty, thirty years, until they retired, and thought they made it.

There were other kids who came from families who weren't working in factories, who were already dentists or whatever; they had different expectations, I'm sure. But the average in the Valley came from families where the fathers worked in factories, and some of the mothers did, though not every one at the time.

As awful as it was being factory workers, it seemed there was even a class division there. There were failures who didn't quite make it, those who never got into one of those larger factories and worked for Hershey Metals or Charlton

Press. Some people did get jobs and stayed forever, for their whole lifetime, in those small shops, and got barely over minimum wage. Most of the time it was a stepping-place; younger people got jobs there, until they got the jobs in the better factories.

[For women] in our house, it was very clear; the expectation of the family was that you would finish high school, and then you would get married to someone who had one of these good jobs in one of the factories. If you were going out with someone who wasn't working in one of the better ones, but worked in the small ones, it was almost like, "What are you doing with that bum?" But if they came home and they were working at American Brass and had been there for two years: "Oh, this is great! He's made it already. So you're going to be secure." That's what it was. You finished high school and you got married to someone who had a steady job in a factory and you had kids.

[The expectations were:] Get married, raise children, eventually buy a home, have this little corner that's yours, clean your kitchen floor, and raise children to do the same thing when they grow up. Build yourself up by having your husband stay in the same factory job long enough that he gets a decent enough wage that you can wear a suit once in a while and go to a PTA meeting looking decent. That's it. You made it.

Most of the women wanted to work. Most of them after high school got jobs, as waitresses, in the offices, or in the smaller factories that were primarily women. You got minimum wage or just above.

Women more hopped around in jobs. They would have a job in a small factory for a couple of years, then they would go on. A lot of them would would work for Christmas money, or if they wanted to go on a trip, they would get a job and not tell the boss that was their intention. They would just build up enough funds for whatever they wanted and then they'd leave the job. Not so many women you would find in a place stayed there forever like the men did. I see that changing, because more and more women are heads of households.

In my generation, the ones who couldn't work, whose husbands said, "No you can't; I want you home," resented that; I felt that from many of them. Many of them had to stop when they got married. I don't think they showed [their resentment about being forbidden to work] to their husbands so much; maybe in just withholding sex. But in talking personally, they would say they don't like it—they aren't working because *he* won't let them, and they say that with a lot of resentment. "He won't let me work; he won't let me do this or that."

Most of the time, it's after they

have children. Most of them that I remember did work, until they had kids. And then, once they had that child, that was it, until the kids were grown.

[The husband's domination was] by verbal order most of the time. There may have been physical abuse, but I wasn't aware of it. It was just an acceptance, too, that this is what you're supposed to do. He has the right to say: No, I don't want this for you; I don't want this for *my* life, that my wife be working. Therefore you cannot work.

I saw a lot of anger. I saw a lot of marriages break up. The reasons were complex. But a lot of it had to do with that, because there was a whole different place that each one was at then. The wife was at home all the time with these little babies. Very often two or three really quick. That was their whole life, which the husband came in and out of once in a while. He was out in the world, doing things, stopping at the bars after work; he had a whole separate life away from the wife.

That would make him see the wife as something not worldly anymore, and not of interest anymore, because she's losing some of her worldliness and interesting qualities, because of this mundane life she's forced into. The wife has this resentment, and understands and sees that he's getting into this whole other world that she's not a part of and not allowed to be part of.

I'm sure many of [the women] began to build their own separate lives in one way or another. The ones who could. Many of them could not, and those were the really devastating divorces, where the woman is still just there with these kids, and doesn't quite know what to do, doesn't understand it, and doesn't have any other connections, and is still stuck there. And now there's no husband bouncing in and out. She's just there with these kids.

Those women usually go a little wild for a while. They shove the kids in the corner, and that's it for a year or two. I guess it's a normal reaction. I saw quite a bit of that.

While they were married, they tried to build networks with other women and do things. That had its limitations, too, because husbands resented that, and if they had the power to stop them from doing anything else, they also had the power to do that.

In general it was just peer group, the kids you went to high school with and now are in the same situation you are. You get together; I remember doing that when I was very young and married, going out with just the girls. It always seemed sort of weird, though, because at that point, when you're married and not doing anything much else than being married, your whole life was "being married," you were not much of a person. You would get together with these women, but

there wasn't much you could do. That's why this didn't fulfill much of the need the women had.

A lot of women would start to go to school or do other productive things. A lot of them didn't tell their husbands they were doing this, but they would do it. They saved, tucking away the grocery money and building up the funds. My sister studied for medical technology. She did it out of her grocery money. She started without her husband knowing it. In the midst of her going to school, he gradually became aware of it, and chose to ignore it like it wasn't happening. There was one woman from Ansonia who started working with Planned Parenthood during the day, when her kids would go to school. She went to nursing school. I don't think through most of it her husband knew about it. She eventually divorced him; I think that was probably the ultimate plan.

Some of my friends didn't make it. One of them ended up in a mental institution, after she had her baby. She got married when she was fifteen. She was very dominated by her husband, but that followed being very dominated by her father. When she was twenty-one, she had a baby. That was the end of it. To this day, she's still institutionalized. The baby is about twelve. I think it was just a lifetime of oppression. She was just dominated so much by everyone. She had an overwhelming desire to please everyone constantly; her only thing in life was that she had to please everyone. It just got to be too much, because you can't always please.

Her husband used her as just a separate piece of his life, and had his whole other life. He did everything else in the world besides be home and be a husband. She wasn't a part of it and wasn't allowed to be part of it, and was restricted from doing other things, from seeing friends. She worked off and on before they had the child. But any time anything happened on the job, or anybody even looked at her, he would pull her out of the job and she'd be back home again. But he did whatever he wanted.

[The husbands] didn't want [the wives] in a social world that didn't include them. If it was mutual friends and they all were together, that was acceptable. But for the woman to leave the home with a friend, or to have a relationship with a friend, that didn't include the husband, that was something you couldn't do. I don't know why that was. I think, historically, that has been the way it is. Women are seen as property, extensions of the husbands. So the males do whatever they choose to do, and the wife is supposed to be there, available at all times, for his needs and his wants. If she has these other relationships that don't include him, then she may not be available, or, heaven forbid, she may

ask him to watch the baby while she goes and does it. This is totally unacceptable.

[In general, the husbands didn't help around the house.] Their fathers didn't help around the house. It's almost as if they would be laughed at if they were caught at it. The woman always had the need for individuals and society to love her, and this is what you had to do to fulfill the role, to be loved by society, to be considered a good woman. If you hear people talk about what is a good woman they say: She always cooked well for her family and kept everything neat and clean. Maybe went to the PTA, but she was rated by how clean her kitchen floor was.

Taking care of the home, and what's expected of you in being a homemaker is so enormous; it's a never-ending, hopelessly unrewarding job. You can never even be considered good at it or thanked for it because you never finish it, because it's never finished. It's so oppressive in that way that, no matter how badly a husband may have acted in any situation, you're always guilty, because your work is never finished. Because it never can be finished. That's where the guilt comes in, too, of never being a good enough housewife, of never being a good enough mother. That's a loss of power for the woman, and power for the male.

Birth control was illegal till not that long ago. I remember when I was young and married and had

my two kids. One of the friends I knew got the pill. I talked to a few of them, and a few others had gotten the pill. And it was illegal, still. But the doctors were still giving it out. I went to the doctor, and he actually decided for me and said, "Now you go on the pill."

When I was given the pill, I wasn't given any options or told about anything else that might be available. I was just given that.

When birth control was in the open and anybody could use it, married or not, no matter how many kids you had, when abortion started to become a reality to everyone, people made better choices because they saw they did have choices.

Birth control did more than to give you the right to decide whether you were going to have this particular baby or not. It made you think about whether you wanted a child or not or when you wanted one. Everything else falls in line, too, then. When do you want to do these things? Instead of: They're just going to happen anyway, so I'd better be married. If I'm going to get pregnant, I'd better be married first.

There was a lot of nondiscussion about [sex]. If you did it, you were bad; however, little things people would say would tend to make you think they were doing it. It was somewhat acceptable, because the ones who were doing it were not the ones who had the bad reputations, but were, in fact, the wholesome, popular girls who were cheerleaders and all those things. They would have denied to the death that they were doing anything sexual, but they would let out little hints that they were. It was something that nobody talked about.

A lot of girls got pregnant. Several, while I was in high school, got pregnant and left school. Everybody got married. If you were pregnant, you got married; that was just routine. You were bad, all of a sudden, even though everybody else was doing it. You got caught. That whole thing has totally changed now because there are so many alternatives and choices.

[For the women I was growing up with,] the wedding was the big thing. They would plan that all through high school. Most of them picked the partner out during high school. It was a big deal, this whole show.

[It's still a big deal,] more to the family than to the actual couple, now. I'm sure it's still an important event to them, but in just the time that I've seen it, couples are older and more established now than they used to be. It used to be right out of high school and, zap, into the gown, have this big party, and that's it. Women have changed now, they're getting more into careers and thinking more of themselves, and waiting a bit before they do it. It's now a piece of their life instead of *the* big event, the en-

tire life: Everything depends on this.

The criticism [of the older expectations] was always there, and the desire to fight it was there, except that the pressures were so great that this is what you should do in order to be a decent person and make everyone around you happy. I don't think it was until after I got out of my marriage, was forced out of that situation, that I really looked at it and saw: Maybe I'm glad to be out of this. Maybe it's better than being in a situation in which you have no control over any part of your life, everything is controlled for you, decided for you. It's a little scary, to have all the responsibility, sometimes you want to revert to being a child again. I don't think that's exclusive to women; I think men have that, but just don't express it.

It's something that people see as not natural for you. I'm always considered a failure because I'm not married. According to my family, my aunts and uncles and everyone. No matter what else I do in life, I'm a failure because I'm not married, haven't established my home and husband and everything that's going to be there for eternity.

Divorce was something unheard of in my father's family. I was the first one to do it. In my mother's, it had happened a couple of times—to my grandmother and to my aunt. My grandmother, I'm sure, was considered a failure be-

cause she never got married again. But my aunt got married again; she got out of a rotten marriage and married a police officer. So she had made it, she was O.K.: acceptable again.

I look back on it and see all the oppression that was there, that I was accepting as just "natural," something you had to do, had to put up with. You think you're happy, but it's pretty awful, looking back on it. It's not happy at all; it's smiling, because you're supposed to look happy.

When I talk to other people one-to-one about it, even relatives who ask those questions, they have the same feelings of oppression. But they're measuring it to what's expected of them. That sort of makes it O.K. for them. They've done what they were supposed to do, so they can be that "good" person, that "good" woman. And if that's what you want in life, to be remembered that way, then that's what's important, whether or not you're happy.

Economic pressures played a major role in making the working wife the norm.

Paul Garatoni: One thing you could do then that you can't do today. When my children were small, my wife wasn't working. We ate good; we managed. The husband working, the wife taking care of the home and the kids. Today, I would say a man on the same job, with his wife working, and six kids, could never make it. It's impossible today with the same job on which I was supporting a wife and six kids. At that time, the cost of living was based on a man supporting a family. Now it takes two, and you can't make it.

Terry Longo's parents came from Italy. They settled in the Reidville section of Waterbury. Terry was born there in 1948. "We've always been in the Reidville section. It was basically all Italian when I grew up. Everybody knew everybody else in the section I was in. My grandparents lived down the street. It was all one big family, even if you weren't related." Her father was a self-employed carpenter. Her mother "worked for as long as I can remember, mostly for Scovill's." After completing her training, she went to work as a nurse in nursing homes for six years, until she was fired by her last employer for complaining about the treatment of the elderly patients. She then went to work as an inspector at Century Brass (formerly Scovill). She has had poor experiences with the union there, and is glad that her present job is technically part of management. She is very active in the Junior Women's Club, a service organization of working and middle-class women that provides aid to the elderly, the handicapped, and other groups.

The rising proportion of working women is gradually forcing changes in other aspects of sex roles.

Terry Longo: When I was growing up I went to Catholic High, so it was all girls. Most girls got out of school, got married, and had a family. That was it. You were a housewife. But as you got older, a lot of women aren't satisfied. Motherhood and wifehood is not everything to them; they have other things they want to do.

When I was growing up, the husbands went out and worked, they came home—Don't bother them. Whereas a lot of our friends with children, the husbands are really good fathers. They take the kids all over. You don't have to work forty-five or fifty-five hours a week; you have a family time. When I was growing up, I don't ever remember the fathers in the neighborhood taking all their kids, girls and boys alike. They took the boys fishing or to the ball game. But nowadays I find that, with my friends, the fathers take a big part in bringing the kids up. The fathers take the girls to the ball games, and the girls are playing ball. It's really opened up a lot. It's become a situation where you're both involved. It's not: "Hey, you're pregnant, you take care of the kid now. When he's twenty, I'll send him to college." The fathers take a more vital role.

Maybe the wives told them to get off the track and get on the train here, let's get moving. Maybe because the wives are working, too.

Mary Fatelli (a pseudonym) was born and raised in Derby. She attended high school there, and worked in a variety of jobs at small factories, nursing homes, schools, stores, and social service agencies. She was married to a brass worker for ten years.

Work pressures often took a serious toll on family life.

Mary Fatelli: When I first got married, my attitude was probably more like my mother's attitude. I was pregnant, I was going to stay home and have a child and take care of the house and the only people that really existed or mattered to me were my husband and child and a close friend of mine. That started to change because it wasn't enough. Later on, I started going to school, I started working, I started getting into doing different things.

Things were changing as far back as my daughter being a baby. I can remember my husband being a zombie, him working second shift and overtime, coming home at one or two in the morning and just needing time to unwind and me being on a totally different schedule, being home and dealing with a child and the house and that whole thing, not having money or transportation to get around.

Later, when he got on days, my day started at ten minutes after four in the morning. The alarm would go off. My husband would get up and leave for work. I would make sure that he got up and left so that he wasn't late, then I would go back to bed until six. I would get ready for work, get my daughter ready for school or daycare, do laundry, start a meal so that it could be heated, and drop my child off.

When my husband came home from work he was very tired. He would start supper because I usually came home later. He would watch TV while he was doing that. He would sleep afterwards, talk about the job during supper all the time. He was just too zonked out to do anything else. Things just did not get done unless I did them. He would always say it's a fifty-fifty thing, but he was always too tired.

At times, I was making less than half of what my husband was making. I felt that my job was secondary. It was considered a supplement to his income. As far as punching the clock, I would work forty to forty-five hours. He might work as far as sixty. But I was still working maybe sixty hours a week because if you added the time to do the laundry, the dishes, to clean the house, to make business phone calls, to do the checking account, do all those kinds of things, I was right up to par with him. I didn't get the dollar for it.

We both worked so many hours, whether it was the job or home or both combined, and we both had to get up so early so we had to go to bed quite early. The only real time we had alone was after my daughter went to bed. That gave us, at times, maybe an hour. By then our energies were drained. It didn't do much for our sex life. I always felt like there was a clock, a time limit, on how long we could really enjoy each other, because after all, we have to get up and do this whole number again the next day.

Even if we went out, there was always work to consider the next day, or other responsibilities, things that had to be done because there was only one day off. We're not that rich that we can just hire somebody to do our work. It was like at a certain hour you would turn into a pumpkin.

Where vacations were concerned, there was a lot of pressure there, too, because when you're going crazy for a whole year and then you get one week off, it isn't easy to shrug off all the hassles and responsibilities and problems that you had throughout that whole year. It was like trying to cram into a week everything that you missed out on in a year.

As far as financial pressures, you worked all this overtime and therefore felt I should have this, that, and the other thing. But of course, with the cost of living, you use credit. You figure you deserve it. So you wind up paying for all these material things and you get in a worse rut, because now you have to work the overtime to pay for the washing machine you put on charge.

It was one big rut. It didn't enable us to move, to experience other life styles, do other things at any great length, to get more involved in other issues, because the job took up so much time. I was also going through a lot of changes myself. I was so young when I got married, I didn't really know myself. I needed answers that I had to find out on my own, that I couldn't find out while I was living with him. I got divorced. I can't say it was all because of his job, but the job did have a lot to do with it, at the time.

Compulsory overtime had an effect on a lot of people's lives. There would be men in there who would work sixty, sixty-five hours, and they'd refuse one time and they'd wind up with a warning. It didn't matter that they couldn't see their wives, and grow up with their children, or have any kind of life together, which is why they got married or had kids to start with. They had no choice but to choose their job over their family.

THE WORK

Industrial unionism gave workers some influence over day-to-day life in the plant. But it explicitly recognized "management's right to manage." The basic decisions about what would be done with the wealth created in the work places of the Brass Valley remained with the large corporations that owned them.

Generally, these companies adopted a two-pronged strategy. On the one hand, they selected a few plants and product lines in the Valley into which they invested money for new, automated production processes. On the other hand, they let the great majority of brass plants deteriorate to the point where they were no longer profitable; the wealth produced in these plants was reinvested elsewhere. Thus the brass workers of the Valley experienced the loss of jobs both through automation and through plant closings. By 1980 there were fewer than 5,000 workers in Naugatuck Valley brass plants, where there had once been more than 50,000. In the Waterbury Labor Market Area, employment in the brass industry declined from over 5,000 in 1970 to barely 2,400 in 1978.

5. Decline of the Brass Industry: "Then One Day the Factory Closed Up and We Were All out of a Job"

From the 1950s on, the Naugatuck Valley brass industry went into a sharp decline. A common belief in the Valley is that this happened because "workers became too greedy."

John Hollingworth: Let's talk about American Brass leaving Waterbury. Chase leaving Waterbury. Union.

They had old machinery in Waterbury. American Brass built a factory out in California. They bought Brown Brass in Canada. New machinery. Rolling mills. The unions were so demanding here they just let it die. That's what happened to Waterbury.

There is little evidence, however, that high labor costs were responsible for the decline of the local brass industry. The real causes are not hard to find. Hollingworth himself pointed to one of the principal reasons: "The companies are so huge now, and there's such a big demand for stuff, that they can afford to spread out."

Bill Moriarty: One of the things that was probably the major factor in the brass industry going sour in Waterbury is the fact that these were all once locally owned plants. Then Kennecott came in and took over Chase; Anaconda took over American Brass. The only semilocal plant was Scovill's; it also had tentacles out all over the country. These conglomerates came in, and they just ran these plants into the ground.

They were smart enough to know that brass was out, plastics and aluminum were coming in. But in order to [convert the plants], they would have to retool and put a lot of money into the plants. For instance, in the Chase plant things were so bad that people in that plant had to wear hard hats because chunks of bricks would fall from the ceiling. They wouldn't do anything to keep up that plant. They had buckets of water, rather than fix a hole in the ceiling. They just bled it dry and wrote it off.

Tony Gerace: We felt, when Kennecott took over [Chase], it was a

An American Brass plant in Waterbury, once the tube mill of Benedict and Burnham, being torn down in 1961. Courtesy Waterbury Republican-American.

Part of an antique rolling mill. It lies abandoned near the building that once housed the Chase Metal Works. Photo: Jerry Lombardi.

TABLE 28

Manufacturing in the Waterbury SMSA, 1939–1973

Year	Number of production workers	Value added by manufacture ($)
1939	28,537	81,371,000
1947	36,386	206,291,000
1954	33,970	307,565,000
1955	33,923	293,310,000
1956	33,798	332,360,000
1957	31,293	310,547,000
1958	28,329	298,308,000
1963	28,500	421,600,000
1964	28,300	448,000,000
1965	27,400	453,200,000
1966	29,200	509,800,000
1967	32,500	503,800,000
1968	31,200	546,800,000
1969	30,700	593,000,000
1972	25,500	570,600,000
1973	26,000	629,100,000

Source: Compiled from U.S. Census data by Peter Rachleff.

good sign because we had a bigger corporation behind us. We didn't realize that the bigger corporations could unload a particular plant without any feelings, where the Chase family did everything possible to maintain the operation.

People have said that [the 1956 strike] was the reason for the downfall of Waterbury Mfg. [division of Chase.] I don't believe it. That was a monstrosity of many floors. In those days the concept was to one-level buildings. The Chase Co. had been taken over by Kennecott. To Kennecott, it was something expendable.

A second major problem—one shared by much of American industry—is that foreign companies built more modernized plants which could produce more cheaply, while American companies invested less in new equipment.

Paul Garatoni: I remember in the postwar period, I got involved in the 1950s and 1960s taking people around the mill. We had visitors from all over the world. They'd come to engineering and say, "We're going to build a brass plant." We'd show them around. "This machinery is old; don't do it this way. If we were starting from scratch, here's the way we would do it." The Spaniards, the Japanese, the Indians, all went back home and did it the way we told them to. And we kept on running

The Chase Metal Works. Built in 1917, it now serves as a warehouse. Photo: Jerry Lombardi.

with the same old equipment. Now they're beating the pants off of us.

The tubing for ball-point pens was made out of brass. We had machines going like crazy. That was at a plant near the Waterbury hospital, called French Small Tube. The Germans thought, "Gee, this is a lucrative market." They designed lines that were completely automated to make it. We lost it.

The high price of copper makes brass an expensive material. Cheaper materials were often substituted.

Frank Pochron: There were so many substitutes that came into the picture. We used to do a lot of tubing, a lot of conduit work, a lot of metal for the automobile industry. But then they came in with plastics and everything else. After

a while they found out it doesn't last as long. In the long run it might be costly, but in the meantime, it was hurting our industry. Brass and copper are more expensive than plastics or other substitutes. That's what hurt us for quite a while.

Bill Moriarty: After the war, the brass industry people, in my opinion, completely missed the boat. They didn't try to go into other areas of production. They just knew brass and they weren't really interested in anything else. We could see it going down the drain but couldn't do anything about it.

John Mankowski: These companies might have done a lot better. They're supposed to be astute planners; this is one time they just neglected to do something about a situation. A lot of these plants had such obsolete equipment that

they probably didn't want to do anything to get up-to-date or improved equipment.

Mike Vernovai: A lot like the railroads. They never put any money back into machinery; they took it out in profits.

Finally, the concentration of the brass industry in one small region could hardly last forever. The decline of industrial specialization and "mono-industry" regions has been a basic trend of the U.S. economy.

Since the companies had no local stake in the Brass Valley, when they did invest in new facilities they were likely to do so in areas nearer their markets, rather than in the older Connecticut plants.

Paul Garatoni: [When companies decide to build a new plant, they consider] where's the land available to build a plant and where's the market? And the work force?

Do you remember the big plant that had the big sign, Anaconda, on top of the building on Meadow Street [in Waterbury]? We had gone hog wild in the strip business, going really heavy. That was the Waterbury plant proper, where they had the rolling mills. That building was an automated strand annealing. A terrific piece of equipment. But then the powers-that-be decided we'd better do something better than that. They decided to expand Buffalo, go in for a 25,000-lb. bar, which would

TABLE 29
Metal Manufacturing in the Waterbury SMSA, 1947 and 1977

Industry	Number of production workers		Value added by manufacture ($)	
	1947	1977	1947	1977
Primary metals	8,702	1,200	47,606,000	96,600,000
Fabricated metals	8,515	2,900	42,567,000	59,900,000
Machinery	1,883	800	10,773,000	12,700,000
Instruments	5,773	3,300*	28,601,000	83,900,000*
Costume jewelry	2,168	1,600*	10,535,000	34,700,000*

* 1972 figures, since 1977 was n.a.
Source: Compiled from U.S. Census data by Peter Rachleff.

TABLE 30
Brass Manufacturing in the Waterbury SMSA, 1958 and 1969

Industry	Number of production workers		Capital expenditures ($)		Value added by manufacture ($)	
	1958	1969	1958	1969	1958	1969
Primary metals	4,878	4,100	7,786,000	7,600,000	59,261,000	94,200,000
Nonferrous rolling and drawing	4,463	3,600	7,736,000	6,900,000	55,519,000	86,100,000
Fabricated metals	5,833	5,400	3,926,000	6,200,000	51,224,000	106,800,000
Machinery	2,427	2,100	3,742,000	1,100,000	28,228,000	34,500,000
Instruments	3,912	4,600	784,000	1,800,000	33,591,000	94,700,000
Watches, clocks, and cases	2,535	3,200	275,000	900,000	17,993,000	65,500,000

Source: Compiled from U.S. Census data by Peter Rachleff.

knock everybody else out. In the brass business, 25,000 lb. is tremendous.

[They expanded in Buffalo because] it was a matter of market. Harrison Radiators, General Motors, is right next door to the plant, practically. They'll continue to use radiators in cars for a long time. Things of that nature help them decide where they're going to expand.

A Puerto Rican, Juan Petros (a pseudonym) started working at Anaconda in Waterbury in 1974.

Although he was laid off several times, he was still working there in 1978, when this interview was conducted.

Many operations have been moved to low-wage areas in the South and overseas.

Juan Petros: I know they were making money. Suddenly, [top American Brass officials] called us—which is unfair—all the workers to a meeting inside the shop. They told us that we must tell the union to sit down and talk about business, because according to him they were losing money, they were losing five million dollars. This was in 1976. They can't afford to keep losing money. The wages were too high; we must go to the union and tell them. He gave us until August 20.

They sat down a couple of times, but the union said: No, we don't go back. We want just what we've got. On August 20, they said the place will be closed November 30. They kept laying off people. October first I was laid off. I stayed laid off for nine months. They shut the whole mill down. I don't know where they sent the business; I heard they opened up a place in Virginia, a new plant.

They're investing in Asia, Saudi Arabia; they just built a plant over there for twenty million dollars. They've got people working there for a dollar-and-a-half an hour, doing the same work we're doing here. That's what we can call runaway shops. They just get out of Waterbury, leaving the people of Waterbury without hope, without work. Moving away to other places.

They have places in my country they are exploiting. They can go over there, work twenty years

Anaconda's Waterbury rolling mill. The sign, put up in 1961, was removed when Anaconda closed down the plant in 1980. Courtesy Waterbury Republican-American.

without paying any taxes. They pay half of the wages we get here for the same work. The same thing when they move to the South, to Taiwan. That production costs them half of what it used to here. That's why they're moving down there.

The process of economic concentration we have traced through the history of the brass industry continues today. Just as the American Brass Company, formed from a combination of the early brass plants, was bought by Anaconda, the largest copper producer, so Anaconda has now become a subsidiary of Atlantic Richfield (Arco), one of the largest oil companies in the world.

Arco is a company of truly

global reach. It holds oil and gas rights covering more than twelve million acres in the U.S. It has oil interests from England to Indonesia, and is exploring for more in Australasia, the Philippines, Chile, Somalia, Colombia, and the North Sea. It operates thousands of miles of pipeline and owns thirteen tankers. It manufactures hundreds of chemicals. It mines copper, uranium, silver, molybdenum, and other metals. It holds leases on more than thirty thousand acres of coal lands and a large interest in Jamaican bauxite. It makes economic decisions and organizes its operations on a global scale: It recently closed its copper smelting and refining operations in Montana, for example, and began shipping copper concentrates to Japan for processing. Arco employs over fifty thousand people. Subsidiaries of which it owns over 95 percent include:

Anaconda Co.
 Chile Copper Co.
 Greene Cananea Copper Co.
Atreco, Inc.
Companhia Atlantic de Petroleo
Empresa Carioca de Productos
 Quimicos, S.A.
Thunder Basin Coal Co.
Sinclair Venezuelan Oil Co.
Tanker Transport, Inc.
Griffith-Consumers Co.
Hondo Oil and Gas Co.
Major Petroleum Co.
Venezuelan Atlantic Refining
 Co.
Atlantic Richfield Indonesia,
 Inc.
Buckley and Scott Co.
Four Corners Pipe Line Co.
Partly-owned affiliates include:
Alumina Partners of Jamaica
Anamax Mining Co.
Condumex, S.A.
Compania Minera de Cananea,
 S.A.
Anaconda-Ericsson Inc.
Industrias Nacobre, S.A.
Sociedade Anomina Marvin*

Brass making is only a minor line for this huge multinational corporation. Metal fabricating provided only 5.2 percent of Arco's pretax income in 1980, and brass was only a fraction of its metal fabricating business. Arco owned or

* Standard and Poor's Co., *Standard Corporation Descriptions*, April 1981.

held interests in metal fabricating plants in the U.S., Canada, the Netherlands, Mexico, Brazil, the United Kingdom, Argentina, Colombia, and Ireland.

A company like Arco can plan its operations on an international basis, without regard to local or even national impacts. In 1980, for example, its annual report stated that Anaconda Industries "launched a strategy to improve and strengthen its market position by diversifying and modernizing its metal fabricating operations." This included installing new equipment in Ansonia, Franklin, Ky., Kenosha, Wisc., Buffalo, N.Y., and Waterbury. "More than $200 million have been allocated for a five-year program to streamline manufacturing operations by upgrading seven brass mill plants." This investment will no doubt help keep Anaconda plants in the Valley competitive. But at the same time, Arco is moving the Anaconda Industries headquarters from Waterbury to Chicago, and one of its affiliates is opening a large new tube mill in Mexico.

During the 1950s and 1960s, with each downswing of the business cycle, more jobs were lost in the brass industry. By the end of the 1970s, there was little left of the Big Three in Waterbury.

As of 1968 Waterbury was in an industrial boom. Five thousand were working at Scovill, largely on Vietnam-related production. Be-

tween 1970 and 1974 the Waterbury area lost 4,500 jobs in fabricated metals and 1,200 in primary metals. Chase closed shop in early 1976 after a nine-month strike, leaving 600 jobless. In 1976 Scovill sold its brass operations to a group of investors. At the American Brass tube mill, management demanded a two-dollars-per-hour cut in wages and benefits; when it was denied, the plant was closed and 460 jobs were eliminated.

In each of these cases, the threat of closing the plant was used to demand union concessions, and the closings themselves were blamed on union refusal.

In the 1960s, Scovill Mfg. Co. entered an extended period of acquisitions, becoming a multinational mini-conglomerate. No longer dependent on its aging brass mills, in 1975 it decided to close or sell them.

The threat to close the mills has twice been used to force workers to accept a wage freeze. The first time involved the initial divestiture by Scovill. The Scovill brass plant was valued at $80 million. A group of investors, headed by a scrap dealer who supplied the mills with much of their raw materials, put up $2 million in cash and agreed to take on the company's unfunded pension liabilities. The Connecticut Development Authority, reflecting tremendous local and state pressure to keep the plant running, agreed to guarantee a $10

The remains of the Oakville Div. of Scovill Mfg. Co. Photo: Jerry Lombardi.

million loan to help them buy the mill. Before closing the deal, however, the purchasers insisted that the workers accept a three-year wage freeze.

Mike Vernovai: The [state] Labor Commissioner came in and sat down with us. He said, these guys are going to move; once they go, the plant's gone. The company's going to shut down. The [local union] committee voted that night eleven to five to reject the [wage freeze] offer. [The next afternoon someone said to me,] "Hey, I see you settled the Scovill thing." He said he had heard on the radio they

had a meeting in the mayor's office with the governor and [the state Labor Commissioner]. I called [the Scovill local union president]. He said, "Yes, we had a meeting this morning in the mayor's office." He said he told them the offer was a lousy offer, but he had voted the night before to accept it and he was willing to accept it now.

It was about three months before they had a ratification meeting. I said, I recommend that they not accept the offer. It was a lousy one to begin with. They voted to accept it anyway. That was it. They've suffered for it.

The new company, named Century Brass, took over the old Scovill brass mill. Between 1976 and 1981, about 500 workers were laid off, leaving about 1,500 employed. In 1981 contract negotiations the company demanded cutbacks in benefits, including abandonment of the pension plan. It threatened to close the plant rather than give increases in wages or benefits. Century workers struck, then accepted another wage freeze.

Although the company has repeatedly threatened to close, it has been profitable for the top officials who are its principal owners. In 1979, the only year for which fig-

Assembling brass garden hose couplings at Century Brass, 1982. Photo: Jerry Lombardi.

Hand skills were still required in this buffing operation on a forged brass aqualung valve at Century in 1982. Photo: Jerry Lombardi.

ures are available, Century's five top officials received more than $1 million in salaries, bonuses, insurance, and retirement plan payments. Further, Century purchased for half-a-million dollars cash and $1.5 million in Century stock a company called Central Metal, all of whose selling stockholders were either officers of Century or their relatives. Century's owners have, within the first five years, recovered their initial $2 million investment several times over.

Bill Moriarty: It was so frustrating because you could see what was happening. I was negotiating the final contract at Chase. In the four months we negotiated the contract, I negotiated with five different personnel directors sent in from Cleveland. You'd try to make some sense with this guy, try to salvage something—next thing you know, he's gone. No explanation. Another guy sits across the table. Start all over again.

We knew—some of the Chase executives admitted it in contract negotiations—that they had made the decision to close out the Chase plant in Waterbury two years prior to the negotiation of this contract. But rather than do it cleanly and close it out, what they wanted to do was force the union into a strike by refusing to do anything.

We had given Chase all kinds of things. Chase was far behind the rest of the brass industry. Next year they came back and said they needed more and more. It gets to a point where you can't do it. I couldn't agree to that contract at Chase, while [another international representative] is over at Scovill's fighting to retain their benefits; I couldn't give things at Chase and go to Bristol Brass and say, "No, you can't have it." It got down to the point where even other managements were complaining: "You're giving our competitors all kinds of breaks." And we knew that Chase was going to fold.

We asked the company: If we would accept a contract that we negotiated with them, would they assure us that they would be in business for one year? They refused to give us that assurance.

We had a strike. It was a horrible thing. It was a real tragic thing. The boss was saying, "If the union would only give a little more, it would be all right." A guy with a wife and family figures, "Well, even if I take a ten-cent-an-hour cut, it's better than not working at all." We had a terrible job. We knew it was all downhill. Even if we had taken the minimal contract that Chase had offered, they were going to close that plant. But they would say, "Here's a UAW contract at Chase Brass and Copper and now we want you to give us the same thing because we're competitors." That was the game. It was a terrible game, a heartbreaking thing to go through.

The strike went on and on. It

was disastrous. Finally, they decided to close out Chase's. They tried to steal their pensions, not pay their pensions. We had to go to Washington, invoke every law and threat; we had suits against the company.

[Chase made] a final offer. They put out all the propaganda they could to accept it. Feeling was so intense, there were a police lieutenant and five other policemen [at the union meeting]. The committee was excellent, but they were so frightened when they got to the meeting that they refused to make a recommendation. They were against accepting the thing. [The meeting voted to reject the contract about sixty to forty.]

If they had voted to accept that contract, people would have lost their pensions. It gave the company carte blanche to do almost whatever they could do. That was just before the new pension law came into effect. We knew that something was going to happen. We stalled as much as we could. Finally, we made the best deal we could.

At the beginning of 1976, unemployment in Waterbury reached 15.5 percent. The human cost of the layoffs and plant closings was enormous. Lea Harvey, who had worked at Chase since World War II, describes what life was like for her after the plant was closed.

Lea Harvey: Then one day the fac-

tory closed up and we were all out of a job. I went job hunting. I was at an insurance company in Hartford for an interview. At the end of the interview, the man said to me, "How come after all these years you're now looking for office work?" I said, "I've always been interested in office work. But when I got out of school, they weren't hiring Black girls in offices. I got a job in a factory. The factory is now closed. Now I thought I'd look for a kind of work that I'm interested in." He said, "Oh, I see." And maybe he didn't know.

[I wasn't able to get a job for] six months. I had just bought a car six months before they closed. The man who bought the credit union account was very good to me. I was only getting forty dollars a week on unemployment. When I could, I'd send him a few dollars. He said, "Pay as much as you can, when you can."

I worked in Hartford. I had to buy gas. My take-home pay netted thirty-five dollars a week. We got paid every two weeks. My unemployment check was forty dollars a week. [The gas station owner told me,] "Anytime you need gas, you can get it. And when you get paid, you can pay me. If you can't pay me all, you can pay on it." It was like manna from heaven. I still do business with that gas station.

I'd drive to work for two weeks with ten cents in my pocket. If anything happened, I could make a phone call. That's all. It wasn't easy.

Parts of the former Oakville Div. of Scovill are now used as warehouses. Photo: Jerry Lombardi.

The plant closings also create fear among those who are still working.

Terry Longo: A lot of people at Century: a lot of the older people are just waiting for retirement, a lot of the younger people are praying the place doesn't fold. Anything in Waterbury—it's really terrible. You hear of all these factories moving out. You go into work and you say, "Geeze, what's going to happen?" Naturally, there's 5,000 rumors going around. If you listen to the rumors, we were going to be closed up last year. The younger ones are just holding on to their jobs and hoping that nothing is going to happen, because then what do you do?

A lot of the older ones, where that's all they know, wouldn't feel confident—I know a lot of times I wouldn't feel confident going out and saying, "I'm a Class A inspector and I can do this and that." So for these people, that's all they know, that's all they have to fall on, I think it would be very devastating for them to go somewhere else and start all over again. Even the younger people. You find a kind of notch in a place. You get to know the people and it's hard to leave. If they just closed it down, it would be even worse, because now you would be competing with all these people that you worked with. There's not enough of that kind of work in this area.

My husband was working at Century, too. At times it would get scary: here are the two of us out of work again, together. That's rough. You're used to having so much money coming into the house; you're running your household, and the next thing you know you're down to absolutely nothing compared to what you were making. Plus your benefits—your medical insurance will put you right into poverty row. That's frightening.

Frieda Ewen discusses the impact of job insecurity and plant closings on community life.

Frieda Ewen: I don't remember things being all that great ever here. It seemed to be more affluent while the war industry was going on during the Vietnam war. After that things were not so good, and it was difficult finding employment. A lot of people were unemployed. In the early 1970s, I remember going to the unemployment office with friends. It was completely packed. There were eight lines with twenty people.

For the young people then, that was the way it was. You were collecting unemployment; it was what you had to do, there was not much choice. They had a better attitude because they didn't have families to support. It was much more devastating for the people with families. It was generally depressing at the unemployment office except for the young people, because they were into laughing at it all anyway and laughing at the system, and taking the money because they were ripping you off so badly that, if you could rip them off in any way, it was worth it.

People who have been relatively comfortable take it as a given that, if you want to do something, you just do it. Maybe you'll have a little less in your savings. That's not the reality of the people who live here and work in the factories.

Valley people are not comfortable; they're always on the edge. It's not just Valley people, it's people who have that kind of life where their dependency is on that facility that supplies their job for the moment and may not the next moment. It's not unique to the Valley.

The factory can get up and go, and people know that. It's happened. It can happen anytime. Then you're just blown away, because that was your whole life. You don't have a career that's independent of anything, that you can just move on to the next place. You're totally dependent on that building. When that leaves, you're left there all alone and with nothing, except people who are dependent upon you. People are really nervous about it's not going to be there someday—the tension and day-to-day pressure of that knowledge is pretty awful and pretty stressful.

Most of them who are working in places like that have, at one point or another, been through it already and know the reality and the horror of it. And now, especially with the government doing the horrible things it's doing, they know it's going to be worse this time than it was last time. Plus everything's more expensive now.

There are not the other support structures that used to be there. You survive on your own, because I don't have enough to help you, whereas it used to be that people helped each other more.

The Battered Women's Project is thriving, unfortunately, with clients, with battered and abused women. I'm sure a lot of it has to do with the pressure. The feeling of failure and frustration that goes along with it, too. That you're so dependent on something like that that, if it goes, you're utterly a failure. You've worked all those years and not made it, and now you're down to nothing.

Alcoholism is extremely high in the Valley. One of the main male activities in the Valley is that after work you go to the bar, and that's where you stay till you go home, for many of them.

People are realizing how little control they have over everything that they do. [People are trying to take control back] by organizing. That's why it's more acceptable to come out of the closet and admit that you're poor. People didn't admit that a while ago. Valley people especially. Everybody is, but nobody says they are; to admit it would be horrible. But people are beginning to see that the only way to control anything is to get together and do it yourself, because certainly nobody else is going to do anything for you, because they haven't done it in the past, and they're making it worse now. People are [organizing] because they want the power back any way they can get it.

One of the reasons people don't want to deal with [multinational corporate power] is that it's so much out of their control and the consequences are so devastating. People don't recognize that it directly affects all the daily things that are happening to you. If you get laid off, it's because of the whole picture, what's happening all over the world, this whole corporate construction. It's not because of your deficiency, it's not because of the town's failure to produce; it's because that's the way that the people on the top decided that it should be. Your getting laid off, whatever happens to you, is a consequence of all that. You have nothing to say about it.

At a point people choose not to do that anymore, not to turn away from it all, to look at it squarely and decide that they don't want it anymore and get with other people and spread that around. I don't think that the powers can hold up any longer. The people can stop everything. They have the power to stop everything. They can put their own being out of work in their control. And where would all the big guys be on the top? They've lost control. They don't have it anymore. There's nothing they can do.

If you stop producing—they're not producing on the top; they're only collecting the money from

what you produce. They're not making it. If you stop making it, they don't have any money anymore. If women stopped producing babies, where is their labor power? They don't have it anymore. If people said, "I'm not going to go fight your war; I'm not going to go there," they can't pick up the phone and order troops over there, because there are no troops to order over there; they won't go. There's a lot of power that people have. They have it individually, but they cannot exercise it unless they're together with it.

With what the government and the corporations are doing now, they're making people face that this is what it's all about. Making it clear that the reason everything exists and goes on is for profit. They say it almost outright now. They used to be subtle about it; now they're being very clear. It's almost like the king in his kingdom, the emperor in his empire, claiming all his properties. Everyone else is slaves. Everyone is becoming slaves. They're going to give you enough food and shelter to survive, but they did that for all the slaves through history. Now they'll throw in a few things like TV to keep you docile and noncomplaining. Make you think you're happy with it. Make you think that that's what you should expect and now you've got it. No reason to fight back.

But very quickly, when you

can't get heat in the wintertime and you don't have the electricity anymore to watch the tube—I think they're destroying themselves at this point.

6. Working Conditions: "One Man Could Run the Whole Machine Himself"

AUTOMATION

Even while much of the production process in the brass industry was becoming antiquated, many jobs were being transformed by automation. It often made the remaining work lighter, but it eliminated large numbers of jobs.

Russell Hunter: On certain machines, say there were four guys on some machines. After the war they had new machinery come in that cut down on the help. Where they used to have five guys working they'd only have two guys working. We knew that was coming. You'd see these new machines coming in, something was up to put people out of work.

Russell Sobin: After they got automation, it was all push-button. One man could run the whole machine himself.

They took all the old machines out and brought everything in new. They started all the automation around the 1960s. Big rolls, furnaces. You'd put it in the furnace and it would come out and go

Workers at the New Haven Copper Co., 1981. New Haven Copper is one of the few plants where women perform mill work. Photo: Jerry Lombardi.

An automated flat wire mill, New Haven Copper, 1981. Photo: Jerry Lombardi.

way up fifty feet in the air, come down and around, then back into a coil. That would be finished. It would be bright without pickling. You didn't have to acid it anymore.

Now they've got a big extruder coming in from Germany. It's going to eliminate I don't know how many men. They're putting it over in the brass rod department where I used to be.

Eddie Labacz: In the old days we had what we called the open-hearth furnace. We had to load the pans with metal. We had a hoist to pull it in. When we pulled it out, it was hot metal. We had to take long prongs and push it out of the

way. We didn't have jitneys like you have now. Now it's easier. You just load the table; it goes in the door, which closes behind the furnace. It comes out cooled. There's no more handling of hot metal. Annealing processes have changed something terrific. We had three men on a furnace; now we've got one man doing the same job. It takes more skill to run the equipment; you have to be knowledgeable if something is not cycling out properly. But the buggy lugging is not there, the back breaking is not there. Years ago it was all buggy lugging. You were just a big mule.

As crews were cut, the pressure of the work could be intensified.

Russell Sobin: It was easy when they had two men and they used to take a break, a half hour each. On a hot summer day a guy would have a chance to sit down for half an hour to have a sandwich or cool off and go outside. After, they made it so there was only one man. Then they made it so there was only the roller and the guy in the back, the catcher. Automation eliminated from five men down to three men.

Some new jobs were created by automation in other areas. William Freeman went from working in the shop at Scovill to the office.

William Freeman: I started attending business school in New Haven for computers and computer-programming operations. At the end of the first semester, I applied for a job as a computer operator and got it. That was my way out of the mills. This was from within the company.

Paul Garatoni was in the engineering department at American Brass when rolling was first automated. He explains how the companies go about designing automated equipment and how they decide to introduce it.

Paul Garatoni: We were the first ones in the world to have automatic control on rolling of metal.

A new casting machine at Century Brass in 1981. It transforms molten metal into two semi-finished coils of brass sheet under computer control, thus eliminating several steps that formerly took place between casting and rolling. Photo: Irene Salvatore.

At the Waterbury plant, one of the engineers started it. We had an X-ray machine send X rays down through the metal. At the other end there was an eye sensitive to those X rays, and the variations in thickness would show up. The roll would open or close to get the correct thickness.

On some of your pictures, you might see a rolling mill with a huge wheel off to the side. The roller would grab that wheel and pull down on it or raise it. He had to know his machine and how much to turn. You're talking half-a-thousandth sometimes.

Instead of using a hand wheel to raise and lower the rolls, they were motorized [in the new system]. So from the signal received from the X ray showing the variation, that would feed to pulsing timers that would jog the motor clockwise or counterclockwise which, in turn, would raise or lower the rolls. That made it into a less demanding job in the required skill of the operator. And you could do a lot better.

[To automate a process, you] combine as many operations as possible into one line. That's basically it. How many functions have to be performed on this item? You make a continuous flow. When this function is performed at this station, it continues by conveyor, or if it's a long piece, it just

Women assembling an automotive part on a dial press, Century, 1982. Photo: Jerry Lombardi.

keeps on going, until it has completed the last function that's required.

Born in New Haven in 1953, Danny LaFortune grew up in Ansonia, the son of Leon LaFortune, the executive secretary of the YMCA, and Thelma Morrison

LaFortune. Danny was always a "YMCA man," and traveled extensively as a YMCA youth counselor on Y-sponsored trips. "I've been to every state in the U.S. except Alaska and Hawaii, and to the Caribbean, Canada, and Mexico." He is an avid skier, tennis player, swimmer, racquetball player, and sports car fan. He graduated from Ansonia High School and attended Housatonic Community College for a year and a half. Like his friend Quentin Garatoni, he worked at B.F. Goodrich and left there in 1974 to work at Anaconda on the extruder and later in the packing

Assembling small automotive parts at Century Brass, 1982. Photo: Jerry Lombardi.

room. He was married for two years and has one child. He recently married again, this time a woman from a large Polish family.

One of eight children, George Magnan was born in New Haven in 1956. He grew up in Bethany, and graduated from Amity High School. His father was an engineer

Assembly of brass hypodermic syringes, Century Brass, 1982. Photo: Jerry Lombardi.

at American Brass, and now works as supervisor of maintenance at a plant in Beacon Falls. His mother works as a salesperson for an office systems concern. George started traveling in 1974. "I've spent time in every state of the union except Alaska. I would stop, work, travel, go another two hundred miles. I think I must've had a hundred jobs. I've worked as a tour guide and a lifeguard in Hawaii; assembled mobile homes in Boise, Idaho; worked as a receptionist at a Howard Johnson's in California; unloaded boats for a fish market in Hawaii; done maintenance work

for the National Parks in California; cleared land; done construction work; installed in-ground pools; and worked in restaurants, hospitals, and convalescent homes as a chef." He lived in Hawaii for several years, where he served in the Hawaii Air National Guard. He was married for a short time, had a daughter, and was then divorced. In 1979 he left Hawaii for Connecticut, because "the islands were economically depressed. There was no work. You could be comfortable, but you couldn't get ahead." He got a job at Anaconda in Ansonia, where he works on the draw bench in the shape area. He has studied cooking for many years, first at Questa College in San Luis Obispo, California, and then at adult education courses. He is presently taking courses at a

school for psychic development in Bristol, Alpha Logics. He says, "My experiences have given me a smaller fear of the unknown than other people." When asked when he thought he would take off again, George says, "I never know when I'm going to leave until three or four days before I go."

Along with automation have come automatic clock charts and increasingly sophisticated forms of time study and work rationalization.

Danny LaFortune: There are certain guys who are on clock charts. If your chart stops, [the company] wants to know why.

Quentin Garatoni: Once you know your chart, you know what your delays are. You're allowed so much every day. See how they're turning us into computers, though? You have to be as good as their computer. You've got to know all the symbols, you've got to know everything to make your money. It doesn't matter how much work you do; it's how much you act like a computer to make your bonus. You could do more work than me, not write it on your record right, and get fired for low performance, whereas I'll be making ten or fifteen dollars a day bonus.

George Magnan: If you know how to push the pencil right, you'll make more money. Every record in there should start: Once upon a time. . . .

Born in Bridgeport, Connecticut, in 1942, Fred Smith grew up in the lower Naugatuck Valley. Divorced, his mother raised him and her three other children on her own. "It wasn't an easy life," Smith recalls. When he was nineteen, Smith went to work at Anaconda. Right after his probationary period, he became a union steward, and has been involved in the union ever since. He has worked as a hand-straightener, a helper on the band saw, a helper on the draw bench, and as a die man and an operator on the extruder. For the last seven years he has been a scrapman/receiver in the Rod Mill. In 1976 Smith was elected vice-president of Local 6445, USWA. When the president, Pat Uva, retired, Smith finished out his term, and in 1979 he was elected president of the local. He served on the negotiating committee during the 1977/78 strike, and again in 1980/81 contract negotiations. During the 1980/81 negotiations, Smith was the first local union president to serve along with representatives from the international on the negotiations subcommittee. Smith lives in Beacon Falls with his wife, the former Mary Ann Widziewicz, and their two children.

Fred Smith: Everybody in there has what we call piggyback jobs. There isn't an employee in there that doesn't have two or three jobs today. Everybody has more than one job to do in the course of a normal eight hours' work.

When I got there sixteen years ago, we had a little over a thousand employees, today we've got 450 people. In the rod mill, we're putting out twice as much work with half the employees we had ten or fifteen years ago with the same equipment. We've made this plant operate not on new equipment. The employees have kept this plant running on productivity.

I've got three jobs. Years ago when a guy retired, the job went out for bid. Today, before that guy is going to get out, they're looking around, who could they add that job onto. Maybe we'll throw him five or six cents an hour, maybe we won't throw him anything.

Productivity has doubled. A furnace operator was on a two-hour cycle, now he's down to an hour. They knocked one hour off. We used to put a pan in every two hours, have one operator in the back and while he was loading a pan it would give the other operator time to breathe before he had to go down to the other end and unload. They took away the second man, and from two hours' annealing time they cut it to one. The next thing they'll do is have the operator put the coils on his back and run through the furnace with them.

Sid Monti: Despite all their screaming, American production is better than the world average, for each hour worked, including Japan. Our guys got a lot of pride in what they do, but when they're told you gotta push it out, what the hell can they do about it? In

Operating a cut-and-draw press, Century Brass, 1982. The machine makes the shell of a diesel engine injector tube. Photo: Jerry Lombardi.

brass especially, in the casting shops, that's the core of the whole operation. If you don't mix the material properly to get a certain alloy, you're going to wind up with scrap. If you try to speed up the rolls, you're going to get scrap. If you try to speed up the piercing machines for tubes, you're going to wind up with scrap. Again they don't care, as long as they get the tonnage out. When they get the tonnage out, and they get the tubes or the sheet metal back, they blame the workers. They don't blame the people who were forcing the stuff out, with nothing in mind except to get the tonnage out, so we can get the cash flow in. That's their whole concept and it's wrong.

When this interview was taped in April 1978, Pete Chevarella, Jr., was a safety steward at Anaconda's Ansonia plant. He's worked for Anaconda for about ten years, and presently works in the indirect extrusion department as an operator. He is a member of the executive board of Local 6445, USWA.

Pete Chevarella, Jr.: I've worked 80, 90, 100, 110 hours a week in there. If you don't they're telling you, you're going to get a warning, or three days off, or we'll take it to arbitration, or you go out and when we want you we'll call you. If it's 120 degrees outside, we'd like to have the option, the right to say if we want to stay or not, not

Checking an automotive assembly for leaks by immersing it in water, Century Brass, 1982. Photo: Jerry Lombardi.

say, well you're on ten hours, you gotta stay. We had an incident down there last year. The five men on the extruder, they couldn't walk, they were falling down, almost, they couldn't move anymore, it was so hot. I asked if the crew could go home early. They told us point blank that if we walked out, we'd be wildcatting. I never heard of such a thing before.

Fred Smith: After ten hours, an individual is basically fatigued. I don't think he can properly func-

tion. After ten hours, you're prone to injury a lot more than on an eight- or ten-hour day. When you start working twelve to fourteen hours a day, you just don't watch what you're doing and you start going through the motions, and that's when a person gets hurt.

Quentin Garatoni: They'll try and eliminate certain things on the job, things a worker might think need to be done. A lot of times they *need* to be done. The quality will be a lot poorer, but it'll get more

production out, more weight out. That in the end is what they're worried about.

Plus, they'll constantly retime your job, try to pick up any little trick an operator learned, which is *his* trick. He doesn't owe it to the company. But they figure you work there, you owe everything to the company. We're unskilled labor. They tell us how to do a job, that's all they can expect of us. But they expect they own our minds when we're in there.

Operating a sizing machine, Century Brass, 1982. The machine makes sure the product is perfectly round; the hand straps pull the worker's hands away from the machine when it operates. Photo: Jerry Lombardi.

HEALTH AND SAFETY

Accidents have become less common since the days when some plants had more accidents in a year than they had workers. The decrease is due to safer equipment and the pressure of insurance costs, government health and safety regulations, and union influence.

Russell Sobin: You don't have as many accidents now because you have more safeguards. Your equipment, too. You had to catch the rod in your hand; now they have tables where you [raise and lower] the table. You don't have to handle the rod; you just guide it along. Cranes to lift metal. In those days,

unless you were picking up 150 lb., they didn't give you a crane. Everything was done by hand. Same way with the machines; they have safeties. OSHA has helped a lot. Maybe sometimes they are too strict, but I'd rather have them more strict than not. These companies don't even like the idea of OSHA coming near the place.

Nonetheless, accidents remain a serious threat to the lives and well-being of brass workers.

Quentin Garatoni: They'll break a man in on a job for three, two hours. They had a guy break in on the saw today for two hours, then they put him on his own. This guy

is a health hazard to himself and everybody else. But he's going to say that he knows the job because he's a new hire and he doesn't want to lose his job. He's going to get on it and he's going to hurt himself.

I saw one guy come in. He was running a block. They broke him in for two days. Then they put him on a twelve-hour, seven-day shift. He lasted about three weeks and then he went around the block. He busted himself up real good. It pulls you in. It tore him all up. He was a big, heavyset guy, too. He went spinning around a merry-go-round where a coil fits. He was just wasted; his glove got caught and it pulled him right in.

George Magnan: He was about three days shy of being in the union.

There was something wrong with the emergency shutoff on his machine, too. I went and saw him in the hospital about five days after the accident. "I know I hit that sonofabitch," he said; "I know I hit it, but it didn't stop."

Another time, another guy cut off his thumb. He got an assigned job. They needed him somewhere else, so they told him to go over to this other job. They showed him how to do it for a couple of days. They never showed him how to shut off the saw that spins behind him. He was banging this thing with a hammer. Me and [another worker] were right behind him; we thought he had pulled a muscle or something.

Quentin Garatoni: [On an extruder furnace] a guy turned on the pilots—he thought. But he didn't have the pilots on. So he was loading the furnace with gas. One pilot was lit, and it just blew the top off the furnace. It was lucky it blew *up*. If it had blown out, it would have got the guys. But it blew up in the air. It's a good thing the furnace was in disrepair; there was a weak section and it worked as a safety valve. If the bricks in that furnace had been good, it would have blown that section of the mill out of there.

George Magnan: They were extruding metal. There was a semi-new operator. It comes out of the machine, and it has a track that gets it going in a straight line. But [the metal] had a hook to it. It caught the outside edge of the track and came whizzing around past me. I didn't have time to jump out of the way. It hit my leg. I knew I got burned; I could feel the burn sensation. But I didn't think it was bad. It was early in the morning. I'd just got my coffee; I wasn't really into working, anyways. I started walking toward the nurse. Halfway up it started to hurt a little more, so I got Danny Bialek, the vice-president of the union. Then I could feel blood in my socks. "Wait a minute; let's take a look before we go any further." He could see there was a pretty deep gash. To the bone.

Fred Smith: In the summer, when it's 98 or 95 degrees outside, it's got to be 140 degrees on that extruder. Even in the summer, the operator has to wear safety glasses, long sleeved shirt, buttoned all the way up, a hat on his head, because these chips fly, and they get on your head and your skin, and they burn.

I've seen on the No. 5 Extruder, extruding nickel silver, 776 alloy: that'll heat up, and it'll never heat up even. It'll be a dark color red when it comes out, and right in the center of the billet it'll be white hot. When you hit that white hot spot, it just blows out. I've seen a chunk of metal, about a pound, fly out of that machine and go as much as 150 feet and hit the back of a saw, a steel plate, and knock it right off.

William Freeman: I was working with another person who loaded the billets on the ramp. He would load at one end; my job was to get up and straighten out the billets on the other end. The lift was timed; it went in every three minutes or something.

One day I was sitting there; there was something like an hour downtime on the machine. All of a sudden, I noticed that everyone was running toward the other end of the press that I worked on. The person who was loading from the jitney onto the ramp had climbed off his jitney and was pushing the billets down, so they would slide. He had to give them a push. As he climbed off the jitney, either he had forgot to put on the brake on his jitney or the brake had slipped. The jitney had crushed him between the ramp and the jitney. He died a couple of days later.

I've often wondered. I didn't feel responsible because I had no business being at the other end of the ramp. But it seems strange that people from the other end of the factory would arrive at this man before I did.

There are a lot of things to take into consideration. The noise factor—I don't think anyone heard him scream. It was a matter of someone finally seeing him.

After the accident, they put a brace, like a sleeve, on the ramp. If the jitneys ever slip their brakes again, you don't have to worry about that particular accident.

Among the other hazards was heat prostration. There were many people who passed out; people constantly passed out. That used to scare me. You were exposed to the heat of the metal. The job was to stack the hot metal. I've watched people fall and pass out. I always thought, "My God, what would happen if they ever passed out toward the bench, instead of the other way?"

Other hazards are only now coming to be understood.

Tony Gerace: The Wilshire Foundry, now part of Century, has a problem with lead poisoning. They have to make modifications in a lot

Repairing a machine in the eyelet room at Century, 1982. The ear protectors indicate the high noise level in the room. Photo: Jerry Lombardi.

of equipment and they're being lead-tested.

Alex Lopez: It's dangerous. The worst part is the fumes. You've got acid. They put work in the fire; if it's not clean, the oil smokes for a couple of hours—you can't see. I think they're against the law; the air is not clean in there. Fans are no good; they send the hot air from here to there and back, circulate it. It has nowhere to go. There's a lot of heat out there; they have eighteen furnaces.

Stress, too, is increasingly recognized as a threat to health, and factories are admittedly a high-stress environment.

Danny LaFortune: I wasn't really planning on working in this place. I was going to go to school, finish what I'd started. Each time I thought I had it all together, they would lay me off. Maybe by this time I had bought a car or I had a rent to pay. Then we had a strike—six months out. I went down the tubes. I pay child support; there was no way I could pay it. I was in the hole again, so I had to go back. How many times I wanted to check into school!

I was on second shift, shell shear. I was going out with a girl, working six or seven days a week, three or four weeks at a time. I started having a little trouble with my girl. At 11 o'clock at night I might go out, start drinking. Nothing else to do. You start drinking, you go home, you sleep, you wake up, mess around a little bit, you've got to go back to work. Every single day. It got to me after a while. I found myself really hitting the bottle. I didn't want to admit it then, but I did. My eyes were sagging down to my stomach.

George Magnan: One common thing among everyone in there is frustration. You can tell, I know in myself: The majority of the people know they could do a lot better, if they only had—all the ifs and buts involved. It's the same with management, too. Even people who are like a fresh opened bottle of champagne most of the time, you can tell when they're into that cycle. Maybe it's once a year, maybe it's once a month. It's something that everybody in there goes through at

Preparing hypodermic syringe bodies for chrome plating in the plating room at Century Brass, 1982. Photo: Jerry Lombardi.

least once a year. Where the ifs and the buts and the if onlys overshadow everything else, and the whole situation seems really hopeless.

7. A Changing Work Force: "They Don't Want to Tote That Barge and Lift That Bale Anymore"

WOMEN WORKERS

Although many women were pushed out of the plants after World War II, many more continued working.

Mary Diogostine: I think you had to [keep working after the war] because you were living on a different scale, and you had to keep up. I couldn't think of quitting my job. I would do without this and that: I might as well work.

Faye Marie Orvetti was born in 1923 in Durant, Oklahoma. She was a childhood friend of Jewel Lucarelli, and came with her to Connecticut to work in the World War II defense industry. She was a roving inspector at Casco in Bridgeport. After working at W. E. Bassett in Derby, she went to work at Autoswage in 1953. She is still there today working as a forelady. She has one son, and lives in Plymouth.

TABLE 31
The Waterbury SMSA Workforce, by Sex and Industry, 1950

Industry	Men	Women	Total
Labor force (aggregate)	47,783	22,103	69,886
Employed	44,412	20,296	64,708
Unemployed	3,335	1,802	5,137
Construction	2,503	74	2,577
All manufacturing	25,782	10,822	36,604
Primary metals	9,704	2,263	11,967
Fabricated metals	4,276	1,430	5,706

Source: Compiled from U.S. Census data by Peter Rachleff.

A great many women worked in small plants that remanufactured brass.

Faye Marie Orvetti: I've been at Autoswage twenty-eight or twenty-nine years; I went there in 1953. I worked days for four years in assembly work. Then I started night shift. We use lots of brass there. I work in the assembly department. We take chain, cut it to the length the customer wants, put whatever gadget it calls for—we have links, couplings, end rings. We do thousands and thousands of keychains that are put on rabbits' feet or whatever novelties. We also do plumbing chains from brass that we assemble in the assembly room.

It's all women in the assembly department, except for one man who doesn't do the assembly work; he works around the machines. There are a lot of women in the machine shop, also. There always have been from the time I went there; that particular company already had women on machines thirty years ago when I went there. Where they'd have a couple of men as mechanics, they'd have a couple of women as operators.

Jewel Lucarelli: I got a job at Autoswage. There I got involved with machinery that I liked. At first we were on the foot presses, but eventually I got on the machines, and I really enjoyed the work. We made all kinds of things on the machines. We made the little keychains, like the Army uses for dog tags. They do different parts for IBM, Timex.

Women are still far from receiving either equal work or equal pay.

Jewel Lucarelli: They brought in men, right off the streets, and they'd tell me to train them right from scratch. They'd just bring them over, this is John or Bill and

TABLE 32
The Waterbury SMSA Workforce, by Types of Employment and Employer, 1950

Occupation	Private wage-earner	Public employee	Self-employed	Total
Wage-earners (aggregate)	55,584	3,571	5,377	64,703
Men (aggregate)	37,502	2,168	4,694	44,418
Professional and technical workers	2,248	330	560	3,138
Managers and officers	1,935	168	2,236	4,341
Clerical workers	2,582	488	18	3,088
Sales workers	2,205	4	302	2,515
Craftsmen and foremen	11,288	168	715	12,174
Operatives	12,151	122	198	12,480
Domestic servants (private households)	48	n.a.	4	52
Service workers	1,896	616	221	2,740
Laborers	2,481	252	42	2,779
Women (aggregate)	18,082	1,403	683	20,285
Professional and technical workers	1,498	972	110	2,590
Managers and officers	290	31	268	596
Clerical workers	4,984	306	29	5,339
Sales workers	1,225	n.a.	71	1,338
Craftsmen and foremen	384	4	10	398
Operatives	7,415	6	31	7,459
Domestic servants (private households)	705	n.a.	16	722
Services workers	986	75	111	1,185
Laborers	357	3	1	365

Source: Compiled from U.S. Census data by Peter Rachleff.

we'd like you to teach him to run these machines. At first, I was flattered, I got a kick out of it. Then after a while, I said "Hey, what's going on, I'm teaching these guys and they're getting this much money, and I'm only getting this much, and I've been here all these years, and I've even got to teach them to start and stop the machines." They weren't mechanics or anything, they were just guys off the street who come in. It got on my nerves. If I can do it that well, how come I don't get paid for it? And this is why I ended up quitting.

Frieda Ewen: I can recall working in shops where the employees were primarily women, and they would be working on lines or on machines. They would be there, all day long, doing the job, chug-a-chug, all day long. The few male employees that they had would be machine operators, or who knows what they did, because they didn't do much of anything. The men would get a decent wage. The women got minimum wage and had to pay union dues out of it. That's when I thought unions were for nothing. You were paying union dues and you weren't ever getting anything except a turkey at Christmas. The union was doing O.K. for the men, but forgot about the women, who were the main people in the place.

The men used to come around and tell us how awful their job was and how hard they worked, but I never saw them do any work. They usually spent their day walking around the section where the women were and hanging their arms on them and just talking, while the woman was working away. Every once in a while, a woman would turn around and say: "What are you doing here? Why aren't you doing any work? You're getting paid so much more than me." The response from the man would be: "I get paid for what I know, not what I do." You'd just keep working.

While I was working at Pen-Keystone, I was in the midst of shop courses, learning how to make tools. I went to the bosses there and asked: How do I apply for a job over there where the guys were working in the other room? They shuffled around a bit, they all got together, and then they came back and said, "You can't get a job in there because the insurance won't cover you." This was in 1965. It took away my desire to finish this course.

In the larger brass plants, the mills remain a male preserve to this day, despite Affirmative Action requirements. Union seniority, job-bidding systems, and a decreasing work force often mean that only the most back-breaking jobs are advertised outside the plants. Some workers believe that the absence of women in the mills is attributable to both company practices and the attitudes of male workers.

Quentin Garatoni: Occasionally, they bring women into the shop. First, the company hasn't really put any effort into it. Second, the guys are scared that women are going to come in and take their jobs. Third, they say women can't do the job, that they're physically not strong enough. I consider myself strong enough, but there's a lot of jobs in there that I can't do. They're looking at it in the wrong terms. They're not saying, this *person* isn't strong enough, they're saying women aren't. They've had women come in there and they get harassed. It takes a really strong woman to make it because guys will make all sexist comments all the time. They won't give her the break they give another guy coming in the mill. So, they're keeping the women out of the mill, the men in. They're keeping men and women fighting, Blacks and whites fighting, and who wins? They do, they sit up in their office and laugh.

In some of the smaller shops, women have managed to break the sex barrier and obtain the better-paying jobs traditionally reserved for men. Stella Horoshak worked a "man's job" during World War II, and today she is one of a few women working at Bridgeport Brass.

Stella Horoshak: I worked on presses for twenty-eight years. One time they took the guard off because they couldn't get the materials in. I lost my thumb there. So they took me to the doctor and he sewed the skin on. I came home. My mother said, "Good! I told you not to work in a shop." That was her attitude then. Women in those days didn't do things that we did.

My kids think it's great I'm driving a jitney now. They get a kick out of it. My son-in-law has a big picture of me driving the jitney on his wall. If anyone comes in he says, "That's my mother-in-law."

When I first started, they wouldn't show me anything. They didn't like the idea. I sat on a bench for two whole weeks. Finally I said to my superior, "Let me go back on my shift." I went outside with the jitney and I learned how to drive the three jitneys. Even up to today: Anything is banged, "Stella did it." I get blamed for everything. If I wasn't there, I still get blamed for it.

Sandy Kay is the Shop Chairperson at the New Haven Copper Co. in Seymour and the Financial Secretary of UAW Amalgamated Local 1827. Born in 1940 in Central Falls, Rhode Island, she moved to Connecticut in 1961 after a stint in the Air Force. She was hired at New Haven Copper in 1972, when the government began to require the company to hire women. "I'm just one of those people who be-

lieve you can do anything if you set your mind to it." She got active in the union, serving as steward, vice-chair, and finally chairperson. "I fought for all the things I believed a union should be and what I thought the people over there wanted." In a shop in which the majority of the workers are male, she encountered "quite a bit of opposition" in her bid for union leadership, but finally won "by a male vote, not a female vote." She brings a tremendous amount of energy to everything she does, from fighting for the workers on the shop floor to playing softball in the Valley Women's Softball League.

A new generation of women entered the brass plants in the 1970s.

Sandy Kay: The first woman in my shop to be hired lived on my street in Derby. She told me they were

Running a slitting machine at New Haven Copper Co., 1981.
Photo: Jerry Lombardi.

hiring because of the government making the company hire so many women. So I came up to apply for a job. I started on the packing floor. That was a fairly simple job. Male or female, anybody could do it. The jitney job came up on the board later and I bid for that. I found that to be an easy job. We have girls who do rolling over there. They do just about everything in our shop. All the machines. Of the seven girls, only one or two have not been on machines at one time or another. They're mostly on machines now. They are the operators, not just the helper. They do the finish gauge and that sort of stuff. We have one on a Nash four-high roller. One's been a slitter. They've been on the blockers. They've done just about [everything]. We've had girls come in and look at the job. I feel that the company made it sound a lot tougher than it was. They refused to take the job because they thought it was a lot tougher. Some of the jobs are heavy, no ifs, ands, or buts about it. They'd say, "It looks too tough," and I could tell by their explanation that the company was more or less discouraging them on certain jobs that they felt a girl couldn't do. I feel there's not a job over there that we can't do.

Some of the coils, if it's a heavy gauge, you have to pick up the tail to begin to set it through the machines. That's definitely heavy—sixty, eighty, a hundred pounds. It's not just lifting it waist high; it may be up over your shoulder to get it where it has to be fed into the machine.

A few of them took the jobs to get into the shop and proved that they could do them. Of course, when an easier or a better-paying job came up, they bid off it.

Average pay is around seven-fifty.

I had to join [the union] when I first got there; it's automatic. Since I was in it, I came to the meetings. With that, I learned more about it. Then the steward job came up on my floor. When I became the steward on my floor, I think I had nine months there. From there I was vice-chairman for three months, and when the regular election came up, I was voted in as chairman of the union over there.

[The opposition] felt a female could not do the job or stand under the pressure that they felt was necessary. I'm going on my third year, so I guess I must have made [it].

[Women have special problems getting involved in their unions because] a lot of women don't have time. They have kids; after they go home from here. Even though the men have families, they get out more. When the woman gets home, she makes supper, she takes care of the kids. I'm single and I don't have any ties, so it's a little different with me. I can get involved and I can spend thirty hours a week on something else besides just going to work. That does make a difference. That is probably why a lot of women don't get involved.

I myself wouldn't be one to go out with a sign. I will have to say that [the women's movement] helped me get into the shop. I wouldn't be over there probably if it wasn't for the government and the fact that they pushed the government into letting us get over there.

Born in New London in 1950, Avis Grant grew up in Ansonia. "I'm a foster child, and my foster father worked in American Brass some twenty-odd years. He never talked too much about the work there. My foster mother was just a regular housewife. She raised forty-seven foster children, all generations." In 1973 Avis got a job under Affirmative Action at the New Haven Copper Company, where she worked as a Nash roller and then as an assistant operator on the Z-mill. She is active in the union, serving as secretary for three years and presently as steward on the third shift. She lives in Ansonia with her foster mother, sister, and son.

Avis Grant: I needed a good-paying job. [Before] I was doing secretarial work during the day; I was a barmaid during the evening. A fellow came in and said they needed help at New Haven Copper; "Just go and tell them I sent you." I said O.K. I went up there the next day. They interviewed me. They hired me. It was about eight years ago.

I've been on various jobs in there.

[Under Affirmative Action they needed women.] And then I think they needed a minority in there. They couldn't decide what I was. "Is she Black? Is she Puerto Rican? Is she Italian?" After a while they realized I was Black.

They hired me on the packing floor. That wasn't bad; it was easy. Packing goods that had to be shipped, loading the trucks up with the hand truck. Unloading the parts that would come out of annealing. The job was O.K., but it was boring at times; then, when they had the work, it was too much work for me. I don't like to work that much.

After my probationary period was up, I had bid on the pickle tubs. They felt a woman couldn't

do it. They had hired two women for the job; they had quit. They didn't even stick out their probationary period. I was determined I was going to stay on the pickle tubs. With luck, the foreman there liked me. So when we had to take things out of the acid and wipe them in sawdust to make sure they were dry, if it was a hot day I would say to the boss, "Do we have to use sawdust?" "No, just dry them well," he said. So it wasn't as bad as everyone said it would be. I stayed on that a few months. We got laid off then. In 1976, 1977.

When I got hired back, I was on the four-high rolls. There was another girl and I worked on it. That was fun, but back then I didn't understand it. The machine was so big and I felt this machine could do a lot of damage to me if something happened. So I think I was scared of the machine; there was a lot of tension because I was scared of it. It was putting 8,000 lb. of copper on the back end; the sticker would stick it through, and then I would take it down to a specific gauge.

I just got off it now, after being on it for two-and-a-half years. I understand it a lot better. It was nice. I thought I was a little older now, so it was time for me to settle into something that, if New Haven Copper laid off, I could go elsewhere and probably get a job pretty easily being a roller.

It was getting hot. I wanted to

get off the rolls, because when you're rolling that stuff, the rolls get very, very hot. You're sweating and everything. I don't like to get dirty! It's that simple; I work in the factory, but I don't like to get dirty. I normally go into work pretty clean, and when I come out, I try to be clean.

Now I'm on the Z-mill, which is a rolling job. But I'm not the operator; I'm just the assistant. Now I just load the machine up. When the fellow finishes rolling it down to the gauge, I rewind it and take it away. That goes on all night.

You can tell that the men are— what's the word you use—male chauvinist. They feel that a woman can't do the job. When I was on the rolls the first time, I didn't understand it. This time I was determined to prove to them that I could do the job. I was out to prove to the men that I could do the job, and that's what I did.

Plenty of time material would jam up in the machine; that's rough; you're working with heavy gauge, and when it jams up, you've got to pull and tug and cut. You've got to use shears that cut metal more than a quarter of an inch thick. You're shaking, while this thing is going across the shop chopping the metal up. It was rough. I was determined. They would say, "You can't use that; that's too heavy." "No, I can use it." It was heavy, but I had to prove to them that I could use it.

When I had a job on the second

shift, the maintenance fellow wouldn't let me do anything heavy, so I didn't have to worry about that. But on days, "You've got the job; you do your own job."

What I like best about my job is the money. I love money! The least I like about it is getting dirty; I don't like to get dirty.

[I am working 7 o'clock at night to 7 o'clock in the morning.] With my mother living there, my sister living with me, my son is not really neglected. On the weekends I'm with him and we'll go out to dinner. He understands that I have to work. He understands that I like money; and he likes money.

A NEW GENERATION

During the 1960s and 1970s, the generation of workers who had entered the brass mills before World War II began to retire. Despite the decreasing overall employment, many younger workers began entering the plants. They differed in a number of ways from the previous generation of workers.

The older generation of factory workers had rarely completed high school.

Eddie Labacz: The kids coming in today are more educated. We have a lot of them who have two, three, four years of college. Coming in because of the money.

The new labor force had distinctly different attitudes about the work

A gate at Anaconda's Ansonia plant in 1982. Quentin Garatoni is on the left of the group in the center. Photo: Jerry Lombardi.

itself. As Grace Cummings put it, "They don't want to tote that barge and lift that bale anymore." Management, and some older workers, greeted the changed attitudes toward work with disapproval.

Russell Sobin: My son-in-law is a pretty big wheel at American Brass. He says that they're having problems with these kids because they won't work. They'll work eight hours; when you tell them to work overtime, they won't do it. And now they haven't got the right to can them like they used to. Before, when they told you you were on a ten-hour schedule, you had to do it or else they would get rid of you. A lot of the kids don't want to work. They'll take a day shift or a third shift, but they won't work the second shift because they can't fool around.

[People haven't wanted to work so much] ever since, you'd say, the hippie movement. They just don't want to work. They come in, they work a couple of days, and they're gone. They don't want to work.

George Magnan: In terms of work, the younger people are really apathetic. Why you're there tends to escape you often. [The older workers] seem more dedicated. I don't think it's out of any kind of love or loyalty toward the place; it's just the way they were raised. To me, I know I'm wasting my time being here. So I don't kill myself.

Alex Lopez: Of course, there will always be somebody in there who doesn't want to work or doesn't want to do the job. Especially these days. Some of the young kids are very tough. The young kids sit down in the middle of the job. If they have twenty minutes for lunch and they take half an hour, they don't care if they see the boss go by. Before, we used to take that time off, but if you saw somebody come, you moved because you didn't know who that person is; maybe it's the big wheel. But today, they answer back all the time. They are not great workers, like it used to be. Especially since they know the job is not that great, the money isn't that good. "Why kill myself?" that's what they say.

In part, this change in attitudes reflects a change in aspirations. Many younger workers express the desire that their work lives be creative, interesting, and fun.

George Magnan: What would I do [if I didn't have to work here]? Cooking, because that's my hobby. I spend three-quarters of my free time reading cookbooks and things like that. I know that's what I would do. I'd love to.

Danny LaFortune: The ideal job for me would be park ranger at Yosemite Valley, with my family, up in the mountains, taking care of the bears and the moose. Or Yellowstone. Or to run raft rides down the Colorado River.

MINORITY WORKERS

An increasing proportion of workers are either Blacks or recent immigrants, either from Europe or from Puerto Rico, Ecuador, and other parts of Latin America.

They continue to face discrimination on the job—and resent it.

William Freeman: I didn't want to go to a trade school because I had no interest there. I wasn't going to college. So that left me with the brass mills. So I went and filled out an application and ended up in the mills. That was in my eighteenth year, about June. I went to work in the mills as an unskilled worker. I was employed in the rod mill as a strand man. As the billets of metal were put in the presses and compressed out in long rods, it was my job to take tongs, hook them onto the rods, and pull them down benches.

I didn't like the job. It was hot. It was dirty. It was very noisy. It required taking a lot of salt tablets. It required taking a lot of water breaks. We worked in fifteen-minute shifts; you worked fifteen minutes and got, maybe, half an hour off, then worked another fifteen minutes.

I did that for a while. I wanted to do something else there. One of the jobs that impressed me was the coiler. I spoke to my foreman about it. He said no, I couldn't do it. There were college students in the mills for the summer allowed to do this coiling; I felt slighted.

Avis Grant: There's a Puerto Rican fellow over there. The people give him a rough time, which I think is a shame. He's in there, like everybody else, to do a job. They pick on him. He goes in the coffee

room; he sits there, no one wants to sit at the table with him. It's bad. If there weren't so many Blacks there, they probably would do the same thing as far as Blacks go. We had three or four of them in there since I've been there. They've treated that whole group like that. Call them porkchops and everything. It's not right. The white workers thought they were a piece of trash.

Grace Cummings: I'm going to tell you why my daughter didn't stay in the office at Scovill's. In an office of about seventy-two women, there were three Blacks. My daughter said there was a subtle harassment from the floorlady over the office. It's not harassment directly because you're Black. But you notice that you are being harassed and the white girls are not. She left; now she's with Colonial Bank. They don't have that kind of harassment, but they have favoritism harassment; she can live with that.

An example my daughter told me. [Scovill made] parts for Ford. Something went wrong with the computer and the Ford order went out with 1,000 too many parts one month. The first thing they did was come jump all over her because she was in production control in the office. It wasn't even her that did it. But the head guy did not wait to check and see who did it. He just walked over to her desk and laid her out. Of course, she's young; she's impressionable. She

A toolsetter and his foreman at Century Brass, 1982. Photo: Jerry Lombardi.

ran in the bathroom to cry. Later on, when he found out the real girl who did it, he just beat her with a wet noodle. He had threatened to fire my daughter if she made another mistake like that, threatened to put it on her record. Even after he found out that she did not make the mistake, he did not come over and apologize. That hurt her even more. She could cite other, similar incidents for why she's not there.

This is why she thought it was racial: Because he picked on her. There was another little girl who was Black who was younger than her; they kept her in the bathroom crying every other day because of the harassment. Anytime there was a mistake, they didn't check to see who had this particular order; they'd come straight to her.

The average young person nowadays will not stand subtle harassment, even if it means quitting.

Alex Lopez: I started work in Scovill's August 11, 1953. I worked two-and-a-half years in there. What I was doing was not like in the foundry, but I didn't know how to do anything; I didn't learn anything in that place. So I was a floorman; he assists somebody who brings the work to the guys, the operators.

About fourteen months later I got married. We got married at Our Lady of Lourdes. I decided to stay [at Scovill] because I got good benefits, insurance. I didn't want to jump around. I've been in that place twenty-eight years now.

They had a union, but halfway. Not everybody joined. There was not a closed shop. But somebody told me, and I joined the union because I think that's good. I didn't know much about unions, but I realized the whole idea of union— you've got to be united, and I believe in that. I knew the union was good. I had heard about unions before. I knew unions tried to do good for the working people. I knew these people suffered. Sometimes they lost their lives. So I joined the union.

After that there came a closed shop. Some people say they want money. I believe that, too. It's very hard to find a rich man with a good heart. Especially when you work in a company like that, you don't know who you're working for. It's a bunch of guys out there. A company that belongs to a bunch of people, and they don't want to know nothing. When you work for somebody, the owner knows what you're doing. I know a guy who says, "It's just like home." He's got all the benefits, he gets a bonus, they put some money in the bank for him; a small place. This guy says, "I hate unions." I say, "You don't know what it's like to work in a big place. In a big place you need a union."

I started working [at Scovill] in 1953. You don't learn much up there. You can spend all your life doing the same. That place is old, old machinery, old systems. They have a very poor training program. You have to do so many thousand hours, and you only get paid about four dollars an hour for all this time, before you learn something. At the end of your training, they may not have a job for you. You go back to the hole.

One day the boss told me, "We were talking about you upstairs. We were mentioning about supervisors and I put your name in." I said, "What happened?" He said, "[The superintendent] likes it that you are a minority group member." I got mad. I said, "You're not supposed to say that."

What really bothered me was, that's a very old-fashioned idea. You can't put that to work today. I told him, "Don't you see in the entrance, it says Equal Opportunity?" You see that paper in there? I know they put that there to make it look good. But inside here, it's a lot of difference.

For a period of about ten years [I was the only Puerto Rican at Scovill], except for somebody who worked in the mills. A good ten years went by without [any other] Puerto Ricans. There was a lady who used to work there also.

After that, they hired. What's happened out there now is that they have to post the jobs. If nobody wants the job, after a week they have to hire somebody. Nobody wants to do this job. So they hire a Puerto Rican looking for a job. There are a great many Puerto Ricans working in there now. From 1965 up.

Before they passed the civil rights law, they didn't hire many Puerto Ricans. After that they started hiring Puerto Ricans. There are not many problems like discrimination, because if we see anything like that happen, with the union we put it through, right away. If anything looks like discrimination, right away we put in a grievance. So they've got no chance.

There is a [Puerto Rican] guy in the mill who is foreman at night. He's running that department. I brought a friend of mine up there to work; he's a toolsetter, he makes good.

[Puerto Rican women] come and go. I know three or four. But they leave or they get laid off. Now I know one works in [the manufacturing division]; there are not many. That place is not like it used to be. There's nothing left in there.

8. The Labor Movement: "I See All the Companies Testing the Unions"

Brass workers and the rest of the community in the Naugatuck Valley faced serious problems in the 1960s and 1970s. Tens of thousands of relatively well-paying jobs were eliminated in the region's industries. Remaining companies demanded that workers take pay cuts and give up working conditions won long before. With a declining economy, it became difficult to pay for community services.

The principal means workers had developed to protect their conditions of life were the industrial unions established in the 1930s and 1940s. Many of the trends we have seen at work in the period from 1950 to 1980 seriously weakened the ability of the unions to respond. The companies have used their power over basic decisions in ways that have greatly undermined union power. Automation and plant closings have reduced Valley brass workers from a major power in the community and within the brass companies to a relatively small group which could strike forever without significantly hurting the multinational corporations that now control most of the brass mills. The economic and social power of the brass workers has been reduced to a fraction of what it was.

At the same time, the work

The first day of a strike by UAW Local 1078 against American Brass, Waterbury, 1967. Courtesy Waterbury Republican-American.

force itself has become more fragmented. The decline of ethnic neighborhoods with their dense web of social relations has weakened the social roots of industrial unionism. Urban reorganization has severed the tie between the work place and the community, so that workers at any given plant may now come from many towns and cities, and those in a particular neighborhood rarely work in the same plant or even the same industry. Unions built by an older generation of white males had difficulty passing on their heritage while adapting themselves to the needs of the changing labor force, with its increasing proportion of younger, minority, and female workers.

The present adversity of the unions by no means spells the end of the labor movement in the Brass Valley. Working people continue to have important needs that can only be met through collective action. To thrive, the labor movement will have to meet the challenges of a greatly changed social context. But as we have seen throughout this book, this, in itself, is nothing new; working people have repeatedly had to change the forms of their organizations in order to deal with a changing world.

Helen Johnson: I've seen the labor movement go right down the drain, and I'd say we didn't have any. But something would happen. I can remember when we first re-organized Scovill. We had thirteen people. They grew and we got a union shop.

Workers continue to use direct action to influence conditions on the job, both independently of the union and with its support.

Quentin Garatoni: The guys used to refuse to work [any overtime]. The negotiations weren't going the way they [should have]. The company tried to blame [the refusal of overtime] on the union. The guys were the ones who did it. They said: "We aren't going to work. That's it." There was no overtime for the last month of the contract. The guys figured the company wasn't bargaining in good faith and, till they did, they weren't going to work.

George Magnan: Another aspect was that they didn't want the company to stockpile. Within forty-five days of the end of the last contract, I was told by two foremen in my area that unlimited overtime [was available]: "As many hours as you want to work." If you want to come in at 5 in the morning, that's fine. You could just see it coming; they were going to try to stockpile up.

Avis Grant: Some workers, if there is a health problem, might just stop working and tell their steward or someone. If [the union representative] says, "I'll go to the foreman and we'll shut this down till the problem gets fixed," that's fine. But there are workers in there who, to make that dollar, will work right through a safety hazard. Sandy [Kay], being the chairman, will try to stop it. She's shut a couple different parts of the floor down. She told them, "Hey, until you get this fixed you're not going to be loading up over here." She has a pretty good voice over there; they listen to her now. The people in the union are starting to respect her as the chairman. If she says, "This is shut down," then it's shut down.

Where [the workers] are mad about something, they'll slow down. [Once] they had it so nobody showed up for work.

Danny Bialek was born to third-generation Polish parents in Derby in 1941. His father died when he was eight years old, and his mother worked in garment sweatshops to

support his brother and him. After graduating from Shelton High School, he worked in the garment industry for two years. "I saw a real sweatshop environment. I remember women being so sick, but too terrified to go home." After a stint in the service, he was offered a job as a foreman in a sweatshop. He refused the offer, and went to work at Sikorsky's instead. He was laid off after three months. In 1962 he got a job at Anaconda, where he worked as an operator on the extruder and then on the turning and polishing machines. For the past seven years he has been a forming die setter, a self-taught trade. In 1974 he was appointed union steward, and was subsequently elected steward in his department. He served on the local's job evaluation committee, and later was appointed recording secretary. When

Fred Smith took office, Danny Bialek was elected vice-president of the local. He was re-elected in 1979. He is married to the former Marilyn Tomek, and they have two children.

Many unions gave up the right to strike during the term of their contracts.

Fred Smith: We used to have the right to strike after the sixth step of the grievance procedure, the step before arbitration. We had very few arbitrations then. We lost that right in 1974. I think it was the year that COLA came on the table.

Danny Bialek: When our predecessors gave that up it took most of our power away.

Fred Smith: Our present contract forbids walkouts, wildcat strikes, or concerted action in any form. Under the contract the union officials have an obligation to prevent those kind of events from happening. The courts gave the companies the right to single out individuals and fire them if a walkout or a wildcat occurs. So the local officers and stewards are really on the hot seat when there's a walkout or a wildcat. The companies can also sue the local and the international. When we gave up those things it really hurt labor. The only thing we have is our labor, and the power to withhold that labor.

Significant gains are still sometimes won through regular grievance procedures. Young workers at Anaconda describe the impact of a recent arbitration decision abolishing compulsory overtime:

Quentin Garatoni: We never really had it clear how many hours we had to work. It started off that the extruders were working a lot of hours. So they hired people and told them, if you go in on the extruder you're going to work a lot of hours. So people kind of took it for granted, you had an extruder job you worked a lot of hours. But then they started with all the jobs. No matter where you were you had to work ten, twelve hours a day. Six or seven days a week. You'd work thirteen days and then have a day off. It just got to the point where people were ready to walk out of the mill. And finally, they gave warnings to some guys for not working ten hours one day. The union couldn't take it any more and decided to take the company on, and took it to arbitration. We were lucky enough to win that. Now we have voluntary overtime. I don't think it hurt the company that much. I'm on voluntary overtime. Today I worked ten hours; I worked last Sunday. The economy the way it is you can't survive on forty hours, you have to work the overtime. People need it. Just knowing that you can refuse it helps a lot. When you have something to do, you don't have to

work it. It's a lot easier on the brain to work overtime if you know you don't have to tomorrow if you don't feel good.

George Magnan: The nice thing about this new overtime thing is that you can ask us today what we're doing this weekend and we'd know. Six months ago we couldn't have told you till Thursday, because that's when they put up the schedule. Now you can plan your weekends as far in advance as you want and know that you're not going to be required to work. That comes as a real convenience.

It's changed things for the younger people. I turn down a lot of overtime now that I was forced to work then. You can be selective. If you have a lot of bills or you're going away and you want to have a lot of spending money, you can accept it at will. It's almost always there.

Quentin Garatoni: You can use it as a bargaining chip, too. Remember, before the strike, everybody refused to work. It gives us a little bit of leverage to play with. Which is nice.

But official procedures are often seen as very limited in their ability to change workers' conditions.

Quentin Garatoni: People get cynical. It's very hard to get anything accomplished. It just takes so long. Like arbitration cases take six months to a year. They just don't see any end to it. They figure what little you accomplish, what's it worth? Especially Black guys feel there's no hope anyway, they're just going to get beat no matter what they try. They think it's a waste of time.

Many older union activists believe younger workers are less committed to the unions.

Eddie Labacz: My own kid, after he worked in our plant for about a year, told me, "What do we need a union in here for? The company gives us everything we want." "The company doesn't give you anything," I said. "The only reason they give it to you is because the union is here. If the union wasn't here, all these things wouldn't come." He figured the insurances, vacations, were all just given by the company. I said all these things were fought for, negotiated for, even threatened to go on strike for. We had to strike sixteen weeks to get a pension plan.

Many younger workers, conversely, consider themselves more active and militant than the old-timers. Sandy Kay is unit chairperson at the New Haven Copper Co. in Seymour.

Sandy Kay: I'd say it's the younger people [who are most active in the union]. My vice-chairman, who just resigned because he's retiring, he's got forty years. He was the only old-timer we had on any com-

mittee or anything over there. Only one other person has more seniority than myself that's on any of the committees.

Women have rarely been encouraged to take leadership in male-dominated unions.

Helen Johnson: The role of the women in the union is not good. They're a little better than they were, but women are used. Women do the dirty work and aren't recognized. And that goes on today. Women weren't active too much in the early days of the union. Some of them tried. They were pretty good as stewards, but when it came to attending meetings, or going further, most of them were raising small families. They were good in this way: if you told them, "Look, next meeting we've got to have you, get down there one way or another," and explained to them what was going on, they'd be there. But to take leadership, no, and we were not encouraged.

Many plants in the Valley remain nonunion. In some respects, the unions have become the representatives of the better-off part of the work force.

Frieda Ewen: When American Brass was having their last strike, one of the union officials was expressing his anger at the company and explaining why they should get an increase because their work

was so dangerous and hard. He made a remark that was the feeling of most of the workers who worked in the big shops: "What does the company expect, us to get paid like those people who work in Hershey Metals? We're not like them." In other words, those are nothing people over there; we're important over here, because we work in the big shop.

This made me very angry. [The worker in the big shop] just happened to walk in one day and fill out an application, just like the guy walked into Hershey Metals, only it was the right day and he got hired there. I don't understand why people in positions like that can't see that those people in the small shops *are* working hard too, and help them get better wages. Those people are just the same as them, and deserve better than what they're getting. That's what a union should be, it seems to me. To go and reach out to people who are not getting what they should be getting and deserve to get. Not only look to yourself and how you can improve yourself, but reach out to everyone else. If that's not there, you're almost as bad as the company, just trying to grab for yourself.

Rank-and-file control of the unions themselves has not been automatic.

Stella Horoshak: I've also found that once there's a clique—not a clique—once the ones elected are in there, they keep them in there all the time. They don't give anybody else a chance. I've seen that at meetings. "You're a friend of mine; you're in there; you're going to stay in there." You see a lot of that, too, which isn't right.

King David Holmes: You find unions that say, "We've got a contract, but it doesn't mean anything." You find unions that get fat and bureaucratic. You get tied up. There's an arbitration thing. The executive board gets together: "What cases are you going to send to arbitration? Are you going to support me?" He'll call employment. "I've got to have this one." "Well, let me have this one." So the union becomes a part of the system. I've seen it happen. I was on the executive board.

Helen Johnson: I can think of some of my old friends when they first got active in the labor movement, they were really lean, now they really need outsized girdles to keep the bay window in. They've lost touch with the little guy, and that's bad. You have to keep in touch, and you have to take time to listen. We don't listen, and I think that's very bad.

In many cases, unions and management have worked out an accommodation. This allows union leaders a voice in what were once management decisions. But it also involves them in responsibility for administering conditions which the rank and file might not otherwise tolerate.

Eddie Labacz: The management people have changed. They sit down and discuss things with the union committee before they make a move. They come in and say: "This is what we want to do, what's the union's attitude towards it? Do you approve it, disapprove it, or what?" They have an open door; if I want to go up there, I can go see the vice-chairman anytime I want. There isn't this fighting, always having to write a grievance and wait for an answer for two or three weeks, process it all the way through to get it resolved. You can get it resolved in five minutes now.

Years ago they used to say: "This is it. You're going to do it this way. If you don't like it, grieve it."

They started bowling leagues, which the company sponsors with the union, half-and-half. We've got a golf league where management and union play golf together.

But many workers view labor-management accommodation in a less favorable light.

Quentin Garatoni: We need the whole union system in this country to change. You get the Steelworkers run by people like McBride. Those guys are so far away from the third shift in Brass Rod, it's ridiculous. They might as well be sitting up in General Motors with all the other executives. At one time they were really radical and really for the worker but now they're more for the status quo, for the country running the way it is, because it fits their pocketbook the best. They're not really interested in the workers anymore. I'd like to see a labor movement where the people who work down in Pittsburgh for the international also keep their jobs and have to go back in the mill and work. Let them go back every three years when their term is up.

While many employers have moved toward cooperation with unions, the late 1970s also saw an effort by many companies to eliminate the gains that unions had won. How successful these efforts will be remains to be seen.

Sandy Kay: The company used to try to run things the way they thought they should be run, even though they were going against our contract. We had to keep fighting them tooth and nail till we showed them we really were going to stick to that contract. We still do that.

When I first took over [as head of the union, the company] made my job extremely hard for me, figuring that, along with the ones that ran against me and the company all giving me a hard time, I would probably resign. Because at the time I became the chairman, we had had three men resign prior to me.

With me, I think it was definitely to see if they could make me resign. They felt that I believed in the union very strongly, which I did. I didn't believe in playing hanky-panky. Once they found I was staying, they did a swing-around and decided to live with me as a chairman and to work with me, instead of against me.

They would call me in, any little thing I did I was nailed for. I was looked at constantly for ways to be fired. I just made up my mind: In no way was I giving up.

The biggest battle with us was just getting management to sit down and talk with us and finding out that we aren't just numbers, that we are people. We wish to be treated as such, all of us. No special cases; we all want the same equality. I think they are finally learning that we are people, just like they are. That we do have brains, most of us, and that we are capable of thinking for ourselves, that they don't have to babysit us twenty-four hours a day.

I see all the companies testing the unions right at the moment. They tried us and found it didn't work. I see them doing it over at Bridgeport Brass. I see them doing it across the nation: All companies are testing the unions. Actually trying to break our backs is what I think they're doing. They were giving me a hard time over there: They felt that if they broke my back, maybe whoever took my place wouldn't have the gumption

The first day of a strike against the Metal Hose Division of American Brass, Waterbury, 1977. Art Muzzicato and Art Finelli are second and third from right. Courtesy Waterbury Republican-American.

they thought I had. They don't want anybody in there that will fight or that the people will follow and stick with.

Workers are going to have to stick together more now than ever. If they feel that they can separate, like they tried to separate us there: If they could have succeeded, they definitely could have beat us. Let's face it, if you're all together and you have the strength, no company is going to win. They need you as much as you need them.

The testing of the unions has been most evident in a series of major strikes that have marked the era of brass industry decline. We will look at two, one at the largest brass company, the other at one of the smallest.

On October 1, 1977, after six months of negotiation, employees of Anaconda's Brass Division went on strike. The coalition of unions, including the Steelworkers, the UAW, and the IAM, which represents employees at Anaconda plants around the country, sought wage and benefit increases based on the copper mining industry contracts that had been negotiated earlier that year. Anaconda's response was to offer to continue wages and benefits at the level of the current contract until the end of bargaining in the brass mill industry, at which point they would adjust the level of their brass workers' wages to be in line with the average of the industry.

In a time of inflation, extending current wages and benefits meant a cut in real wages. Parity with the rest of the brass industry, mostly small shops, would mean an even larger cut. Workers found it hard to believe it was necessary for them to take a wage cut to keep Arco, the country's thirteenth-largest corporation, competitive in the industry.

Long before negotiations began, Anaconda mounted a campaign to convince the workers to take a cut in their wages and benefits. By citing wage and benefit figures from other shops, company letters and newspaper advertisements tried to convince workers that they were overpaid. In Ansonia and Waterbury, where Anaconda had already closed down or transferred many of its operations and laid off thousands of people, the company threatened a shutdown or transfer of its current operations. The campaign was designed to influence not only the workers, but the community as a whole, since Anaconda was a large taxpayer in Waterbury, and the largest taxpayer in the city of Ansonia.

Fred Smith: The main cause for this strike is the company wanting a parity clause in the contract which would have given them the unilateral right to adjust wages and benefits to the average of the industry which they would decide. It would apply for a three-year period.

[The companies] are never happy with the amount of profit they make. All they think about is how can we make more? If they can't make it off the product, we're at the day and age when they say, we gotta make it off the employees. If they can't get it in productivity, and our guys work their butts off, then the other way is to take it out of [the worker's] pocket. This is what it amounts to today. It's a concerted action of all the big corporations in this country today to cut wages and benefits.

They call it parity, all kinds of things. They've been trying to sell this to us for the last two years. The only thing that stopped them was the contract they gave us in 1974. They tried to brainwash the people over the last two years with all the propaganda you can imagine, letter after letter after letter, trying to convince the average working man in their plant that he's overpaid. The company must've spent thousands and thousands of dollars on propaganda over the last two years. With what they spent on thirteen-cent stamps alone, we could've had a contract for the last ten years.

Danny Bialek: The companies are becoming so diversified and so strong you cut one leg off, they've still got a hundred to walk on. You'll never hurt Arco. They took it upon themselves to buy this company, and it's for profit in any way they can.

Fred Smith: We have a new sign up front. It says: "When Atlantic-Richfield cuts gas to thirty cents a gallon, the union will take a wage cut!"

In past strikes, Anaconda had always agreed to an orderly shutdown. In 1977, they decided to keep the plant gates open, and operate the mills with salaried personnel, some of whom had been reassigned from plants around the country.

In the early days of the strike, the Ansonia local, USWA Local 6445, set up mass picket lines at the plant gates. The company installed TV equipment, lights, and extra guard shacks to monitor the strikers. In the first week of the strike, Local 6445 filed charges with the National Labor Relations Board related to the company taking pictures of the strikers. These charges were subsequently withdrawn. The following week, Anaconda sought and obtained a temporary restraining order limiting the number of pickets to five, and requiring that the pickets stay two feet apart, keep moving, not use abusive language and allow people to enter and leave the plant.

On October 22, Fred Smith, the president of Local 6445, and another striker were arrested and charged with "reckless use of a highway" after they allegedly stopped two Anaconda trucks on Route 8. Anaconda charged the union with violence, and the union denied the charges. On October 27, Superior Court Judge Henebry issued a permanent injunction limiting the number of pickets to five, and enjoining the strikers from preventing anyone from entering or leaving company grounds. Violation of the injunction would result in $5,000 fines for union executive board members. In Fred Smith's opinion, the company maintained, but did not prove, the strikers were engaged in illegal activities. The union viewed the injunction as a travesty of justice.

Fred Smith: It was the first time, and I'm thirty-five years old, that I was ever in court. And you hear so much about the American justice system. Myself, I'm a right down the middle of the road type of person, and you say, well, it can't be that way. But I'll tell you, they disillusioned me. When I came out of there, I said now I know what some of these people have been crying about for years. How could a man give an injunction without saying, "Is this true?" to the other party. It's like me going down to the police department and saying "Janet has done this and this and this" and boom, they run right out and lock, key, and throw you away without hearing your side of it. And that type of thing to me isn't being very American, that's leaning to the other side.

After the injunction, now they got us out of the way. Then they put on a campaign to get the people to come to work: "The gates are open, come right in. It's your constitutional right to go to work."

In November, Anaconda placed ads in the local papers inviting their employees back to work. Smith was arrested again in January, this time charged with reckless endangerment in the second degree. It was alleged that he threw a rock through the windshield of a truck leaving the plant. The propaganda war continued, with both sides placing ads in the local papers. Negotiations broke off several times during this period.

In February Danny Bialek, the vice-president of the Ansonia local, was arrested and charged with disorderly conduct when he allegedly refused to allow cars to leave the parking area of the plant.

Danny Bialek: Five Ansonia policemen threw me against a police car. They handcuffed me, and they took me for a good long ride too before they took me to the police station. I was really afraid. I was searched, booked and locked up for six or seven hours until Freddy got me out.

Later that month, Anaconda made what they said was their final offer to the union: A continuation of wages and benefits at the level of the last contract, a capped COLA totaling seventy-five cents over three years, along with many changes in contract language. The Ansonia and Waterbury lo-

DANCE BENEFIT 754

For

Waterbury Rolling Mills Strikers

Friday, February 27, 1981 — 8 P.M. to 2 A.M.

Featuring Mr. Funky D.J. Himself "KEN REEDER"

CASH BAR — DRAWING

OUR LADY OF FATIMA

2071 Baldwin Street   Waterbury, Conn.

Sponsored by:

Community Labor Support Committee and U.A.W.

Price: $3.00 — $5.00 Per Couple

Ticket to dance benefit for Waterbury Rolling Mills strikers, 1981. Courtesy UAW Amalgamated Local 1251.

cals turned this offer down resoundingly, as did the rest of the coalition.

On March 31, after six months on strike, the union coalition and the company reached a tentative agreement: There would be some small increases in benefits, a capped COLA amounting to $1.05 over three years, and substantial changes in contract language. Because of the changes in contract language, the Ansonia local turned down the company's offer, 228–105. The Waterbury local accepted it, however, 199–5, as did the majority in the coalition.

When the settlement was reached, the company dropped all charges against members of the union, with the exception of the charges against Fred Smith. Smith ended up doing six months' accelerated rehabilitation.

Anaconda workers returned to work April 4. The members of the Ansonia local were bitter about the contract language. Fred Smith summed it up: "We had to buy a million dollars' worth of contract language for $1.05."

Joseph Soda worked in Anaconda's power house and boiler room for many years. He remembers the days before the union came in, when "if you didn't bring the boss a box of cigars, a bottle of whiskey, or a chicken, or stuff like that, you didn't work." Soda was active in the union until his retirement in the late 1970s. This interview was taped in April 1978.

Joseph Soda: The contract language is awful. They're driving labor back at least fifty years. I've been working for this company for thirty-seven years, and I've never seen language such as this put into a contract. It's dictatorial, and it's very harmful to the working people. This company, for many years, if we signed for a job, that was our job. Now they want the right, if you've been on a job for thirty years, to take you off, and put somebody who's been in the plant for two years and take your job. They say, well, "That's your choice, either go do this or we'll fire you." Their greatest weapon up there is: "We'll fire you. No matter what we tell you to do, you have to do." That went out fifty, sixty years ago. We are willing to work, we are good workers. But they want the right to push you around, as if you were sitting on a chess board or a checkerboard. This is what we're against.

The Waterbury Rolling Mills is a small shop, employing about seventy-five union workers. In May 1980 their contract expired and they voted to strike. After three months they returned to work with an extension of the old contract; in January 1981 they struck again for three months. During a year of bargaining, the company presented a series of proposals for takebacks that give a good indication of the conditions brass industry employers would like to impose were there no worker opposition. They included:

WAGES

Reduce wages 75 cents per hour.

A 10 percent reduction in personal and/or job rates.

Rally in support of striking nurses at Waterbury Hospital, December 1980. This rally helped lead to the formation of the Community/Labor Support Committee. Helen Johnson is wearing the quilted coat. Photo: Dennis Guillaume.

Community/Labor Support Committee rally in support of Waterbury Rolling Mills strikers, February 1981. Photo: Dennis Guillaume.

35-cent per hour cap on COLA.

A starting rate of 30 cents per hour below the regular rate.

HOURS

Cut ten days off vacations.

Cut ten-minute wash-up time.

Eliminate all vacations in excess of three weeks.

Compulsory overtime, even if no advance notice is given.

Establishment of a "continuous work schedule," under which employees would normally be scheduled for four consecutive twelve-hour days, with overtime pay only after twelve hours of work.

WORKING CONDITIONS

Erosion of seniority and transfer rights: "The Company shall have the right to make temporary transfers. . . . Employees required to work in a temporary position may be excused from such temporary work only for medical reasons or other extreme emergencies."

PENSIONS

Put pension plan into "deep freeze" and curtail future benefits to the extent legally permissible.

BENEFITS

Eliminate health care riders for maternity; dependent children 18 to 25 years old; prescriptions; vision care; dental care.

The Rolling Mill strike saw the creation of a new coalition, the Community/Labor Support Committee. It sponsored a big fund-raising dance and a support march in which hundreds participated. A song was written for the occasion:

Hard Times, Rolling Mills

Uncle Mal said "Let's be fair;
Give me time, you'll get your share."
It's a shaft, and we know where!
Hard times, Rolling Mills.

CHORUS:
Hard Times, Rolling Mills
Hard Times, Rolling Mills
Hard Times, Rolling Mills
Hard Times everywhere.

Wants us all on overtime
Birthdays, he won't spend a dime
Lies and takebacks are a crime
Hard times, Rolling Mills.

Ten percent he'd cut our wage,
Throw us out when we're old age;
Working folks aren't in a cage!
Hard times, Rolling Mills.

All the bosses look alike,
Union's not afraid to strike;
Uncle Mal can take a hike!
Hard Times, Rolling Mills.

Scabs come out and scabs go in,
They don't know that it's a sin;
Uncle Mal knows WE WILL WIN*!!*
Hard times, Rolling Mills.

People know our cause is just,
In our strength we put our trust
We're a Union Mal can't bust!
Hard Times, Rolling Mills.

To the tune of "Cotton Mill Girls." Words by Dennis Guillaume, politics by UAW 1251 members.

According to Tony Gerace, this represented the first major community support for a brass workers' strike since the 1950s. He saw it as the product of "a different era," resulting from new coalitions with citizen's action organizations, the women's movement, and similar groups.

Tony Gerace: These things bring people into a common bond. More people get involved. If we help people on E.R.A., they help us. There is a common thread of social justice. We had not only labor unions but community groups, E.R.A. groups—people who are concerned about people. It welded a group of people who are now in a position to assist each other on a quasi-formal basis.

The settlement also represented a new departure. The union accepted a one-year wage freeze and benefit cuts, with limited increases thereafter. In exchange, a profit-sharing plan was introduced and a former U.A.W. international vice-president was placed on the Board of Directors. Whether or not such agreements become widespread, they indicate that new issues and new approaches will be necessary if the labor movement is to have a future.

P A R T V

In Conclusion: "You Get Up against the Wall and There's No Further to Go: You Have to Start Fighting Back. Right?"

Their numbers and economic power decreasing, workers in the brass industry have also seen the power of their unions decline. They have been forced to take wage cuts and to give up working conditions that they had established in earlier struggles. The problems of the brass industry have been compounded by the more general problems of the American economy in the 1970s and early 1980s.

If they are to again make a change in their conditions of life through collective action, there are a number of problems workers in the Brass Valley will have to deal with. While ethnic divisions have become less important, divisions along race lines remain a major block to cooperation, especially with Black and Hispanic workers becoming concentrated in the inner city and white workers in the suburbs. While ever-increasing numbers of women have gone to work in plants and offices, unions

remain primarily a male preserve. As multinational corporations operate on a global basis, they are able to pit workers in different countries against each other, just as they once did with workers in different regions of the U.S.

In the last twenty years the Brass Valley—and the rest of the country—has seen major industrial changes. Rather than huge plants with tens of thousands of workers in the same industry, there are smaller plants with diverse products. Rather than a predominantly blue-collar work force, there are now large numbers of white-collar workers. And today, instead of working in the home, most women are in the outside work force.

Finally, the problems facing working people today are much less amenable to being settled between one group of workers and their employer. A union contract means little if the company can simply close up the plant and move away. Health benefits can't

protect against environmental pollution. It is hard for company pensions to provide protection against inflation.

Will the working people of the Naugatuck Valley again create new forms of organization and action to deal with the new problems they face? The answer is not yet given. However, over the past few years, there have been some developments which could provide the seeds for such an effort. One has been the development of community organizations in low- and moderate-income neighborhoods throughout the Valley. These have focused both on neighborhood issues, such as decent public services, and on broader issues, such as utilities and tax policies. Significantly, the 1980s have seen the beginning of a coalition between such organizations and the unions, both in response to community issues and in support of the strikes and job actions of local workers. These actions already show some of the characteristics required by a future labor movement: They address issues beyond the particular work place, but draw on workers' power and organization within it; they cut across lines of race, ethnicity, and sex; they coordinate the efforts of people who work in different industries.

Are conditions ripe for a further development of collective action by working people?

Helen Johnson: You get up against the wall and there's no further to go: You have to start fighting back. Right? That means revolution in my book.

I have always been of this opinion: We don't have money but we have the bodies. I haven't seen it yet, except in rare cases like our labor movement while the threat was there. Or in wartime we have that cohesion. And that's what we have to do; we have to stick together. I get very annoyed when people say you can't fight City Hall. I say: "Yes you can. But I can't fight it alone; you have to stick with me, and you have to stick with me. This is what we have to do. Don't meet with your neighbors and moan. Get with a group that wants to do something and let the group grow. Then, make them listen to us."

How do we do it? We could do our share, but the next ten don't do anything except moan. But if they get hurt enough—and the time is coming, it's getting closer and closer—they're going to have to do it. They're going to have to say, "Hey, we tried other ways and we got nowhere, so let's try these people's way and see what we get."

Rents are going sky-high and they're getting scarcer and scarcer. Deregulation of gas—you need gas, you need electricity, they've got you there. Everything.

The main concern should be what's going on: our livelihood, our survival, really. I think it's gotten where it's just plain survival. We should direct ourselves more to that. There's a lot of bodies there, right? We should direct ourselves to the community as a whole, to make it better—to survive.

I think we're going to see some bad times, real bad times. I hope to God I'm wrong. We're going to be fighting each other before we learn that that's not the way to go. We've got to have a common cause, and we have. I think the 1980s are going to be a rough, rough time. I don't think we're going to have all the things we have today. I think life is going to be a lot simpler. But we'll learn to live with our neighbor, and if we

don't love him, at least admire what he's trying to do.

We go to church—I remember Fulton Sheen used to talk about Sunday-going Christians. It's so true. We're so pious when we go to mass or whatever service. Monday morning we're ready to cut our neighbors' throats. If only a little bit of that would carry over.

My grandfather always said, "Each generation owes a better living to the next generation." It was up to the present generation to try to make it better. We haven't done that. We've lost a generation, I think. We have a lot of making up to do.

If you like people and you see injustices, you have to try and do something. This brother against brother, Blacks against whites, Italians against the Irish, Polish against the Lithuanians—this is wrong. We all bleed when we get cut; we all suffer, so we should be one.

APPENDIX

How This Book Was Made

Background

Recently, a student at the University of Connecticut learned of the massive strike in the Naugatuck Valley in 1920 and decided he would like to know more about it. He wrote,

"I live in the city that this incident occurred in and yet had never heard about it. When it was mentioned during the class lecture . . . it immediately aroused my curiosity. Upon looking into the matter, I found that there was nothing said in *any* of the books concerning Waterbury's history (approximately 15 books included this period of time)."

John Yrchik, whose family has worked in the brass industry for three generations, and who has an intense interest in labor history, when told that there had been a large, general strike in the area, replied: "I never even heard about it. It's interesting how your own history is concealed from you."

This experience is quite common. Over the past few years, fortunately, strong movements have arisen to tell the story of those previously left out of the history books:

Many historians have ceased to focus primarily on "great events," "great men," and formal political arenas and have begun to study the daily lives and struggles of women, Blacks, workers, immigrants, native Americans, and other groups whose history has often been ignored or distorted.

Historical research has ceased to be the property of an elite club of well-to-do white men. Women, Blacks, and those of immigrant backgrounds have begun to make their own contributions by writing the histories of their respective groups.

Many people have begun using new techniques, notably oral interviewing, to recover realities that exist only in the memory of those who lived them.

An even greater departure from conventional history has been the development of history projects in which workers or other community members engage in studying and presenting their own history. In England thousands of people have participated in local "history workshops" which explore the histories of particular neighborhoods; in Sweden thousands of workers have taken part in the "dig-where-you-stand" movement, tracing the histories of their own work places and communities. In the U.S. a number of efforts of this kind are under way, ranging from history workshops on the English model in Lynn and Lawrence, Mass., initiated by the Massachusetts History Workshop, to the Beaver Valley Labor History Association, started and run primarily by retired steel workers in the Pittsburgh area.

These movements form the background of ideas, values, and experiences out of which the Brass

Workers History Project emerged.

The Brass Workers History Project was initiated by four people:

Jan Stackhouse spent most of her childhood in Middle Eastern countries. She came to Connecticut in 1973, where she has been involved in the labor movement and the women's movement. In 1976 she was elected vice-president of a union she helped to organize, Local 1173 ACTWU, which represents employees at the Yale Co-op department store in New Haven, where she worked as a clerk. She has lived in Derby since 1977. She was instrumental in founding the Valley Women's Center, where she organized many educational programs on women's issues including a series on working women's history.

Jerry Lombardi grew up in New Haven, Connecticut. For five years he was a motion picture projectionist, and was active in Local 273 of the International Alliance of Theatrical Stage Employees (IATSE). He has lived in Derby since 1977. In the Naugatuck Valley, he and Jan Stackhouse produced videotapes on a number of labor-related issues, including one on a major brass strike in 1977/78, and a series of three tapes— sponsored by the Connecticut Humanities Council—about unemployment in the region. The International Association of Machinists and Aerospace Workers, the UAW, and the New England Hospital and Health Care Workers Union (District 1199) have utilized his talents as a video maker, photographer, and scriptwriter.

Jeremy Brecher grew up and lives about thirty miles from the Naugatuck Valley; however, he did not know the Valley well. A freelance writer and labor historian, he is the author of *Strike!*, a history of rank-and-file activity in peak periods of labor conflict in the U.S., and *Common Sense for Hard Times*, a look at contemporary working-class life in the U.S. In 1977 he started research for a book on the social history of the working people of Waterbury.

Hank Murray, who had studied history in college and worked in the Fafnir Bearing plant in Connecticut, was Education Director for Region 9-A of the UAW, which represents the majority of Connecticut brass workers.

We came together at a showing of the Stackhouse/Lombardi Unemployment Tapes in Derby in 1978. Since Stackhouse and Lombardi already wanted to make videotapes on Naugatuck Valley labor history, and Brecher was already doing research on the subject, some kind of collaboration seemed natural. At a subsequent gathering, Hank Murray suggested that we focus on the workers in the brass industry, who formed a clearly defined unit and whose story seemed in danger of passing into oblivion. We decided to frame such a project.

The initiators' own orientation was important in shaping this book. We see this kind of history, not as an academic exercise, but as a social act, a way people can communicate with each other about their experiences, needs, aspirations, and potentials. We believe that social movements are essential to social progress and that those who are powerless in society need to organize and deal with their problems through collective action. Naturally, our beliefs affected the way we conducted research and, ultimately, helped determine the content of this book.

Our first difficult decision involved community and worker participation in the early stages of the project. We wanted to draw many local people into the planning of the Project, so that the project could reflect their interests and needs from the start. We decided not to do so, however, because we felt it would be destructive to get people involved and then have the project peter out through lack of funding. We did discuss the project with a few people in the Valley we already knew well and with leaders of community institutions, such as the unions, senior centers, and historical societies, whose support we needed for a grant proposal.

We drew up a grant proposal and submitted it to the National Endowment for the Humanities. It proposed "to develop a model for the collaboration of workers and historians in preserving workers' history; to use this model to recover the history of brass workers in Connecticut's Naugatuck River Valley; to use this history as a case study for introducing basic themes of the 'new labor history' in formats accessible to the widest possible audience." The principal products were to be a videotape documentary, a guide to worker participation in preparing labor history, and this book. The Institute for Labor Education and Research in New York served as grantee for the project and helped provide liaison between the project and the National Endowment.

Many months of back-and-forth discussions followed. We repeatedly revised the proposal in the light of NEH suggestions. In March 1980, the project received word that the grant was approved; in April 1980, work began.

Jan Stackhouse served as project director, Jerry Lombardi as media coordinator, and Jeremy Brecher as historical coordinator. In practice, we met regularly and made decisions by consensus or negotiation.

During the spring and summer of 1980, Brecher conducted background historical research for the project, visiting archives that held papers of major unions and companies in the brass industry. In September 1980, we opened an office in Waterbury and began working full time. In order to establish ourselves in the community, we made the rounds of senior centers, retired workers' organizations, ethnic clubs, community organizations, and brass worker union locals. We explained the project, suggested ways people could become involved, and asked for people to interview. We almost always received at least a few names. Some of the senior centers organized group interviews. Interested individuals set up interviews with their friends. Sons and daughters of retired brass workers helped interview their parents.

A brochure describing the project and several feature articles in local newspapers elicited calls from people with stories to tell and documents to share. A few people expressed an interest in working directly with the project. Hyotha Hofler, for instance, offered to develop maps. Alannah Nardello, the secretary-treasurer of Local 45, URW in Naugatuck, became very involved in seeking out new people to interview, and, after assisting on a number of interviews, began conducting some on her own.

After initial outreach was completed, we invited twenty-five people who had worked with us to become members of our Community/Labor Advisory Panel. The panel consists of six brass worker union presidents, five retired brass workers, one union steward at Anaconda, an employee of the Retired Workers Council, a general contractor, a marketing consultant at a local bank, the economic developer of the city of Ansonia, a paralegal worker at a legal assistance office, a Waterbury poet, the directors of the Waterbury and Derby historical societies, the president of the Waterbury branch of the University of Connecticut, the son of a Seymour brass worker, now a graduate student in sociology, and a professor of urban planning.

The panel operated informally. All of its members were busy people, so most consultations took place on an individual basis. Individual panelists helped locate interviewees, documents, and photographs. Some helped publicize the project. Others reviewed the first draft of the book. The diverse perspectives of the panelists were essential for developing a book which could speak to a wide variety of people in the Naugatuck Valley communities. Their interest and support helped keep us going when things were difficult.

The Interviews

The first round of interviewing took place from October to February. About 75 percent of the interviews were conducted by Brecher, about 25 percent—including the majority of those of women—were conducted by Stackhouse. In most cases, a second person (generally a staff person, but sometimes a relative or friend of the interviewee) went along, took charge of the recording equipment, and asked an occasional question.

Our approach to interviewing is described more fully in our *Preserving Workers History: A Guide.* It can be summed up by saying that we approach each interviewee as an expert on the world in which he or she lives. We were not studying people as objects; rather, we regarded them as individuals who had much to teach and from whom we wanted to learn. We let the discussion go into whatever spheres people seemed willing to talk about, but didn't try to push into more intimate or sensitive areas if the interviewee seemed unwilling.

The first twenty or thirty interviews gave us a strong grasp on many parts of the story; they also allowed us to identify gaps that needed to be filled, such as older immigrant women, young people who were working in the brass industry at the time, people who would remember the strike of 1920.

While we aimed for a wide range of interview sources, those interviewed by no means constitute a random sample of brass workers in the Naugatuck Valley. First of all, interviewing was largely limited to people who stayed in the area— and a large proportion of those who worked in the industry at one time or another have left the region. Our sources are probably unusually deeply rooted in the area. Second, we naturally tended to get people connected with our own contact networks, particularly unions, senior centers, and ethnic clubs; those in other networks, or those who are more socially isolated, are no doubt underrepresented in the sample. Third, while we interviewed many people who were never leaders of any organization, the group as a whole is weighted toward what might be called rank-and-file leaders, people who played important roles in ethnic, union, or other organizations, even if they were never presidents or professionals in them. Fourth, we were looking for people who were regarded as observant, thoughtful, and articulate. No doubt there are other ways as well in which those interviewed are not fully representative.

The interviewees had rather diverse motives for working with the project and different messages they wished to convey. Some regarded the project as an attempt to gather knowledge about "life in the old days" and were pleased to have the value of their memories and experiences recognized and to be able to contribute to their preservation. Some, notably those in ethnic organizations, felt a responsibility to help preserve a disappearing heritage, and saw participation in the project as one way they could contribute to passing on that heritage and winning respect for it. Some who had participated in social and political activities, notably the labor movement, felt that they had indeed taken part, if only in a small way, in something of historical significance; they felt its preservation to be important, and believed that what the Project was doing would make a positive contribution to carrying on the movements of which they had been a part.

About the Illustrations

Media Coordinator Jerry Lombardi had primary responsibility for supplying the photographs in this book. Using leads from Brecher, he pored over the archives and photo collections of the Scovill Mfg. Co., located at the Baker Library of the Harvard University School of Business Administration; the International Union of Mine, Mill and Smelter Workers, located at the University of Colorado Library; the Waterbury *Republican-American*; the New York Public Library; and the Connecticut State Library. In many cases he reproduced them on the spot, using a portable copystand and lights. These sources provided the bulk of the eight hundred photographs Lombardi collected. The rest were loaned or donated by interviewees or friends of the project, and obtained by Lombardi, other staff members, and volunteers.

An old photo contest, coordinated by Alannah Nardello, produced several rare photographs. The photo contest, and two subsequent exhibits at senior centers, while not a grand success in terms of producing photos, proved to be an excellent way to create community interest and involvement in the project. Mrs. Nardello made the rounds of senior centers throughout the Valley to talk about the project and the contest, and came back invariably with new contacts and stories. The exhibits proved to be good informal ways for people to share their experiences, and talk about the old days.

Lombardi and others found that more than one visit to people's homes was often necessary to obtain photos, many of which were lying forgotten in a drawer or family album.

Some people loaned us photographs they had taken of contemporary events, and Lombardi himself took photographs of present-day conditions in the Naugatuck Valley. He also took all but a few of the portraits of interviewees which appear in the book.

Making the Book

In February 1981, Brecher began to transcribe an estimated 5 to 10 percent of the taped interview material. He selected the material that, in his judgment, shed light on the social history of the community, made a cogent, understandable statement, and did not contradict what was known from other sources. He then sorted the material into a rough manuscript of 420 pages. Ten of the Community/Labor panelists were given this draft or relevant sections. Many not only read it but passed it on to friends and co-workers. Half a dozen academic experts reviewed the manuscript; the authors and literary consultant Jill Cutler edited and reorganized it. Meanwhile, we analyzed gaps in our interviewing and decided to conduct another round of interviews, including more Blacks, women, younger brass workers, and members of the Cape Verdean and Puerto Rican communities. These interviews were incorporated into the final manuscript. Biographical sketches of the speakers were prepared, and the speakers were asked to review and correct their quotes.

The Form of This Book

The book that emerged from this process differs sharply from traditional history and from the collections of interviews that are often published by oral historians.

Unlike traditional history books, this one is not simply the product of a historian who has conducted research, weighed evidence, and then presented his own conclusions concerning events and their significance. Indeed, most of the book consists of statements by people whom a traditional historian would regard only as raw sources. These people provide both their own accounts of events and their own interpretations of their meaning.

Yet this book as a whole is quite different from a collection of interviews. First, the material used has been selected for its historical value from a much larger mass of interviews and documents. Second, it has been arranged by topics and periods as they are conceived by historians, not as they are lived by individuals. Third, the materials have been framed by introductions and commentaries intended to provide a historical context and an interpretation of the larger features of the story.

The book deliberately takes the form of a dialogue between individual experiences, as lived and thought about by the participants, and their lives as viewed in a larger historical context. Ideally, it should allow readers to see both how people's lives fit into the broader developments of history and how history is actually composed of people's lives—shaped by, as well as shaping them.

Weaknesses and Strengths of Oral History

Documents of oral history, like other historical sources, cannot be thought of as simply accounts of "what really happened," or even of the source's direct experience. In reading these accounts, it is important to keep in mind the many factors that color them.

First of all, there is the frailty of human memory itself. Memory of long-ago events is bound to be full of gaps, distortions, and outright errors. But for those aspects of life which are not recorded in other ways, it is the best source we have. In this book, we did what any historian does: We selected accounts which seemed plausible, rejecting those which didn't accord with known facts or other more plausible accounts. Most of the statements made by people in this book are unchecked and uncheckable, but we did not include material that seemed likely to mislead the reader.

Memory is itself a creative faculty. It doesn't just record what strikes it, like a sheet of photographic paper; rather, it constructs an account of what has happened on the basis of past learning and present purposes. Oral history material must be read in this light. On the one hand, the reader needs to compensate for the fact that sources' accounts are affected by their personal subcultures, by their exposure to the mass media, and by the effect they would like to have on their listeners or the public. On the other hand, the value of these materials is enhanced by the fact that they shed light, not only on what happened, but on the ways that various people organized their understandings of what happened.

The interviewers for this book tried deliberately to reduce the impact of mass-media views of reality. We usually started by asking people about things they knew from direct personal experience—their families, their neighborhoods, their work places. We didn't indicate too much interest in how people felt about the things they saw on the evening news. This, no doubt, limited the range of memories we received, but it also allowed us to "cut under" mass-media perceptions and categories. Where people presented what seemed to be stereotypes that didn't accord with their actual experiences, we asked questions which invited them to reflect afresh on their experiences and think of new ways to look at them. This, of course, did not make their accounts more "pure," but rather added another level to them.

The questions asked in an interview determine, to a great extent, the kinds of answers that are given. Studs Terkel, for example, is a master of questions which elicit private musings and the expression of a personal philosophy of life. Our questions took off from the kinds of issues with which labor and social historians have previously been concerned. Different investigators, asking different questions, might have received far different answers.

The interviewers also influence the results in more subtle ways. Our evident interest in and sympathy with the labor movement, no doubt, led some people to emphasize its positive aspects more than they would have to an interviewer who appeared hostile to it; conversely, labor movement loyalists might have been more reluctant to express criticisms to a more hostile interviewer. By inviting people to reflect on why things happened, to help with the job of figuring out the historical process, the interviewers, no doubt, got very different material than one who simply asked for historical information. The range of such subtle effects of the interviewer on the nature of oral history documents is almost infinite.

There are few controls for these effects. Interviewing must be viewed as the product of a relationship between people, rather than as simply a production of the interviewee; the detached formality of a poll-taker influences the results of an interview as surely as a more involved style. Interviewers did, however, try to avoid leading questions, questions which dictated the answer. And we tried to maintain an atmosphere in which it would be possible for the interviewees to say things which contradicted what we expected—or wanted—to hear.

Our impression is that, in general, people were willing to speak their minds about their employers and the local elite. However, several retirees expressed the concern that, by talking to us, they might somehow jeopardize their pension rights or otherwise bring down trouble on themselves. One worker, out of concern that his pension might be taken away, asked us not to publish his account of how he had caught his employers violating federal pay regulations and had forced them to raise wages. This was all the more dramatic because the incident had occurred during World War I. It is not hard to see how interviewers who did not effectively allay such concerns might come up with more statements to the effect that, "The companies were wonderful to us in the old days."

A Book as a Social Product

If we, as the project's staff, have shaped the book and even influenced the content of the interviews, it is equally important to recognize the reverse process: The way in which those interviewed and those who worked with the project influenced us and our work on the book. Much of our understanding was shaped by what we had previously learned from workers and community members. Further, we discussed with many people what should be in the book and how it should approach various questions. The commentaries in the book, though written out by the historical coordinator, draw heavily on these discussions. Finally, people who had been sources read drafts of the book, commented on them, and made suggestions for changes. The historians involved in the project were "mediated" by community members, as well as the other way around. The book is the product of this entire process of interaction. While the final editing and the commentaries are our responsibility, any insights they express are likely to be the product of this entire process.

Many other factors influenced the shape of this book. The National Endowment for the Humanities, which funded the project, did not interfere in any way. Nonetheless, few people are uninfluenced by the source of their paycheck; and the hope for possible future grants forms an incentive to please the granting agency. The project required cooperation from unions and other community organizations; hence we needed to avoid making enemies in the community who could make things tough for us. Such needs create subtle limits on what a project can and cannot do: Community history is inevitably a political process. (Such pressures are not unknown to professional academic historians, either.) There were our own personal milieus, locally in the Valley, outside in labor history, community history, and other social and political networks of which we are a part and to which we look for understanding and approval. The desire to create a publishable book influences the character of the product, and specific advice from the publisher contributed to reshaping the book. In short, the making of a book, like any other event, is the product of many intersecting personal and social forces.

INDEX

Index of Interviewees

General Index